A Companion To The Lakes Of Cumberland, Westmoreland, And Lancashire: In A Descriptive Account Of A Family Tour, And Excursions On Horseback And On Foot

Sir Edward Baines

CRITICAL NOTICES

OF THE
FIRST AND SECOND EDITIONS
OF
BAINES'S COMPANION TO THE LAKES.

" Travellers to the Lakes have long felt the want of a book which should be written by a person possessing sufficient ability to describe the romantic scenes they exhibit with taste and feeling, but at the same time willing to enter into all the little details and instructions so necessary for the traveller in his every-day toils and perils. The work on our table is very properly termed a Companion, rather than a Guide, and, in a very well written and amusing introduction, it brings us acquainted with three or four characters, one or two of which it is probable will be found in almost every party setting forth on a similar expedition. The very full account which is given of every object worthy of attention, the friendly tone which the author assumes in giving advice to his readers, the complete and useful Itinerary which follows the details, and the excellent Map with which they are pre-ceded, render this not only a very superior guide-book, but a very interesting volume as a descriptive tour. It is rarely, indeed, so much talent and information are employed on such works, and we should have no slight pleasure in finding the author employing his next summer's unoccupied months in preparing a similar guide for us to some other place of healthy and romantic resort. We recommend the work to any one visiting the Lakes, as likely to contribute very much to the pleasure of their journey."—*Monthly Review*.

" With a good map prefixed, this book contains all that is necessary for the information of the tourist, who (with fine weather) may spend a month or six weeks most delightfully in visiting these sylvan beau-ties of England. The Companion really deserves its name, for it is an amusing miscellany, and contains many things to interest the reader, or while away the duller hours that occur on every party of pleasure."—*Literary Gazette*.

" We can recommend this book to persons who intend to visit the English Lakes. The author possesses taste and sense, a just percep-tion of the picturesque, and a wide range of topographical, antiquarian, and general information, of which he makes a good use. The largest part of the book is in the form of a tour by a family party, which is judiciously managed so as to embrace a notice of every thing remark-able, and to combine with this an idea of how the different objects are likely to affect the young and the middle-aged, the lively and the pensive. This is followed by a " Tour on Horseback," through lines partly different ; and after this comes a Pedestrian tour, which differs in some points from both. From internal evidence, we infer with certainty, that the writer has travelled through Westmoreland in all these modes."—*Scotsman*.

" Mr. Baines has succeeded in combining in this volume the accuracy of a Guide-Book with the liveliness and interest of a Personal Narrative. Knowing something of the district of which it treats, we are the better able to recommend the volume with confidence to our readers."—*Edinburgh Literary Journal.*

" Mr. Baines has provided the tourist to the English Lakes with an excellent Companion. Every thing enchanting in their beauties, romantic in their scenery, and interesting in their history, is here faithfully described. To the traveller who visits these delightful scenes for amusement, such a work is invaluable ; and even the fireside tourist, who performs all journeys in his easy chair, will here find pleasure and useful information. The book is accompanied with a full and accurate Map, forming altogether a most agreeable road miscellany."—*New North Briton.*

" Mr. Baines not only gives us a copious Itinerary, but he favours us also with a journal of a personal tour, or family tour rather, in which the various objects of an Itinerary are graphically described. Mr. Baines's book will be found a pleasant and useful companion."—*Spectator.*

" This adds another to the hundred and one already published ' Guides' to our far-famed Lakes: and certainly we must class it amongst the most valuable that have yet appeared. It is in fact what it professes to be, a ' Companion' to the Lakes, and teaches how the journey in this fairy region may be best performed, by showing how it has been performed by a family party. The various beauties of scenery are clearly pointed out; the different lakes, mountains, &c. lucidly and forcibly described; and the most favourable routes for seeing every thing worthy of being seen recommended. When we add that the volume is accompanied by an excellent map of the lake district, and contains a most valuable Itinerary, with the distances correctly marked, and every object upon each road carefully noted, we have said enough to recommend the book to every person intending to visit the Lakes, to which it is an indispensable ' Companion.' "—*Carlisle Journal.*

" As a well-written and highly interesting descriptive Tour, Baines's Companion to the Lakes has great attractions, and will be read with the most pleasing associations by those who can indulge in reminiscences of ' the land of the mountain and flood.' "—*Carlisle Patriot.*

" Every page gives ample proof that Mr. Baines, Jun. has done greater justice to the Lake and Mountain Scenery than any of the numerous writers on the same subject who had preceded him. His plan is novel, and infinitely preferable to the dry and formal style which the Guide-Book writers have hitherto adopted ; in short we have no scruple in pronouncing this Second Edition of ' The Companion to the Lakes' the most useful and interesting guide extant. Speaking from the knowledge which *half a century* of close connexion with the district it describes has put us in possession of, we dare take upon ourselves to vouch for its general accuracy."——*Cumberland Pacquet and Ware's Whitehaven Advertiser.*

Drawn by T. Allom.

Engraved by H. Sands.

1834.

DERWENTWATER AND THE BORROWDALE MOUNTAINS.

A

COMPANION

TO THE

LAKES

OF

CUMBERLAND, WESTMORELAND, AND LANCASHIRE;

IN A DESCRIPTIVE ACCOUNT OF A

FAMILY TOUR,

AND EXCURSIONS ON HORSEBACK AND ON FOOT.

WITH A NEW, COPIOUS, AND CORRECT

ITINERARY.

THIRD EDITION.

BY EDWARD BAINES, Jun.

LONDON:
SIMPKIN AND MARSHALL;

BAINES AND NEWSOME, LEEDS; WALES AND BAINES, LIVER-
POOL; M. AND R. BRANTHWAITE, KENDAL; AND ALL BOOK-
SELLERS AT KENDAL, CARLISLE, PENRITH, KESWICK,
ULVERSTON, LANCASTER, &c. &c.

1834.

14605
.556
.142

PREFACE.

THE favourable reception given to this work has called for a Third Edition within five years after its original publication. The Author has availed himself of the opportunity afforded him by the publication of the Second and Third Editions, to add greatly to the information it contained: he has each time considerably enlarged the useful contents of the volume, and has revised and corrected the whole with the greatest care.

This volume is intended to combine the accuracy of a *Guide-Book* with the liveliness and interest of a *Personal Narrative*. It contains all and more than all the information usually given in the former, but so arranged as to fall naturally into the latter. Avoiding the dry and didactic form of the Gazetteer-Guide, the Author has aimed to produce a readable volume, which may at once serve as a pleasant *Companion* in the carriage, the boat, or the inn,

A 2

and afford the best practical directions to tourists, by giving an actual exemplification of the manner in which the Tour of the Lakes has been accomplished both by a Family Party and by an individual. From this the traveller will receive a distinct view of the most advantageous method of making each excursion,—of the time consumed, the accommodations or inconveniences experienced, and the precautions to be taken. Ladies, in particular, will learn what enterprises they may safely attempt in the mountainous region, and where they would be exposed to danger or excessive fatigue.

Much of the information concerning the objects seen, the families and distinguished men residing at the Lakes, the manners and customs of the inhabitants, and the history and antiquities of the district, is conveyed in the form of conversation ; but, although this has frequently been adopted as the most agreeable method of communicating facts, the Author has never exercised his invention or imagination as to the facts themselves, but has in all cases scrupulously confined himself within the strictest bounds of truth.

The FAMILY TOUR is a narrative of a Tour actually performed by a Family Party, consisting of two ladies and two gentlemen ; the journeys were made as they are described; and the incidents, with a few trifling exceptions, occurred just as they are related.

The EXCURSION ON HORSEBACK and the two EXCURSIONS ON FOOT are faithful descriptions of journeys performed by the Author, and they will be found to contain much useful information for those who may travel in either of these methods.

The Four Parts together contain a full description of all the principal Routes and Excursions at the Lakes; including a particular account of the ascents of Skiddaw, Helvellyn, Scawfell Pikes, Great Gavel, Bowfell, Langdale Pikes, Hill Bell, High Street, and several other mountains.

The ITINERARY is an original feature of this work, and will be found of great utility. It gives numerous statistical details concerning the towns, villages, lakes, and mountains,—the distances of all the places in every stage,—the names of the noblemen's and gentlemen's seats, with those of their owners or occupiers, (a species of information always desired by the Tourist,)—and many other particulars concerning inns and accommodations.

The MAP with which the work is embellished will be found strictly faithful, having

been carefully corrected down to the year 1834.*
It is also engraved with a clearness and distinctness rarely perceived in maps of mountainous countries, which will assist the traveller
in consulting it.

The engraving of *Derwentwater and the
Borrowdale Mountains*, in the FRONTISPIECE,
will be regarded as an ornament to the volume ;
perhaps a more beautiful combination of lake
and mountain scenery is not to be found in
Cumberland or Westmoreland. The view is
taken from Castlehead, near Keswick.

The INDEX of Places will enable the
reader to turn immediately to the page where
any town, village, mansion, lake, mountain, or
other object is mentioned, either in the Companion or the Itinerary.

Leeds, June 9, 1834.

* The volume is sold both with and without the Map and
Frontispiece,—of course at different prices; and the Map is sold
separately in case, accompanied with the Itinerary.

CONTENTS.

FAMILY TOUR.

EXCURSION ON HORSEBACK.

FIRST EXCURSION ON FOOT.

SECOND EXCURSION ON FOOT.

Published by Simpkin & Marshall, London: Baines & Newsome, Leeds, & Wales & Baines.

COMPANION TO THE LAKES.

CHAPTER I.

INTRODUCTION—CHARACTER OF THE LAKE SCENERY, COMPARED
WITH OTHER PARTS OF ENGLAND; COMPARED WITH THE
SWISS AND ITALIAN LAKES—ISLANDS—WATERFALLS—MAN-
SIONS—MONUMENTS OF ANTIQUITY—COMPANY AT THE
LAKES—SEASON OF VISITING—MODES OF TRAVELLING.

THE Lakes of Cumberland and Westmoreland are
allowed to excel every other part of England in the
combined grandeur and loveliness of their scenery.
The general character of English scenery is cheerful
beauty, whilst the sublime and romantic are rarely
met with: and though some of our counties boast
the finer and bolder features of nature, it is no disparagement to them to say that they must all yield
the prize of beauty to the northern Lakes.   Rich,
noble, and picturesque as are the banks of the Wye,—
wild and romantic as are the hills, rocks, and valleys
of Derbyshire,—varied and fascinating as are the

beauties of the Isle of Wight,—luxuriant and opulent as are the borders of the Thames, the Trent, and the Severn,—delightful as are the dales of Yorkshire,—all these tracts yield in some important respect to the region of the Lakes, which may be truly said to combine the beauties of each, whilst it far surpasses them all in grandeur and sublimity.

The fine groups of mountains which cover a large part of Cumberland and Westmoreland—extending about thirty miles from north to south, and as many from east to west—stretch from the Irish Sea to a long chain of hills which has been called the back-bone of England. This chain, of which Cross Fell is the most elevated summit, runs northward to the mountains of Scotland, and southward, along the frontiers of Yorkshire and Lancashire, to the hills of Derbyshire. In Cumberland the mountains rise to a greater elevation than in any other part of England; and in their forms and positions there is that happy mixture of the regular and the irregular, which is most pleasing to the admirer of the picturesque. There is no general elevation of the land above the level of the sea: but the hills spring up directly from plains and valleys scarcely raised above that level, and stand with the full advantage of their noble stature, in groups of gigantic bulk, or in ridges running towards every point of the compass. Enclosed among the mountainous ridges are numerous valleys of considerable fertility, which, being adorned with wood both natural and planted, covered with verdure of the most brilliant green, and intersected by meandering streams or glassed with spreading *lakes*, present a rich variety of the most delicious landscapes.

The last-mentioned feature of this tract is its most striking characteristic, and has given to it the general designation of THE LAKES. Lakes are rarely found except among elevated mountains, and none of considerable magnitude exist in any other part of England. Hence those parts of Cumberland, Westmoreland, and Lancashire, where they are found in such numbers and of such considerable extent, have naturally received the distinguishing appellation of ' The English Lakes.' Water is the richest feature of natural scenery. When spread out in ample sheets, and especially when fringed by wood, sprinkled with islands, and embosomed in the depth of valleys, the mirrored surface is itself most grateful to the eye, and sets off every other beauty of the landscape. The towering crag or mountain looks still bolder when rising from the smooth sheet of the lake : the crisped foliage of the wood, and the emerald carpet of the field or knoll, have their colours heightened, and their outline more distinctly traced, from contrast with the silvery expanse. The water reflects the tints of the hill and the azure face of heaven. It sweeps gracefully round bays and promontories, and ' clips in' the islands as with a loving embrace. When slightly ruffled with the breeze, it assumes a clear lead colour, of the most delightful freshness. The prospects from the surface of a lake are still more pleasing than from its shores, and, whilst enjoying them, the spectator may also have the healthful exercise of rowing, or the amusement of fishing.

Beautiful in itself, the lake becomes much more so when surrounded by mountains of noble form and sublime elevation, like those of Cumberland and Westmoreland. The rarity of lake and mountain scenery in this country adds greatly to its charm in the eyes of the English tourist. Nor would I rank the lakes of England far below those of any other country in point of beauty. It is true that many of the Swiss and Italian lakes are of much larger dimensions, and the mountains and precipices by which they are environed are several times more lofty. In point of sublimity, therefore, our native lakes are greatly surpassed ; yet even in this quality the superiority of the Alpine lakes is by no means so striking as their magnitude might lead us to suppose. Beyond a certain point, increased size produces but a comparatively small addition of effect, owing to the limited powers of human vision. Among the Alps, too, the magnitudes of all the objects are proportionate, and they are consequently the less striking to the spectator. So much do the mountains and lakes of Cumberland and Westmoreland exceed the other parts of this country in grandeur, that they would unquestionably appear more astonishing to Englishmen in general, than Switzerland seen *after* having visited the Lakes. The continental traveller may even return from the Oberland of Berne and the valley of Chamouni, and still visit this delightful part of our native country with high admiration. Such views as that of Scawfell Pikes, seen from the platform of Styhead,— the Old Man, from the surface of Coniston Water,— Langdale Pikes, from the head of Langdale,—and Honister Crag, from Gatesgarth Dale,—cannot fail to impress the mind with mingled awe and transport. In one important feature our native lakes surpass those of Switzerland and Italy, namely, in their *islands*. This ornament is entirely wanting to the continental lakes, whilst it eminently increases the charms of Windermere, Derwentwater, and several of the smaller lakes of Westmoreland and Cumberland. The spectator who views Windermere from Elleray or the Station, Derwentwater from Wallow Crag, or Rydal Water from Rydal Mount, must acknowledge that the sheets of water would be comparatively tame without the beautiful tufted islands which stud their surfaces. It may be difficult to pronounce what it is that gives the last and highest finish to these charming scenes; but if required to offer an opinion, I should say it is the islands.

The *waterfalls* at the Lakes are eminently beautiful, and not the less pleasing to the tourist because he has generally to reach them by penetrating through a rough and tangled glen. The streamlets which supply them are invariably of the most limpid clearness, which gives to the falling waters a sparkling lustre. In point of sublimity these waterfalls cannot be compared with those of Switzerland ; but they rival the cascades of any country in picturesque effect.   Colwith Force is the only one which can claim the character of wild and impetuous grandeur ;* but Stockgill Force, Ayrey Force, the Rydal water-falls, and many others, are distinguished by all that can delight the lover of the picturesque.

The *variety* to be found at the Lakes greatly enhances their charms ; for natural beauties, however splendid, soon pall upon the taste without the aid of diversity.   Every lake has its distinguishing character ; the valleys exhibit all the varieties between rugged grandeur and soft luxuriance.   Sunshine, cloud, and storm, the morning and the evening glories, are perpetually changing the aspect of these mountainous regions, and thus their graces become more fascinating,—as the female countenance is rendered *piquant* from changes in the expression.

When the tourist has exhausted his powers of admiration in surveying mountain, lake, and valley, the beauties of art may afford a new stimulus.   These counties have their *mansions* and *parks*, adorned with all that wealth and taste can furnish, to gratify the wishes of their owners.   The stately castle and noble woods of Lowther, the delicious grounds of Conishead Priory and Holker Hall, the elegant mansion of Storrs, and many other beautiful residences, claim the admiration of the traveller.   It is true that art

* The Fall of Lowdore is magnificent immediately after heavy rains, but at all other times the quantity of water is small.

has sometimes been employed to mar, rather than to mend the scene; but this is not frequently the case; and on the whole the Lakes have gained in beauty and attraction by the residence of men of fortune amongst them.

A source of still greater attraction is to be found in the *monuments of antiquity* which may be seen at the Lakes. These are of three kinds—druidical remains, ruins of ecclesiastical structures and of baronial castles. Near Keswick and Penrith are several interesting relics of druidical temples and places of judicature. Of the ecclesiastical structures, the principal is Furness Abbey, one of the grandest ruins in the kingdom. The castles of Cockermouth, Egremont, Brougham, Penrith, Kendal, Lancaster, and several others, merit the attention not merely of the antiquarian, but of the artist. An ancient castle and a venerable cathedral adorn the capital of Cumberland; and there are many interesting remains of feudal grandeur in the northern parts of the county, where fortresses were in former days unhappily too much needed, from the ravages and hostilities which afflicted the ' Borders.'

To the geologist, mineralogist, and botanist, this district affords an ample field of research. Here are mines of iron, copper, lead, plumbago, and coal, and slate quarries of great extent. There is also an abundance of minerals, collections of which are to be seen at Keswick and other places. The elevation of the mountains and the variety of the soil also make the range of the vegetable kingdom extensive.

Possessing these high and varied sources of gratification, it is not surprising that the Lakes should attract visiters from every part of the kingdom during the summer and autumn. They appear to have been frequented soon after travelling became easy in England, from the formation of turnpike roads. I have been informed by one of the oldest guides at Keswick—an octogenarian—that they were much brought into notice on occasion of a celebrated contested election for Cumberland, when Sir James Lowther and three other candidates brought up friends and supporters from very distant places,* who then saw the Lakes and carried away the fame of their beauties. My informant resided five years, in his youth, at Buttermere, and during that time never heard of a stranger visiting the place. Gray, the poet, Gilpin, Mrs. Radcliffe, Pennant, and other distinguished authors, visited this region of the picturesque, and much increased its celebrity by their graphic delineations. Mr. West, a Roman Catholic clergyman, who resided long at Ulverston, contributed to excite the public interest by the eloquent descriptions of the lake scenery in his " Guide," and by his book on " The Antiquities of Furness." Artists have found here one of the richest fields for the exercise of the pencil ; and the landscapes of the Lakes, seen in

* This was in 1768. Sir James Lowther, Bart. and Humphrey Senhouse, Esq. were returned, but Henry Curwen, Esq. and Henry Fletcher, Esq. petitioned against the return, and were declared by a Committee of the House of Commons to be duly elected. The Sheriff was committed to Newgate for his misconduct.

public exhibitions, or more widely distributed by means of the engraver's art, have doubtless attracted visiters to see the surpassing originals.

For the last fifty years these districts have constituted a favourite resort of the lovers of nature, whose means enable them to travel ; and as the wealth and population of the country have increased, the number of visiters to the Lakes has augmented in a more rapid ratio. During the same period most of the mansions on the banks of Windermere, Derwentwater, and the other lakes have been built, and a great quantity of wood planted. The inns and all the accommodations for travellers have been materially improved, so that now neither comfort nor luxury is wanting ; and the tourist may travel through this mountainous region, either in his own carriage or in vehicles found on the spot, with nothing of discomfort to interrupt his enjoyment, except what may occasionally arise from the crowd of travellers.

The musing sentimentalist, or the fastidious travel-ler who is nice about best rooms and constant atten-tion, might wish that the number of tourists were diminished. But such, I am persuaded, is not the general desire of the visiters, any more than of the inhabitants. There is ample space among these moun-tains and valleys for the rovings of those who love seclusion ; and even in the height of the season the rambler will meet with very few parties in any excur-sion he may make, except in the immediate neigh-bourhood of the towns. There is also time enough for solitude in ascending the mountains, visiting the waterfalls, rowing on the lakes, and passing from stage to stage. Delightful and impressive as it is to contemplate the sublimities of nature in deep silence, undisturbed by the busy hum or the appearance of men, there are few who can long endure the loneliness of such contemplation, and who would not, at the close of a five or six hours' ramble, hail the sight of a friend, a townsman, or even a fellow creature. For my own part, in the course of many rambles in this and other countries, I have found my gratification much enhanced by the alternations of solitude and society: it has given me great pleasure to meet an intelligent traveller on the top of a lofty hill, or in the depth of a lonely valley,—to sit down, after a day spent upon the mountains, at a *table d'hôte* with ten or twenty persons, each of whom had his narrative of wonders, toils, and pleasures,—or (in England) occasionally to join my own party to another, of which the members were well-informed and conversable. Even to look over the book of visiters at a favourite resort, and to see the names of friends, or of persons illustrious for talent or rank, is generally found amusing.

The season at which the Lakes are usually visited is from the middle of July to the end of September;* but they may be very well visited as early as the beginning of June, and (in many years) as late as the

---

* The bustle at the inns during this season, contrasted with their dreary loneliness at all other times, is striking, and caused an old Boniface to observe, that "they were *mad* three months of the year, and *melancholy* the other nine."

middle of October. In the former month the length
of the days is favourable to excursions, and vegetation
then appears in all its freshness and luxuriance.
Though the woods are of somewhat too uniform a
green, the hedges are then decorated with the wild
rose, the honeysuckle, the yellow broom, and innumerable humbler flowers, hung with bells of pink or
purple, or dropped with gold. The birds fill every
grove with melody, the white-fleeced lambs bound on
the mountain side, and all nature appear to rejoice in
the fulness of life and vigour. The atmosphere is
then also clearer than in an advanced period of
autumn, when morning and evening mists begin to
prevail. On the other hand, the woods and mountains
are seen in their glory in September and October,
when the foliage is enriched and variegated with the
autumnal tints, and when the hills, assuming a warm
brown from the sun-baked fern which covers them, or
a bright purple from the innumerable bells which
deck the heather, are contrasted with the yet brilliant
green of the valleys. The evening skies, too, are now
more glowing than at any other period of the year.
On the whole, therefore, the landscape is more rich
and diversified in the advanced part of the season, and
the painter would certainly choose this time for visiting the Lakes,—putting up with the inconveniences
of shortened days and cool evenings. The heat of
summer is unfavourable for pedestrian excursions
either in the valleys or to the tops of mountains, and
the tourist who is compelled to make his visit at this

time would do well to take his long walks very early
in the morning, or in the evening. The view from a
high mountain is clearer just before sunrise than at
any other hour of the day: at noon there is generally
a degree of sun-haziness, which renders distant objects
indistinct.

The modes of travelling are various. Where ladies
are of the party, a carriage is indispensable; and the
most convenient vehicle is a chariot, where the party
is not too numerous, as it gives the opportunity of
seeing the country better than any other kind of carriage, and at the same time affords protection against
the uncertainty of the weather. A party of gentlemen
might find it more agreeable to travel on horseback,
not merely for the sake of the exercise, but from the
greater independence the rider enjoys, and the power
he possesses of taking his horse over tracks which a
carriage could not traverse. Those who have time,
health, vigour, and a disposition to enjoy rambling,
will find a pedestrian excursion the most agreeable:
they will thus be more independent even than the
horseman, and may deviate at pleasure from the beaten
track, to climb the rocks, explore the woods, roam
from mountain to mountain, cross from valley to
valley, sketch, or collect specimens. I have found, by
experience in more than one tour, that two fellow-
travellers may journey very agreeably by taking a
single horse, and riding alternately. This plan, whilst
it allows great freedom of motion, affords the pleasure
both of foot and horse exercise, diminishes fatigue,

saves time, and enables the travellers to convey by saddle-bags or valise the small stock of clothes they may need in those excursions in which they are distant from the principal towns,—the coaches serving to convey a trunk or portmanteau from one town to another. I do not recommend solitary rambling, if pleasure be the object. I have tried it, and found it dull and wearisome. A friend to whom you can express the feelings which the beautiful and sublime of nature excite, whose gratification you can at once partake and enhance by sympathy, and with whom you can converse when there are no objects demanding attention, will increase tenfold the pleasure of the tour.

I may be excused for hinting, as the conclusion of this introductory chapter, that the pleasure of travelling depends at least as much upon the state of a man's mind as on the objects he beholds. Those who set out in good health, with light hearts, and a disposition to be pleased, will be likely to secure a large sum of enjoyment. A peevish or fastidious traveller will find sources of dissatisfaction amongst the highest beauties of nature or art ; whilst the good-humoured man will draw amusement even from accidents and hardships, and will freely indulge his admiration without troubling himself to seek for faults.

CHAPTER II.

PLAN OF THE " COMPANION "—ORIGINAL SCHEME OF THE
FAMILY TOUR—ALTERATION IN THE PLAN—GREAT PRE-
PARATIONS—COMMENCEMENT OF THE TOUR—ORMSKIRK—
PRESTON—LANCASTER.

In conducting my reader through the district of
the Lakes, I believe I shall be able to do it in no way
more satisfactory or agreeable to him, than by re-
questing him to accompany me along the routes I
have myself repeatedly taken. If he will do me the
honour to accept of me as a "COMPANION," I will
take him from stage to stage, and from scene to
sight, in the order and manner in which I have
found it most convenient to visit them. To avoid the
dulness of solitary rambling, I shall also take the
liberty of introducing him to a family party, whom I
hope he will find agreeable and good-natured people,
and whose conversation he may feel to be a pleasant
resource, especially on a rainy day or when the road is
uninteresting. I own they are no heroes or heroines,
but very much like the greater number of families
who visit the Lakes; they eat, drink, and sleep, are
subject to be fatigued by a long day's journey, and do
not always agree among themselves in their opinions
on men and places. But as my reader is doubtless
made of flesh and blood, it can be no objection to him

to tarry for refreshment, to " sleep o' nights," to have moderate days' work cut out for him, and to find that he is not obliged to think in every case precisely as his guide would have him.

A family residing in the neighbourhood of Liverpool, to whom I am distantly related, formed a project, some few months ago, of making a summer excursion to the Lakes of Westmoreland and Cumberland; and as the party consisted of an odd number, two ladies and one gentleman, it was resolved, after great deliberation I believe, to invite their bachelor cousin to join the expedition. To this determination they were led by various reasons. My cousins had been very little accustomed to travel, and the ladies therefore conceived this to be an enterprise of some importance and danger, in which it was highly necessary that they should be protected, as well against banditti and rude men, as in the navigation of unfathomable lakes, and the passage of frightful glens and mountains. And *I* was pitched upon as their companion, partly because I had often been at the Lakes, and by my great prudence and dexterity had escaped all their dangers, bringing back with me extensive knowledge of " men and things,"—partly because I was on pretty good terms with all the family,—and partly because, as a relation, there could be no possible exception taken to me by the censorious, as there might have been to certain other gentlemen of their acquaintance.

When the project was broached to me, as it was

with much ceremony by the senior lady, I heartily
accepted the invitation, with due acknowledgments
for the honour done me.   No sooner was it known
that I should accompany them, than they produced
numerous maps and guide-books, and began to
unfold to me, with something more of eagerness than
of clearness or method, the routes which they had
respectively marked out.   The lead was taken very
decidedly by a maiden aunt, Mrs. Anabella G———,
who, having made a short trip to the Lakes some
twenty or thirty years ago, undertook to direct all our
movements; yet I soon found that she had seen but
few of the Lakes, and had gone rapidly over the
most beaten tracks.   Her niece, my fair little cousin
Matilda, who, though no enthusiast, entered with
unwonted ardour on this scheme, had marked out a
route which excited her aunt's indignation; for, with
a total disregard to roads and tracks, she took the
shortest cut from place to place, dragging the carriage unmercifully over mountain tops and through
the midst of lakes, and showing that she had not
very accurately consulted the geography of the country.   Her brother George had made a far more
reasonable route, but somewhat of the widest: his
showed that he was bent on seeing every thing, and,
what was less practicable, on taking his aunt and
sister every where: but he had sadly miscalculated
times and distances, and he was for taking the carriage over routes never yet crossed by wheels, and
rarely trodden by the foot of fair lady.

On all these plans I made few remarks, but I ventured to offer two suggestions; first, that we should put off the trip till autumn; and second, that we should go at the time of Lancaster Assizes, and stay two or three days to witness the proceedings in the courts. When I uttered the first of these propositions, I was interrupted by a general exclamation of " Impossible !"   My cousins had made up their minds to go in July, and it seemed an age to wait till the beginning of September.   It would disarrange all their plans; the season would be too far advanced; winter would be coming on; Mrs. Anabella's engagements with different Institutions, of which she was a member, would not admit of it; Matilda's Italian lessons would be interrupted; it was incompatible with George's business; above all, the Musical Festival would take place at the beginning of October, and they should need a month to prepare for it: in short, the whole party with one voice reiterated that the thing was on every account quite out of the range of possibility.   It would have availed little to urge any thing about the greater mildness of the season, the mellower tints of autumn, &c. &c., and I therefore called in aid my second proposition—the Lancaster Assizes.   None of them had ever been at an Assize, and I saw instantly that their curiosity was stimulated.   Mrs. Anabella, you must know, has been a passionate admirer of Mr. Brougham* ever since he

* Of course this journey was performed before Henry Brougham, the powerful advocate of popular rights, became Baron

said some very civil things to her at Liverpool, when he was candidate for that town in 1812: she has a wonderful veneration for his eloquence, and she thinks him the most agreeable gentleman in the world into the bargain. She went to hear his speech at the dinner given to him not long since in our Music-Hall; and she was amongst the first to dart into the Orchestra, long before the gentlemen were at liberty to lift their eyes from the substantial banquet before them to the feast of beauty prepared for them on the sideboard. I need hardly add, that the idea of seeing and hearing her great favourite at Lancaster went fast and far towards cutting down the impossibilities which had previously been urged. My cousin Madge, who is a shrewd girl, with not much romance about her, but a quiz, and a lover of the droll and comical, was excessively curious to see how some young barristers of her acquaintance looked in wigs and gowns. She had never seen Mr. Brougham, but, having heard rather more of him than she liked from her aunt, I believe she had a spiteful desire to see him, suspecting that he was not the all-perfect being Mrs. Anabella described, and quite prepared, like the Athenian, to vote him an ostracism, merely because she was tired of hearing his praises. George, though one of the best-natured

---

Brougham and Vaux, the reforming Minister, and sat upon the woolsack. Of all the rejoicing that took place on that event, no exultation equalled that of Mrs. Anabella G——, whose sagacity was thus triumphantly established beyond the reach of cavil or ridicule, and whose ambitious views for her favourite orator were more than realized.

beings in the world, is very romantic and bashful, and he therefore vigorously opposed the postponement of his ramble amongst the Lakes, and deprecated the idea of appearing in a crowded court, where he should probably have to suffer several introductions, and to listen to very tedious trials. However, his pliability and want of self-confidence induced him soon to yield to our persuasions, which he did the more readily as he knew that it was vain to oppose his aunt in any thing on which she had set her mind. It is true that the ladies themselves wavered betwixt the immediate enjoyment offered by their own plan, and the higher though later entertainment proposed by mine ; but after a long, grave, and anxious discussion, the amendment was put to the vote, and carried by a decided majority.

However interesting the detail, it would occupy too much time to mention particularly all our deep deliberations, extensive purchases, and laborious preparations before setting out for the north. Suffice it to say, that we had every thing ready at least a month before our departure, and that we settled our affairs as though we were about to circumnavigate the globe. At length, in the middle of the Assizes, (for I had with difficulty prevailed upon them not to set off the first day,) we quitted Liverpool, after a sleepless night, at eight o'clock in the morning. It was resolved that, though we were to make a short stay in Preston, we should not dine till we arrived at Lancaster ; and never party formed such a resolve with less danger of perishing

from inanition. What with our own foresight and that
of the housekeeper, we had a far greater quantity of
eatables and drinkables than the pockets of the carriage
would hold ; and, after leaving many things behind,
we found ourselves entrenched to the teeth in cakes,
sandwiches, wine, glasses, maps, fans, reticules, guide-
books, note-books, and lead pencils. We had also provided a pocket compass, whereby to steer our course ;
and I afterwards found that George had secreted a pair
of pistols in the hinder part of the carriage, to defend
us against robbers ; though he prudently refrained
from mentioning this to the ladies, who would have
been as much frightened by the contiguity of such
weapons as by an actual attack of highwaymen. It
had been thought advisable to procure a roomy travelling chariot, without a barouche seat, in order that we
might have the fullest possible view of the country in
front and on each side ; but this was attended with the
inconvenience, that one of the party was obliged to
sit bodkin. Matilda, George, and myself took this
enviable post of precedence in turns ; but as Matilda
loved comfort more than glory, and as I had rather too
much length of leg to be easy in that station, we contrived to let George have considerably the longest turn.
He, to be sure, was not at all shorter in limb than
myself, but, being more eager to see the country, he
was content to endure the constraint. When we got
amongst the hills, however, he soon gave us leg bail ;
he walked up all the steep ascents, and often stretched
on for several miles. He annoyed his aunt and sister

by climbing rocks and hills out of the road for the sake
of a view, which obliged us to wait for him; and
sometimes we were even alarmed for his safety, as he
has a most extraordinary proneness to get into awkward
predicaments.

The morning was propitious. A few light clouds,
intended to " deck the sky," not to hide it, sailed
with imperceptible motion from the north, and by
their elevation promised some continuance of fine weather. The tide was up as we passed the mouth of
the Mersey, and several vessels were just sailing out
of the river, destined for the most opposite quarters
of the globe. So clear was the atmosphere, that from
the hill above Ormskirk we saw distinctly the coast
of Wales as far as the Ormes Heads, and the grand
range of Snowdon in the rear. In the ride from
Liverpool to Preston, there is little to interest, owing
to the flatness of the country. We admired the
grotesque appearance of the old church at Ormskirk,
in which a slim spire stands close by the side of a
massive square tower. The church, as Mrs. Anabella
informed us, was built at the expense of two maiden
ladies, one of whom preferred a tower and the
other a spire ; and as neither would give up her
favourite idea, they agreed to erect both a tower and
a spire side by side. Such at least is the tradition
which has descended through many centuries. The
church contains the burial-place of the Stanleys.
Ormskirk is famous for the number of maiden ladies
who reside in it, and perhaps on that account it is a

favourite place with Mrs. Anabella. In going through the town we were amused by the alluring signs over more than one of the shops which deal in its staple manufacture,—*Old Original Best Ormskirk Gingerbread.*

Two miles from Ormskirk, on our right, we saw the solitary Gothic arch which is all that remains of Burscough Priory. A little further we passed within a short distance of the place where once stood Lathamhouse, so gallantly defended by the heroic Countess of Derby against the forces of the Parliament. The house being ruined by the sieges it withstood, it has been replaced by a more modern structure. Lathamhouse was formerly the principal seat of the Stanleys, but now belongs to Lord Skelmersdale. Rufford Old Hall, which is built with a wooden front, curiously painted in stripes of black and white, and with some dozen of gable ends like pigeon-cotes, was long the seat of the Hesketh family; but Sir Thomas has built a new hall, in the modern style, at a short distance from it, where he resides. About ten miles from Preston, we had a good view of the Ribble, where it expands into a broad estuary, and the village of Lytham may be seen on the opposite bank. The approach to Preston is interesting. The old low mansion of Penwortham-hall stands on a steep grassy bank overlooking the valley of the Ribble, which forms a noble sweep round the south side of the town. The valley is luxuriant and beautiful; the woods of Walton-hall are seen to the right, and beyond rises the hill which is

crowned with the ancient seat of Hoghton Tower:
both of these mansions belong to Sir Harry Hoghton.
Preston stands on a gentle elevation at the north of the
river, and looks a handsome town as seen in the descent
of Penwortham hill.

"Proud Preston" is less deserving of its title now
than it was before the late extraordinary increase of
its manufactures, which, though they have added
greatly to its wealth and population, have impaired
its aristocratic claim to peculiar gentility.   It is a
well-built-town, with a delightful neighbourhood, but
has no curiosities claiming the attention of the tourist,
and therefore it did not detain us longer than enabled
us to visit the promenade called Avenham Walk (pronounced *Aynham*) which affords a beautiful view of
the river and valley.   Mrs. Anabella knew much of
the by-gone times of Preston, and could enumerate
many of the " fair women and brave men" who shone
at the last three Guilds,* but most of whom, alas !
had passed away from this worldly stage.

Between Preston and Lancaster the country is still
flat, but fertile, the soil being very favourable for
wheat.   A few miles to the right of the road, and
running parallel with it, is a long ridge of hills,
which we kept in view during the remainder of our
journey.   Their height is sufficient to have gained for
them the name of *Fells*†—a name with which we

* The guild is a festival held at Preston every twenty years, and
celebrated with great splendour.

† Longridge Fells.

became very familiar before we quitted the Lakes. The undulating and sloping ground at the foot of the hills, agreeably sprinkled with wood, affords pleasant prospects from the road.   In the direction of the sea the land is perfectly flat, and contains extensive mosses : it bears the name of the Fylde.   Three miles from Lancaster on our left, we passed Ashton-hall, a seat of the Duke of Hamilton : it is not visible from the road.

Lancaster is not to be seen till you arrive within about a mile of the town, when, on ascending an acclivity, its castled height rises to view proudly overlooking the valley of the Lune : the Lune itself, here a fine estuary, winds majestically to the sea ; and the extensive Bay of Morecambe spreads beyond the town, backed by the Westmoreland and Cumberland mountains.   The magnificent appearance of Lancaster Castle drew forth exclamations of astonishment from George, and excited the admiration of Matilda.   Its numerous towers and extensive battlements, cresting the hill, give it an air of grandeur scarcely equalled by any other castle in England ; and the flag which now waved from the top easily recalled to my cousin's susceptible imagination the days of the renowned John of Gaunt, with the palatine glories of Lancaster. He had very little time to contemplate this object before we arrived at the end of our journey.

We were fortunately not under the necessity of taking up our quarters at an inn, where it might have been difficult to find good accommodation, owing to

We were fortunately not under the necessity of taking up our quarters at an inn, where it might have been difficult to find good accommodation, owing to the crowd of persons attending the Assizes. We had an invitation to spend a few days with some friends who lived about a mile out of the town, and whose house and grounds command beautiful views of the Lune and surrounding country. We arrived there to a late dinner, and remained several days under our friends' hospitable roof.

CHAPTER III.

WHEN we had assembled for breakfast on the
morning after our arrival, our host brought in a fine
salmon, which had just been caught in his nets in the
river Lune.   He informed us that the salmon fishery
in this river was much less productive now than
formerly, as is the case in most of the rivers on
the western coast.*   The diminution of fish in some
of the streams is accounted for by the increase of
manufactories, which pollute the water ; but there are
no manufactories on the Lune, and it has been pronounced by competent judges one of the best salmon
streams in the kingdom.   The prevalent opinion is,
that the fish are frightened away by the steam-
packets, which make a much greater noise and dis-
turbance in the water than sailing vessels.   If this

---

* So plentiful was salmon in former days at Lancaster, that it
was customary for apprentices to stipulate in their indentures, that
they should not be fed upon salmon more than three days in the
week !   The same agreement was common at Kendal.

be the case, it must be said on behalf of the steam-packets, that they have not more disturbed our waters than facilitated and increased our traffic; and that if they have frightened away the salmon of the Lune, the Ribble, and the Eden, they make some compensation by regularly bringing Irish salmon to the fish-markets of England.

After breakfast we walked into the town, accompanied by our host and his lady. Lancaster is a clean, well-built, well-paved, and agreeable town. It lies on the south-eastern slope of the castle hill, and the lower parts of it descend to the river, which serpentizes through the valley, and makes a double bend at the foot of the hill. The houses are all built of stone, and have consequently an appearance of solidity and respectability: several of the streets are genteel and handsome. Lancaster had once a more extensive foreign commerce than it can boast at present. A range of deserted warehouses along the quay speaks of departed trade; the decline has been occasioned partly by the rivalry of ports more conveniently situated in respect to the sea and to the manufacturing districts, partly by a disastrous series of failures among the bankers of the town, and partly also by the fact that the navigation of the river has of late been much obstructed by sand banks. The vessels bound to Lancaster now chiefly unload at Glasson Dock, five miles below the town, and just within the mouth of the Lune.

The ascent from the town to the castle is a short but steep acclivity. In toiling up it our party were repaid for their exertion by the noble entrance to the castle, which is an ancient and lofty tower, flanked by two octagonal turrets. Over the portcullised gateway is a shield bearing the arms of France semi-quartered with those of England; and in a niche is the statue of John of Gaunt, Duke of Lancaster, in complete armour. It was by this illustrious prince that the tower was built and the castle re-edified, in the fourteenth century: it was originally built by Roger de Poictou, in the eleventh century, on the site of a Roman fortification, but was destroyed or greatly injured, by the Scotch invaders in 1322.

The castle stands on the brow of the hill, but descending a little in the direction of the town. It covers a great space of ground, and consists of several distinct buildings. In the centre is a massive square tower, called the Lungess tower, seventy-eight feet high, on the top of which, at one angle, is a turret called *John O'Gaunt's chair*. This tower and the spacious court-yard are surrounded by several outer towers, joined by a lofty wall. A great part of the pile is modern, but the Lungess tower, the Gateway tower, Hadrian's tower and the Dungeon tower on the western side, and the Well tower on the southern, are all ancient. The lower part of the Lungess tower is supposed to be of Roman architecture, and it is certainly of great antiquity. The modern parts are castellated, and made to correspond with the ancient.

As a prison, Lancaster castle is one of the strongest and best-regulated in the kingdom. The courts in which the Assizes are held form part of the castle, and are on the north side. On the western side part of the ancient moat remains.

Walking round the castle, we came to the terrace, which commands a splendid view of the Lune, the sea, and the mountains. We also entered the church-yard, which immediately adjoins, and whence we saw the valley above the town. The church is a fine structure, and harmonizes well with the castle; at a distance, the towers and battlements of both appear as if they belonged to one huge pile of building.

In order that my cousins might enjoy the best possible view of the surrounding country, we entered the castle, and ascended to *John O'Gaunt's chair*, whence we had a prospect not surpassed by many in England for grandeur, beauty, and variety. I could not have wished for a clearer or brighter day, to show them this view, which possesses nearly every feature of a perfect landscape. The hill on which the castle stands rises abruptly in the midst of the vale of the Lune, and commands a complete panoramic view of the country. The river is seen winding round the foot of the hill, and may be traced up the valley as far as the aqueduct, and, in the opposite direction, to the sea. Just below the town it expands into a broad estuary, which makes a sweeping bend through the valley, and at high water has a noble effect. Looking north-

ward and beyond the Lune, the eye beholds the whole
of the extensive Bay of Morecambe, running several
miles inland, and the white houses of Ulverston, at
the distance of fourteen or fifteen miles, on the opposite shore. The fine wooded estuaries of the Kent
and the Leven penetrate the northern shore of the
Bay, and give it a richly picturesque effect. Rising
beyond the Bay is the whole range of the Westmoreland and Cumberland mountains—the ultimate object
of our expedition. To the left, nearest the sea, is the
regular and rounded yet high mountain of Black
Comb, said to command one of the most extensive
views of any hill in England; and further inland
springs up the loftier and more rugged cluster of Scawfell and his neighbouring heights, which, as well as
the range of Helvellyn, further still to the right,
display the pointed and irregular forms common to
high mountains. I thought George would have gazed
his eyes out at this splendid view of the mountains
which he had been so eager to behold: the sun,
resting upon them, showed their barren sides and
bold summits to great advantage, and the slight
degree of indistinctness and softening which their
remoteness occasioned, gave them an almost unearthly
and perfectly fascinating appearance to one who saw
them for the first time. Turning eastward, the eye
follows a long chain of hills till it rests on the broad
head of Ingleborough, the prince of Yorkshire mountains, rearing his enormous bulk over the upper
extremity of the vale of the Lune. The vale itself

is fertile and beautiful, highly adorned by the winding stream, and by a majestic aqueduct which carries the canal across it by five lofty arches, at the distance of a mile and a half from the town. Both the aqueduct and bridge are here in view, and, being very fine erections, they add much to the interest of the prospect. Woods, corn-fields, meadows, villages, and mansions are beautifully disposed on the sides of the valley, and on the long slip of land which lies between the river and the Bay of Morecambe. On the south-east, the town is overlooked by heath-covered hills, but on the south-west a fine expanse of country opens, and runs down to the sea-shore.

Mrs. Anabella gazed with delight on a scene which she had once before beheld, and still faintly remembered ; and whilst she pointed out to her niece the different objects, as old friends which recalled the feelings of her youth, Matilda too caught the infection, and our whole party became quite amiable. Nevertheless, as we intended to visit the courts, it was now high time to quit this beautiful scene ; and we repaired to the Crown Court, which looked sufficiently gloomy by the contrast. This court is plain, sombre, and rather incommodious ; the " dim *judicial* light" shed into it through windows overtopped by the spike-surmounted walls of the prison, seemed not inappropriate to the dismal investigations carried on there. The presiding judge was Sir John Bayley, an amiable, upright, and independent man, but who was thought to err on the side of humanity. The court

was engaged in the trial of a man charged with
burglary, who seemed likely to escape owing to the
stupidity and hesitation with which the prosecutor
gave his evidence; the witness quailed and floundered
under the cross-examination of a noisy counsel; but
the case was helped out by the glib swearing of a
constable, and the prisoner was convicted. This trial
possessed little interest, but the sight of the barristers
in their wigs and gowns afforded infinite amusement
to Matilda, who now saw the legal attire for the first
time. She recognized some of her friends in this
disguise, but with the same astonishment as if she had
seen them in a masquerade dress. It seemed to her
of all things the most preposterous thus to disfigure
and disguise the human countenance, and she pronounced it at least as bad as the tattooing of the
New Zealanders.

From the Crown Court, we proceeded to the Nisi
Prius Court, where Mr. Baron Hullock (since deceased) presided, and where some of the most
eminent counsel of the day were wrangling about the
death of an old horse. This is a spacious and handsome Court, and contrasted very advantageously with
that which we had just quitted. The Nisi Prius
Court is, I believe, one of the most beautiful halls of
justice in the kingdom; for my own part, I have not
seen its equal. It is built after the ancient fashion,
and with Gothic ornaments; but it is exceedingly
lightsome and elegant. The form is nearly that of a
semicircle, and the Judge sits with his back to the

wall in the centre of its base : in the curve opposite to him are half a dozen tall windows, with the pointed arch and handsome mullions ; and above him are two other windows, which, being of stained glass, admit less light, but give great richness to the building. The wall is indented with niches, above which a screen carved in stone, of delicate workmanship, runs along like a string; and upon it rest two full-length portraits, very well painted, the one of Col. Stanley, and the other of Mr. Blackburne, who were the members for the county when the portraits were placed there. The roof corresponds with the Gothic character of the hall, rising upwards in a concave form, and being carved in stone, with several clustered pillars supporting it. The substantial oaken furniture, and the yeoman-like bailiffs in uniform, pacing about with their halberds, complete the venerable appearance of the Court of Common Pleas of the County Palatine of Lancaster.

Here Mrs. Anabella had the unspeakable pleasure of seeing her old friend, Mr. Brougham, and hearing one of his wittiest speeches. Before he rose, she observed to me that fifteen years had made a very perceptible alteration in his appearance. "So many sessions in the House of Commons," she said, "in which, you know, Sir, he often made his great speeches after midnight,—so many years' confinement in crowded courts like this, or in his chambers,—so many years of severe and unceasing labour, in literary and scientific studies,—so much writing, speaking, thinking, and

wrangling,—so much trouble, vexation, and fatigue,—
all undergone, you know, Sir, for the good of his
country and of mankind—all these, Sir, must have
made great inroads upon his constitution." Matilda,
who had been watching Mr. Brougham's meagre and
unprepossessing countenance, and wondering how it
could belong to so eloquent a man, here interposed—
" You know, aunt, Mr. Brougham is the god of your
idolatry—and *(aside)* I marvel at your taste—but
should you not think that, with all his patriotism and
philanthropy, he has some little regard for his
own fame and emolument ?"   Mrs. Anabella declared
with warmth that Mr. Brougham was the most public-
spirited man in the kingdom, and that he had done
more for the cause of education and for the spread
of knowledge than all the other members of Parliament
of his age.   She was proceeding to expatiate on his
great labours and achievements, when she was interrupted by his rising to reply in the horse cause.   The
speech was a series of felicitous jokes, which kept the
whole court in a roar of laughter, and had well nigh
been the death of Mrs. Anabella, who was prodigiously tickled by every pun and happy turn that fell
from her favourite orator.   Matilda, too, was delighted
by Mr. Brougham's wit and drollery, and her opinion
was very much changed in his favour, though she still
declared that he was " any thing, any thing but what
she had expected."

During this trial, George, who sat at the end of the
bench on which we were seated, was remarkably taci-

turn, and I soon discovered that he was engaged in much better employment than conversation with us. He was stealing glances at a very sweet girl who stood near him: for, though exceedingly bashful, he is a passionate admirer of beauty when he can observe it quietly. Matilda was the first to perceive how he was engaged, and she whispering to me, we watched him for a considerable time to our great entertainment. His glances became more frequent and less timid, as he thought himself perfectly unobserved. The lady was very young, with a placid and interesting countenance, and was one of those innocent creatures who can sustain, and even exchange, a look of admiration, without being excited or afflicted. George, therefore, perused her delicate features, soft, clear eye, and brow of alabaster, till it seemed almost necessary for him to speak. His bashfulness struggled for a long time, but at length, when I turned to peep at him, I saw, to my amazement, that he was standing, and the lady sitting in his place. He had plucked up courage to offer her his seat, and with a face of crimson was addressing to her some laconic observation. From want of spirit on his part, and a certain taciturnity on hers, the conversation did not become very brisk; but before the day was over I agreed in the remark which Matilda whispered in my ear, (except as to the libellous part of it) that " George was over head and ears in love with a doll." She rallied him unmercifully in the evening, but I hope he received ample atonement from his dreams.

We remained five days in Lancaster, two of which we spent in the courts. We heard the trial of a young woman, named Jane Scott, of Preston, a monster of iniquity, who had poisoned her father and mother for the sake of obtaining a trifling sum with which to tempt her paramour to marry her. She was first tried for the parricide, but was acquitted from an accidental defect in the evidence. At the following Assize she was tried for the matricide, convicted, and executed; and before her execution she confessed that she had also murdered an illegitimate child of her own, and a child of her sister's. This wretched murderess was a compound of brutal ignorance, sensuality, and hypocrisy,—one of the most awful instances of the depravity of human nature.

In the Nisi Prius Court we heard the trial of an indictment against the Mersey and Irwell Navigation Company, preferred by the Corporation of Liverpool, for nuisances in the erection of extensive works connected with the canals of the Company, which were calculated, according to the allegation of the prosecutors, to injure the navigation of the river Mersey. Mr. Brougham was the leading counsel for the prosecution, and Sir James Scarlett, then the Attorney-General, was brought down by special retainer for the defendants. Both these eminent counsel put forth their strength. Mr. Brougham made an eloquent speech; and Sir James cross-examined, spoke, and manœuvred with matchless dexterity. The evidence for the prosecution was so defective, and that for the defence so strong, that the Jury stopped the examination of the witnesses, and returned a verdict for the defendants. Mrs. Anabella, however, to this day believes that the verdict ought to have been the other way; she commends Mr. Brougham's speech as equally eloquent and unanswerable, and remembers with considerable bitterness the triumphant and arrogant air of the Attorney-General.*

* For various statistical details connected with Lancaster—an account of its population, buildings, trade, inns, distance from London and the principal towns at the Lakes, and the seats of the neighbouring gentry, see the ITINERARY at the end of the volume. The Tourist will find it useful frequently to consult the Itinerary, as it includes many particulars which would have encumbered the narrative and descriptive parts of the work, and are therefore omitted in the COMPANION, but which will materially add to the information of the traveller. He will find there every considerable village, most of the gentlemen's seats, and all the objects worthy of notice, in the stages from town to town, and on all the routes at the Lakes.

CHAPTER IV.

FROM LANCASTER TO KIRKBY LONSDALE—PARTING VIEW OF THE
BAY OF MORECAMBE—AQUEDUCT—VALE OF THE LUNE—
CROOK OF LUNE—SPLENDID PROSPECT—HORNBY CASTLE—
DERIVATIONS OF NAMES—BRIDGE AT KIRKBY LONSDALE—
VIEW FROM THE CHURCH-YARD—UNDERLEY PARK—SUNSET.

AFTER a very agreeable sojourn at Lancaster, we
quitted our kind friends, to prosecute the main
object of our tour, in a visit to the Lakes. It was a
lovely morning, and we were all in the highest
spirits, for we had become weary of sitting in court,
and, the novelty of the thing having passed off, my
cousins found their curiosity fully satisfied with law
and lawyers. Their eagerness to see the Lakes, for
some time repressed, now revived with great ardour.
The fineness of the weather also relieved them from
considerable solicitude, as the preceding day had been
dull and rainy, and they had been alarmed lest they
should enter the hill country without seeing its beauties.
For two days the Westmoreland mountains had been
concealed or dimly visible, and a south-west wind
had driven the streaming clouds just over the tops of
the black hills south of Lancaster, occasionally cover-

ing the highest of them with a misty cap. This morning there were only a few fleecy clouds lying high in the blue heaven,

" In beauteous semblance of a flock at rest;"

and the wind, having gone about to the north, gave us assurance that the weather would continue favourable, at least for some time.

Who has not felt the exhilarating effects of such a change? Who does not know that the mind of him who waits for the sun-shine, sympathizes with the changeful face of the sky?—is darkened by gloomy forebodings when the heavens are overcast,—is cheered by the beamings of hope when the clouds break and disperse,—fluctuates with the shifting wind,—and brightens into joy and confidence when the sun reigns alone in the firmament? But in a mountainous country these feelings are unusually lively: you come there for out-of-doors pleasures, and when the weather keeps you prisoner in the house, you are nearly destitute of resources, and have nothing to do but to sigh for a change. The more beautiful the landscape, the more mortifying it is to see it blurred, and in great part hidden, by dark masses of cloud and streaming showers: and afterwards the more delightful to see the mourning veil uplifted, and the clear eye of heaven and the lovely face of nature shine forth in renovated splendour.

We had had some discussion the previous evening as to the route we should pursue to Kendal,—whether

the shorter one of Milnthorpe, or the more interesting and beautiful route by the vale of the Lune and
Kirkby Lonsdale. The former is recommended by the
fine view it occasionally affords of the sea and the mountains, and by the scenery in the neighbourhood of
Milnthorpe—the parks of Dallam Tower and Levens
Hall. The latter, however, as leading us through
one of the richest and finest valleys in England, and
through the pleasant town of Kirkby, was preferred.
There is still a third route, which might have been
taken with advantage, namely, over the sands to
Ulverston, so as to see Furness Abbey and Coniston
Water before coming to Windermere. George earnestly
advocated this route, which I myself was disposed to
recommend; but such was the terror of the ladies on
being told that they would have to ford two considerable rivers, where the water was so deep as sometimes
to enter the bottom of the carriage, that we were
obliged to keep on *terra firma.**

From a rising ground near Lancaster we had a
parting view of the Bay of Morecambe. The expanse of waters, of a deep lead colour, fretted and
partially whitened by the breeze, looked most refreshing, and at the same time awakened that feeling
of the sublime, which any fine view of the sea

* The route "over sands" is described in the "Tour on Horseback," forming the second part of the "COMPANION." Those
who wish to visit Furness before seeing the rest of the Lakes—
which is desirable for all who have sufficient time—may also go
from Lancaster to Ulverston by Milnthorpe and Newby bridge,
which is sixteen miles longer than the route "over sands.'

inevitably produces. The tide was up, and the sands, which are so firm as to be crossed by carriages, at ebb-tide, some miles below high-water mark, were now entirely covered. So extensive are the sands left dry at the ebb in this shallow Bay, that the portion of Lonsdale Hundred lying to the north of them is called *Lonsdale North of the Sands.* But at present the waves advanced and spilt their foam on the very edge of the green fields; and boats scudded about, with their well-filled sails almost dipping in the water, in many parts of the Bay. The white houses and smoke of Ulverston were distinctly visible, and the eye followed the coast, from the rugged hills of Cumberland and the dome of Black Comb, to the low tongue of land at the mouth of the Bay, on which stands Pile Castle. Further still, in the open sea, we discerned a faint line of smoke, which indicated the passing of a steam-boat.

Leaving this fine view and the noble castle of Lancaster behind us, we took the road to Kirkby Lonsdale. A mile from the town we had a near view of the aqueduct which carries the canal over the Lune. " I understand," said George, " that this is considered the finest aqueduct in the kingdom: it was built by the late Mr. Rennie, the celebrated engineer, and the laying of the foundation alone cost £15,000 : owing to the softness of the earth, it was necessary to drive piles to a very great depth, and to lay a wooden platform upon them, on which the stone foundation was laid. The whole work is said to have cost more than £50,000." "Is not the aqueduct of Pont y Cys-syllte," I asked, "which conveys the Ellesmere canal across the Dee and the valley of Llangollen, in Wales, a greater work? I have only seen it from a distance, but I counted seventeen or eighteen arches, which seemed to me considerably higher than these."*

"I have not seen the aqueduct you speak of," rejoined my cousin, "but this ranks amongst the finest works of the kind in Europe. Its height is fifty-one feet from the surface of the river to the sur-face of the canal, and the length nearly seven hundred feet; and, as you perceive, a vast embankment is made in connexion with the aqueduct, to carry the canal across the valley." "Rennie!" said Matilda, "I think I have heard of him before; was he not originally a poor man?" "He was the son of a Scotch farmer," replied George, "and rose by his own genius, like Smeaton and Brindley, to the highest eminence as an engineer. The celebrated James Watt was one of the first to appreciate and bring forth his merit. Rennie has immortalized himself by the Breakwater at Plymouth, and by Waterloo and Southwark bridges at London: I have not seen any of those works; but I have often heard you say, William,†

---

* Pont y Cyssyllte is both higher and longer than the Lancaster aqueduct; it consists of nineteen arches; its height is a hundred and twenty-six feet, and its length a thousand feet; but it is much narrower than the Lancaster aqueduct, and of a less firm and solid construction. Its cost would probably be less.

† This is the name by which the author is mentioned throughout the book.

that you think Waterloo bridge a sublime monument of art." "It is indeed," I said: "I have seen nothing of the kind equal to it for combined simplicity, symmetry, majesty, and strength."

We soon came to a part of the valley where it makes a bend, and opens out into a finer expanse. Here the river sweeps so completely round as nearly to form a circle, on which account the place is designated the *Crook of Lune.* The view from this spot has long been famous, and, in order to see it to the best advantage, we left the carriage three miles and a quarter from Lancaster, and, passing through a field on our right, climbed up a craggy hill, in the side of which a stone quarry has been worked. The ascent was very toilsome to Mrs. Anabella, but the prospect richly repaid her for the exertion.

The Lune lay far beneath us, sweeping round the foot of a wooded hill, and enclosing within its dark broad circle a peninsula covered with grass and fern. Beyond, for many a mile, stretched the rich and open valley, fertilized by the river, which was seen winding through it in graceful curves. On the left side of the valley rose a high and steep hill, wrapped in a mantle of wood; on the right the hills are more rugged. Some miles before us we saw Hornby castle, on a hill of moderate elevation, on one side of which branches off the valley of the Lune, and on the other that of the Wenning, like the fork of a Y. And, as the magnificent back-ground of the landscape, rises the vast form of Ingleborough, whose broad and lofty head

' The semblance of a royal crown has on,'

which fits him to preside over so noble a scene.

Gray speaks in the highest terms of this prospect; he says that "every feature which constitutes a perfect landscape of the extensive sort is here not only boldly marked, but also in its best position."* He saw it, however, from a field on the left of the road, which must be much lower than the station we climbed to, and cannot therefore have so commanding a view of the valley. Mrs. Anabella informed us that Queen Elizabeth had pronounced this the finest prospect in her dominions. From these two high authorities we felt little inclined to differ.

Passing through several pleasant villages we came to Hornby, a small market-town near the confluence of the Wenning and the Lune, and saw on the hill which rises above the town, the castle, part of which is ancient and belonged to the Barons Monteagle. The keep of the ancient castle remains, but just in front of it a modern house has been built, which conceals this interesting relic of antiquity from the passing spectator. Two miles beyond, we passed Thurland

---

* Gray visited this part in returning from his solitary tour in Cumberland and Westmoreland, of which he gives a brief but pleasing account in a journal kept for the amusement of his friend, Dr. Wharton, who had been prevented by illness from accompanying him. He made this tour in the autumn of 1769, when he was in a poor state of health, and less than two years before his death.

castle, the seat of Mr. North : it is a fine old massive structure, and stood a siege in the Civil Wars of Charles I. The valley continues highly fertile and beautiful, though with no striking objects—Ingleborough being no longer within view—till we come to the immediate neighbourhood of Kirkby Lonsdale.

In this ride George, who had been dipping into a book of antiquities which he found in the library of our friend at Lancaster, enlightened his aunt and sister as to the derivations of the names of many of the places we had passed through or were approaching. Preston, he said, was a corruption of *Priests' town,* so called from being a kind of head-quarters for the Roman Catholics. Lancaster was the Roman fortified station on the Lune, whose ancient name was *Lon* or Loyne ; the town was therefore called *Longovicum,* and also *Lon-caster*—camp on the Lon (whence Lancaster); as *Rib-caster,* (now Ribchester) was the fortified station of the Romans on the Ribble. Lonsdale, the name of the Hundred of Lancashire we were traversing, derived its name from the fine valley by which it is intersected from the borders of Westmoreland and Yorkshire to the sea. The *Dale* of *Lon,* now generally called the vale of the Lune, thus gave name to the Hundred, and also to the town of Kirkby Lonsdale, which signified the *kirk* (church) *town* in the *dale* of *Lon.* Kendal, of which the correct name was Kirkby in Kendal, also signified the *kirk town* in the *dale* of *Ken* or Kent. As for the name of the county we were approaching, Westmoreland, there were, he said, two probable

etymologies, besides many improbable ones ; the first
was, that it implied *the land of the Western moors*,
which etymology was adopted by Camden ; and the
second, which was founded on the ancient spelling of
the word, *Westmerland*, was, that it signified *the land
of the Western meres*, or lakes—*mere* being the Saxon
word for lake, and being retained in many of the
names to the present day, as Windermere, Grasmere,
Thirlmere, &c.

When we came to the bridge over the Lune, at
the entrance of Kirkby Lonsdale, (where we also
entered Westmoreland) we got out of the carriage and
sent it forward to the inn, whilst we proceeded to
inspect and admire the curious construction of the
bridge, and the prospect of the river and valley from
this place.   The spot is truly romantic.   The river, of
considerable width, rolls in the bottom of the valley,
and is overshadowed by the trees that grow upon its
banks.   Its current is roughened by the rocks which
form its bed, and some of which stand up in huge
moss-grown blocks in the midst of the stream.   The
water is clear to a great depth, though of a deep amber
colour, indicating that it has flowed from peat-covered
hills.   The steep grassy banks and the abundance of
trees close in the prospect, and give it an air of seclusion.   This is a good trout and salmon stream,
and, both on account of its fish and its natural
beauties, it would have charmed the scientific author
of "Salmonia."*   The bridge is of immemorial
antiquity : it is a long, lofty, firm, and handsome

* The late Sir Humphry Davy.

structure, but so narrow as almost to deserve the taunt cast upon the " auld brig of Ayr,"'

" Where twa wheelbarrows trembled when they met."

At least no two carriages of a larger size can pass each other ; but, for the security of foot passengers, there are angular recesses in the battlements, corresponding with the projecting piers. The bridge has three arches, which are ribbed, and of remarkable beauty : the centre arch rises twelve yards above the stream.

Like many other very clever works executed in difficult circumstances, this bridge has been ascribed to the devil, who has been a bridge-builder time out of mind. It seems improbable, indeed, as was observed by Mrs. Anabella, that that personage should employ himself in works of so much real utility to men. Nevertheless there is a tradition in the neighbourhood, that he built the bridge one windy night, and that in fetching the stones from a distance, he let fall the last apron-full as he flew over a fell hard by. This very probable story accounts for the huge blocks of stone found on some of those elevated moors.

From the bridge we walked up the hill into Kirkby Lonsdale—a neat, clean, stone-built town, with an excellent inn. Having ordered dinner, we proceeded to the church-yard, from which there is a charming and splendid prospect. On the brow of the hill is a seat shaded with trees, whence we looked down upon a deep and luxuriant valley. The hill on the summit of which we were seated descends headlong to the river, which rolls at a depth of nearly two hundred feet below, and sweeps with a majestic bend through the vale. On the opposite hill, which is higher than that of Kirkby Lonsdale, are the fine woods and lawns of Casterton-hall, (the seat of Wm. Wilson Carus Wilson, Esq.) combining the richness of the park with almost the boldness of mountain scenery. The eye, pursuing the valley upwards, reaches the fells of Sedbergh, and, in the opposite direction, follows a range of heath-covered hills, which are terminated by the bold front of Ingleborough. The noble woods which hang upon the sides of this valley, and the clear winding stream that flows through it, give an uncommon richness to a land-scape the principal features of which are simple and grand.

In the evening we visited the church-yard a second time, and walked forward to Underley-park, the seat of Mr. Nowell. The path leads for some distance along the brow of the hill, commanding delightful views of the valley, and then gradually descends towards Underley-park, which lies nearly on a level with the river. The distance is about a mile. Mr. Nowell's house has been erected only a few years ; it is an extensive and handsome structure, built of the finest stone, and principally in the old English style, but with a Grecian portico. The grounds were in a neglected state, being not yet finished.

In returning we saw a fine effect of sunshine on the heath-covered hills beyond Casterton-hall. A mass of clouds had long obscured the descent of the sun towards the horizon, but a gleam of red light on the distant fells told us that he was to have a glorious setting. We were so situated that we could not see the sun himself, and the hill-side upon which we stood formed a vast shadow; but this only heightened the effect of the glare on the opposite hills, which were lit up with uncommon splendour, less resembling the usual effect of sunshine than the reflection of an enormous conflagration. From Casterton-hall, quite along to the head of Ingleborough, the hills seemed bathed in a flood of crimson light. The clouds above caught the same rich hue, and made the whole scene one of nature's most resplendent pictures. We lingered in our walk, and dwelt with delight on a scene so rarely equalled. I compared it to a sunset in Italy, where, in the words of Byron—

> ——— " Parting Day
> Dies like the dolphin, whom each pang imbues
> With a new colour as it gasps away,
> The last still loveliest, till—'tis gone—and all is grey."

CHAPTER V.

On the following morning we left Kirkby Lonsdale,
immediately after breakfast, for Kendal, intending to
make a short stay in that town, and to reach Bowness,
on the lake of Windermere, in time for dinner. In
quitting Kirkby Lonsdale we had a fine view of the
Sedbergh fells, but the rest of the stage, till we came
to the neighbourhood of Kendal, was not particularly
interesting.

The vale of the Kent is lively and fertile, but by
no means equal in beauty to that of the Lune. As
we looked down upon it, we saw the town of Kendal,
lying at the foot of a steep fell, called Underbarrow
Scar.* It was partly concealed from us by a round
grassy hill, which rises in the midst of the valley,
and on the top of which stand the ruins of Kendal

---

* Scar signifies a *brow of naked rocks*, and is applied to most
of those ridges the summit of which is fronted by a line of perpendicular crags.

castle. Looking up the valley, we saw the high mountains among which the river Kent takes its rise. The most remarkable of them is Hill Bell, a mountain with a conical and verdant summit, which forms a beautiful and commanding object from the lake of Windermere. The hill nearest to us in that direction is Potter Fell. Stretching away to the left is a splendid range of mountains, including those of the Langdale and Coniston districts, and among which Langdale Pikes, Bowfell, Scawfell Pikes, Wrynose, Wetherlam, and the Old Man, were conspicuous ; but I shall not now describe their appearance more particularly, as we afterwards saw the same range from a nearer point between Kendal and Bowness.

As we approached Kendal, a light carriage passed us at considerable speed. I observed that George, who at that moment was sitting forward, looked eagerly at the persons in the carriage, and that his cheek was slightly flushed when he saw them. He pretended, however, not to know who they were, having had a mere glimpse, from which he only saw that there were two ladies and a gentleman. When we arrived at the King's Arms, the same carriage, having changed horses, was just driving off ; but Matilda had time to see the persons within, and exclaimed, almost loud enough to be heard by them— " There's George's flame—I suspected as much by his blushing." George, who I believe had not been quite assured of this happy fact, looked half-pleased and half abashed, but chid Matilda warmly for speaking

so loud, and protested that he neither knew nor
cared any thing about that young lady, whoever she
might be, except that he gave her his seat in court,
rather than see her stand all day. When, however,
Matilda afterwards asked him plumply if he had not
been inquiring of the postillion the name of the
gentleman whose carriage had driven off, he was
obliged to confess that he had, and it was forthwith
voted that all his pretended indifference was a cloak
for a very tender feeling.

We stayed in Kendal about a couple of hours, which
allowed us time to look round the town, and pay a
hurried visit to the castle. Kendal lies, as has been
mentioned, beneath the lee of a scar, or lofty perpendicular cliff, which overlooks the town on the west side,
whilst the river runs in the valley on the east, and
beyond it is the castle-hill. The castle is well worth
visiting, both from the situation, and from the interest
always attaching to the venerable relics of former days.
Its appearance, however, is more imposing from a distance than close at hand. The walls are circular, and
have been surrounded by a deep fosse, over which there
is an entrance on the west. There are remains of
three towers, two of them circular, and also traces
of a keep; but, excepting these, all is a mere shell.
The castle belonged, in the fifteenth and sixteenth
centuries, to the family of Parr, or Parre, one of whose
members, Catherine, the daughter of Sir Thomas, was
raised to the throne of England—being the last wife
of Henry VIII.

Kendal is the seat of an ancient woollen manufacture, to which it was long indebted for a steady prosperity. This manufacture was founded in the fourteenth century, when Flemish weavers were invited to settle in this country, at the same time that the exportation of English wool was prohibited. Kendal was one of the few towns in which these foreign importers of the woollen manufacture took up their abode. The woollens made here were coarse, and, what is remarkable, they went by the name of *Kendal Cottons* at a much earlier period than the real cotton manufacture was known in England. Of late years the manufacture of coarse woollens has greatly declined, owing to the successful competition of the Yorkshire manufacturers ; and a finer kind of goods is now made here, consisting principally of fancy waistcoatings. Leather is also extensively manufactured ; and there is an establishment for the cutting of marble, of which several different kinds are found in Kendal fell. As the country people for many miles round attend the market, this town combines the character of a manufacturing place with that of the centre of an agricultural district.

Kendal contains nearly 12,000 inhabitants, and is the most populous and wealthy town in Westmoreland. It is a neat, clean, and agreeable place ; and consists principally of one good street, a mile in length, running parallel with the river, with a few small streets branching from it at right angles. The church is a handsome and spacious Gothic structure, and contains many monuments of the Parrs, the Stricklands, the Bellinghams, and other old families of the neighbourhood. Near it stands Abbot-hall, the seat of Christopher Wilson, Esq. which derives its name from having heen the occasional residence of the Abbot of St. Mary's, York, before the dissolution of monasteries.

The greater number of persons who visit the Lakes pass through Kendal. The quakers are a numerous and highly respectable body here; and Mr. Brougham's greatest strength, in his contests with the Lowthers for the representation of Westmoreland, always lay amongst the independent " grey coats" of Kendal. For this cause Mrs. Anabella has the highest respect 1or the town, and looked, I thought, upon every person she met in the streets with peculiar benevolence, as probably a fellow-worshipper of the great orator.*

From Kendal to Bowness, a distance of nine miles, the road is excessively uneven, and, after leaving the valley of the Kent, passes over a barren, rugged, and desolate tract. I had not gone by this road on any of my former visits to the Lakes, but either to Newby bridge, or along the Ambleside road, so as to come down upon Windermere a mile or two above Bowness. I had, however, afterwards visited that place, in which I had the advantage of Mrs. Anabella, who, having made a flying expedition round the Lakes, had taken the high road to Ambleside, so as only to see

* Kendal received by the Reform Act the privilege of sending one Member to Parliament; and the first Member was James Brougham, Esq., brother of Lord Brougham; on the death of this gentleman in December, 1833, John Barham, Esq. was elected.

Windermere at its upper extremity. My fellow travellers were not prepared for the uninteresting moorland over which our road now lay, but I ventured to promise them an ample compensation before the day was over. Nor was the journey altogether disagreeable, for, as it lay over the high ground between Windermere and Kendal, we enjoyed very extensive views of the Westmoreland, Cumberland, and Lancashire mountains, which, being harmonized by distance, seemed to form one grand chain, encircling half the horizon. We spread out our map, therefore, and began to trace them upon it,—a task which my cousins found much more difficult than they had anticipated, owing to the great number of hills which rose before us, and their ignorance of the respective distances. I distinctly recognized most of the principal summits, but my companions were generally very wide of the truth in their guesses.

George was unspeakably delighted when he had ascertained the names and positions of these fine mountains. I repeated my lesson several times at his instance—" The lofty and pointed mountain in the distance, nearly opposite to us, but a little to the northward, is Coniston Old Man, which rises over the head of the lake of Coniston, and is the pride of Furness ; more to the north is the broad back of Wetherlam ; then Wrynose ; still further is the pointed and rocky summit of Bowfell, a mountain nearly 3000 feet high, which stands at the head of Great Langdale. The two remarkable peaks which

you see next, one of them pointed and the other
ending in a blunt knob, are Langdale Pikes. Considerably further to the right is Loughrigg fell, at
the head of Windermere, comparatively a low hill;
then the lofty Fairfield, and then Scandale and
Wansfell; which brings us round to Hill Bell, the
conical mountain we saw from the other side of Kendal." "What," inquired George, "are those faintly-
marked and confused summits which seem to be beyond
Bowfell? They must be very lofty." "They are
the highest mountains in England—Scawfell and
Scawfell Pikes, which, you will find from the map,
are considerably further from us than Bowfell: they
stand at the head of Wasdale. Great Gavel may also
be seen more to the right." I soon found that George
had an excellent memory for places and objects;
having once learnt the form and situation of a mountain, he never forgot it: whereas his sister, though
for other matters she had a retentive memory, was
very dull in learning localities, and forgot one day
what she had learnt the preceding. These varieties
in the faculty of memory are rendered very manifest
in a mountainous country: I suppose a phrenologist
would discover that in George's skull the organ of
locality was large, and in Matilda's very small.

During our ride great impatience was displayed by
our party to obtain a view of Windermere—the first,
as well as the largest of the lakes. George sat forward in the carriage, straining his eyes to discover
the wished-for object. When we were only half-way

to Bowness, he suddenly ejaculated "Windermere!" and was pleasing himself with the thought that he had been the first to see the lake; but the postillion damped his joy by telling him that the water he saw was the river Kent at Milnthorpe. The ladies were in great terror at the steepness of some of the hills we descended, which might well alarm persons accustomed to the most level part of Lancashire; but before we had finished our tour, they learnt to view the descents with more calmness, and to trust more to the strength of the horses and the skill of the postillions.

Our first view of Windermere was from the brow of a hill, which looks down immediately upon the lake, and from which we saw it nearly in its whole extent. An exclamation of delight burst from our party when the first view of the water presented itself; but this was immediately followed by silence, and we were all busily employed in looking right and left at the long-expected and interesting object. Very few remarks were made in descending the steep hill to Bowness; for in truth we all felt, though none of us expressed the sentiment till some time afterwards, a little disappointment at the *coup d'œil.* Various circumstances contributed to produce this feeling. Having come upon the lake at its centre, and having understood that this was the largest of the English lakes, my companions had expected to see a magnificent expanse of water. But unluckily this is the narrowest part, and in the very midst of it runs an island three quarters of a mile long, which, being covered with wood, partially conceals the water beyond it, and looks like the further shore. Add to this, the effect of the woody promontories which run into the lake on either side, and of the dark and lofty hill that rises precipitously from the opposite bank, both of which tend still further to diminish the apparent breadth of the water; and it is not surprising that my cousins should have thought that Windermere looked only like a considerable river. Another circumstance still contributed to their disappointment. It was afternoon, and the sun was declining towards the opposite hill, whose shaded side was presented to us; and this, combined with a considerable degree of sun-haziness, gave an indistinctness to the objects which lay below us in the valley. In the morning the scene would have been incomparably finer. Having done much to raise the expectations of our party, I felt some anxiety about the impression which would be made upon them; and, as I knew that the view from the lake itself was far more striking than that from the hill above Bowness, (at least under the circumstances in which we had seen it) I was desirous of getting them into a boat as soon as possible.*

* The hill from which we obtained the first sight of the lake commands one of the finest general views of Windermere, but the best point is nearly a mile north of the Kendal road, in the rear of Bowness. The chief causes of our disappointment were, first, the dimness of the atmosphere, which is always most perceptible in looking down from an elevated situation; and second, the height of the two hills that hem in this part of the lake, and which, to an eye unaccustomed to mountain scenery, makes all objects appear much smaller than they really are.

Windermere (more correctly, but less commonly written Winandermere) is nearly 11 miles in length, and has an average breadth of three quarters of a mile. The lake runs north and south, with a very slight curve near the centre. The middle and lower parts of the lake lie between bold and steep hills : that on the west, called Furness fell, is clothed in woods of larch and fir ; that on the east rises with a rugged surface into crags and heath-covered fells. The lake is contracted towards its foot, where its undulating shores are adorned with forest trees ; and it pours out its waters by the river Leven at Newby-bridge. Towards the head the hills recede, leaving a broad but irregular margin of woods, meadows, and lawns, beautifully spread over a waving surface, and affording the most delightful situations for gentlemen's seats. The lake is a mile in width in the upper part, and presents a very fine expanse of water. Around the head stand lofty mountains, which combine gracefulness with boldness of form. Windermere contains fourteen islands, most of them forming a cluster near the middle. Both the shores are cultivated in the intervals of the plantations, and adorned with handsome mansions, which heighten the natural beauty of the scenery, and contribute to give to the queen of English lakes a character of unequalled richness and elegance.

The village or small town of Bowness,* by far

* Formerly Bulness : the termination *ness*, (*nese*, Sax. *nose*,) which signifies *point* or *promontory*, indicates that the town is *near* a promontory, though it is also situated upon a bay.

the most considerable, and perhaps the most beautifully situated, of any on the borders of the Lake,
stands on uneven ground rising somewhat rapidly
from a semicircular bay.   Its whitened church and
houses, appearing amongst the trees which adorn the
village, have a charming effect; and, as we drove up
to the White Lion, the mixture of rustic simplicity
and irregularity with cultivated taste, in the flowers
and gardens which ornamented the fronts of the
houses, made my cousins pronounce it a very sweet
spot.

We were lucky in obtaining bed-rooms which
looked upon the lake, but our parlour fronted towards
the village.   We ordered dinner immediately on entering the house, and, that being about the usual
dinner-hour, the preparations were so far made that
we were able to sit down to table as soon as the
ceremonies of unpacking and dressing had been gone
through.   An excellent dinner, in which the rarest
and most delicious dish was char fresh from the lake,
was served up.   We lost very little time at the
dessert, but, having made an agreement with a boatman to take us to the Station, we entered the boat
about an hour before sunset.

The very first view of the lake obtained from the
level of its own surface, impressed my cousins most
favourably.   They were now aware that the long slip
of land which lay opposite to us was an island, and,
on observing more attentively the trees on the hill
which formed the actual boundary of the lake, they

found that the hill was considerably higher and further distant, and the lake consequently wider, than they had supposed. Our view of the water was circumscribed by the woody promontories which flank the bay of Bowness, and by a large island called Belle Isle, or Curwen's Island; yet it was a lovely and even fascinating view. The profusion and extreme beauty of the wood upon the island and shores,—the clear and glassy surface of the lake, reflecting all the objects upon its borders,—the majestic hill and forest which rose in front of us,—the perfect placidity and still seclusion of this hill-embosomed view, not disturbed, yet enlivened, by the tiny marine reposing at anchor in the bay, and consisting of a few fishing vessels and elegant pleasure-boats,—all tended to inspire the mind with serene admiration and delight.

For some time after we had pushed off, we were employed in observing the limpid clearness of the water, which enabled us to see the bottom at the depth of several yards. Shoals of small fish, suspended in the pure element, were gliding gracefully about, keeping together like migrating flocks of birds, and, when alarmed by the splash of the oars, darting into the subaqueous forests of weeds, which grow to a great height round the bay. Sometimes large dark-coloured fish were seen alone, pursuing their silent, thief-like course, as monsters of prey prowling round the skirts of a wood, and, when alarmed by the approach of man, plunging into the thicket. Whilst we observed these tenants of the lake, and the rocks and aquatic plants amongst which they were moving, Matilda said this was a sight she had not calculated upon, and she did not know whether the prospect beneath or around was the more pleasing.

When we passed out of the bay of Bowness, the water deepened so as to deprive us of any further observations of this kind. But as we rowed along the channel which lies between Belle Isle and the shore, fresh beauties opened upon us every instant. The island itself is a scene of fairy elegance. Its verdant eminences slope down in lawns to the very brink of the water, which is skirted, for the whole length of the strand, with trees of every form and hue. The graceful willow droops its streamers into the lake; the elegant larch springs up towards heaven; the sombre and matted tufts of the fir-tree contrast with the freely-waving foliage of the yellow ash; and the delicate twigs and silvered bark of the birch set off the sturdy and gnarled branches of the oak. The beech, the plane, and the chesnut also abound among the forest trees; and aged yews and hawthorns are scattered upon the lawns. The green island, thus exquisitely fringed, is set, as it were, in the mirror of the lake, which reflects from its bosom every shape and colour with perfect fidelity. Out of the midst of the trees rises a cupola, which indicates the mansion of Henry Curwen, Esq., the proprietor of the island.* As we passed, all was perfect stillness,

* Mr. Curwen is the son of the late John Christian Curwen, Esq., M. P. for Cumberland, who bought this island from Mr.

except the occasional baying of a large hound belonging to the island, and we felt the calmness of the scene infused into our spirits; but as we returned, a party of Italian musicians were sounding their timbrels and guitars on the lawn in front of the house, and the merry tunes came dancing over the lake, and seemed to fill with melodious sound what before was all harmony to the eye.

Having passed the island, and what I have called the channel, as we approached the Ferry, about a mile to the south of Bowness, the lake opened out on both sides into an expanse which may be termed magnificent. On our right, and to the rear of the island, the waters form a bay which washes the foot of the steep hill opposite Bowness; and on our left the lake makes a corresponding indentation of the shore. The Ferry has been established where two promontories advance towards each other from the opposite sides of the lake, and form a strait, below which there is again a fine sweep of about a mile, to the promontory of Storrs, on which stands the handsome mansion of John Bolton, Esq. The evening was bright and beautiful: all the haze we had seen in looking down from the hill, when the sun was just in our eyes, had passed away; the lake was as clear and tranquil as the blue

English about the year 1790, and laid it out in the present tasteful manner. Mr. Curwen also planted Furness fell with larch, of which valuable tree he had at one time planted a greater quantity than any landed proprietor in the kingdom. Visiters are allowed to land upon Belle Isle, and to walk round it—a circuit of two miles.

heaven which it reflected, and the sun shed his last glory over the scene ere he sank behind the mountain top.

We had time, before the sun set, to reach the Station, a small house of observation built on the top of a wooded rock, which rises behind the Ferry-house, on the west side of the lake.   From this point nearly the whole extent of the "liquid vale" may be seen, from Newby bridge at the southern extremity, almost up to Ambleside at the northern. A richer landscape of wood and water cannot be pictured by the imagination of man.   The glassy lake returns the heaven and the mountains, enriched by the reflection.   The islands, the promontories, the hills are all covered with wood, yet endlessly varied, from the natural thicket which feathers the islets, and the regular grove that environs the mansions on the shore, to the solemn forest of larch and fir with which the hills are mantled.   Southward the landscape is graceful without boldness; but the head of the lake is surrounded by lofty mountains, which are sufficiently near to impart magnificence to the view.   The windows of the Station are partly filled with stained glass of several colours, by looking through which you see the lake as it appears in the four seasons of the year. The green glass imparts to the landscape the fresh vernal hue; the yellow throws over it the full brilliance of a summer's noon-tide; the orange invests it with the mellow tints of autumn; and the light blue gives the pale, chill, snowy aspect of winter.

Perhaps nothing is more impressive, in the contemplation of this exquisite scene, than the perfect calm and death-like stillness which reigns over the whole. At this time not a breeze stirred,—not even the faintest sound reached the ear,—nothing moved ; the lake lay below us clear and bright, but so unruffled that it seemed like one vast mirror without a flaw.   The preternatural silence, combined with the ravishing beauty of the scene, gave us the impression of a vision, or an Elysium peopled rather by shades than by mortal men.   Our party were even oppressed with emotion ; the tears gathered in Matilda's eyes, and she afterwards declared that she felt a mixture of awe and transport which she never before experienced.

We descended from the Station, and returned with the deepening twilight to Bowness, all delighted by the scenery we had beheld, and Mrs. Anabella, Matilda, and George uniting to declare, that their highest expectations had fallen far beneath the reality.

CHAPTER VI.

MORNING VIEW OF WINDERMERE—GEORGE'S DREAMS—TOMB
OF BISHOP WATSON—WATER EXCURSION—THE ISLANDS—
SPLENDID VIEW FROM RAYRIGG BANK—PROFESSOR WILSON
—THE LAKE POETS—HOLMS—BELLE ISLE.

Our party assembled before breakfast in the morning on the grass-plot in front of our windows, which commanded a full view of Windermere. The sun was already on his march, and was busily employed in drinking up the vapour which hung about the tops and sides of the mountains, as if he meant to have " all heaven to himself." When we first saw the hills at the head of the lake,—Fairfield, Scandale, Hill Bell, and others,—they were half enveloped in white clouds; but, as we watched them, the clouds streamed up their sides like smoke; and though occasionally a fleece or two, which hung from the ragged edge of the cloudy mantle, seemed to drop down to a lower position, the tendency on the whole was upwards; and with great delight we saw them slowly uncover ridge after ridge, and summit after summit, till they left the whole cluster of hills without a vapour, and were dissipated in the higher regions of the atmosphere. A gentle breeze produced a ripple on the surface of the lake, and gave us a sensation of delightful freshness. We now saw the hills on the opposite side of the lake, and every object upon them, with the most perfect distinctness; and indeed so much difference does the position of the sun make in such a country as this, by the manner in which the shadows are cast, and the objects brought out, that you can scarcely be said to have the same view in the morning as you have in the evening. When the eye has been long accustomed to the scene, the difference is less perceived, but to a stranger it is very remarkable. A distant boat struck Matilda as a pretty and interesting object: it could scarcely have been discerned but for the long wedge-like track which it left behind in the waters, and which conducted the eye to the dark point at its apex; one felt inclined to pity the insignificance of the object, though, for any thing we knew, there might be, in that nutshell vessel, a cargo of passengers more important in their own eyes, and in their own circle, than all the world besides.

At breakfast George told us that he had scarcely had a quarter of an hour's sound sleep all night. The visions of his imagination had kept him lively and restless. He had been surrounded by mountains reaching up to heaven, and woods richer than tropical forests: he had been wandering up and down in the valley of Rasselas: he had walked under the crystal waters, and visited the grottoes of the Naiads: he had been a willing prisoner in enchanted islands, had heard the song of the syrens, and been intoxicated

by the charms of Calypso : he had peeped through the
windows of Elysium, and seen its immortal bowers :
he had navigated seas of glass in the shell of the
nautilus.   In short, every object he had seen the preceding day had risen up in his imagination during the
night, magnified, coloured, distorted, associated at
random with a thousand objects previously in his
memory, and quite uncontrolled by reason.   When
George had related to us his " visions of the night"
with a copious eloquence which showed that he had
been under strong impressions, Matilda asked him if
he would have the goodness to tell her whom Calypso
looked like ?—what was the colour of her eyes and
the shape of her features ?   George's face was instantly flushed, and, in spite of himself, there was a
smile of pleasure on his lips ; at which we all laughed
heartily, and Matilda said, she did not wonder at his
not sleeping, or at his being intoxicated, or at his
seeing Elysium ; but she wanted to know whether
Calypso was at Low Wood or at Ambleside, because
it was very necessary for us to avoid so dangerous a
personage.   It will be long before George is allowed to
forget Calypso.

After breakfast we summoned our boatman, and
consulted him as to the best points of view on the
lake.   He proposed to take us up to Ambleside, and
recommended us to send the carriage to the same
place ; but, as we wished to have the views both on
the lake itself and from the shore, we declined his
offer.   He then told us that Rayrigg bank, a mile and

a half above Bowness, commanded the most extensive view of the lake which was to be had in that neighbourhood, and we therefore determined to go there in the boat.

In walking from the inn to the lake, we passed by the small church of Bowness, whose whitened exterior and stunted square tower are in accordance with the cleanliness and rustic simplicity of the village. The gate of the church-yard was locked, but as we knew that the remains of the late Bishop of Landaff were interred here, we sent for the sexton, that we might see the burying-place of so distinguished a man. Entering the grass-grown cemetery, we were conducted to a plain grave-stone, raised about two feet above the ground, and enclosed by an iron railing, at the corner of the church. Nothing can be more appropriate to his character than the inscription on his tomb. It is as follows: "RICARDI WATSON, *Episcopi Landavensis, cineribus sacrum ; Obiit Julii* 1. *A.D.* 1816. *Ætatis* 79." No array of titles, no parade of honours, talents, and virtues, offends the character of the place or of the man. In the height of the fame to which his talents raised him, Bishop Watson never forgot his humble origin, and never was ashamed of it.* It may be permitted me to say, that I revere his

* Bishop Watson was the son of a schoolmaster, and his ancestors farmed their own small estate at Heversham, near Kendal. He was Professor of Chemistry, and afterwards Regius Professor of Divinity at Cambridge, and was raised to a bishopric by the Earl of Shelburne in 1782. He advanced the science of Chemistry, triumphantly defended Christianity, and benefited

memory for the services he rendered to the cause of science and of truth, and for the example he set as an independent bishop and an honest man.

Retiring slowly from the contemplation of this tomb, we proceeded to the boat, and rowed out of the bay. Our course lay past several beautiful islands, covered thickly with natural wood. My memory does not present to me any one scene amongst the lakes of Switzerland or Italy so profusely rich, so perfectly delicious, as this part of Windermere. Six or seven islands, of different sizes, are within view at the same moment, all of them crested with masses of the most luxuriant foliage, and some of them presenting amidst the trees bold crags adorned with heath and moss. These umbrageous spots on the lake, situated at various distances, are a relief to the eye, and add exceedingly to the effect of the water; for in a lake without islands the eye glances at once across the water, and rests on the shore, but here it is detained and diverted by objects beautiful in themselves, and heightening by contrast the beauty of the glassy element which floats around them. Islands in a lake answer the same purpose as insects in amber, by setting off the lustre and purity of the material in which they are enclosed.

But, though the *beauty* of a lake is much heightened by being thus varied, it is the unbroken expanse

Agriculture by his experiments in planting. But his politics were too independent to allow of his receiving promotion from Mr. Pitt or his successors.

of water which produces a sense of *sublimity*. And
this, too, you may have in Windermere, when you
have passed the islands which occupy the middle portion of the lake. Skirting the eastern shore, we saw
on our right Rayrigg-hall, in the recess of a quiet bay ;*
and as our boat glided along, the hills of the Langdale
district opened upon us magnificently from behind
Furness fell, which had screened them from our view
at Bowness. We left our boat at a landing-place,
and walked up Rayrigg bank, which is a grassy dome
rising out of a girdle of woods.

From this eminence you see at once the whole of
the upper reach of Windermere—a noble sheet, about
four miles in length and one in breadth. Branching
off from it in every direction are crooked valleys of
inconceivable richness and beauty, leading up to lofty
and barren mountains, from which descend the streams
that feed the lake. These valleys spread out, as they
open upon the basin of Windermere, in little deltas
clothed with wood and verdure ; and betwixt them,
bold ridges push forward their promontories almost to
the water's brink. To your right, as you look northward, is the valley of Troutbeck, running up to the
mountains of Hill Bell and High Street, with Calgarth,
the seat of the late Bishop Watson, (and now of his
son) at its mouth, surrounded by wood, much of it
planted by the bishop himself. On the hill, still further

---

* Rayrigg-hall, the seat of the Rev. John Fleming, has been
thought to resemble Ferney, the residence of Voltaire, near the
Lake of Geneva. The house is a plain, whitened mansion.

to the right, is Elleray, the delightful cottage of Professor Wilson. Beyond Calgarth is Low Wood, concealed by the trees which cover the whole shore; and Dove Nest stands on an eminence above, embowered among woods. At the head of the Lake is the bold and rugged hill called Loughrigg fell, with the mansion and park of Brathay lying at its foot nearly on a level with the lake. On the right of this hill lies the rich valley of Ambleside, terminated by the heights of Fairfield. And on the left of Loughrigg is the valley of Langdale, branching off in an oblique direction from the head of Windermere, and carrying the eye many miles back to the rocky crest of Bowfell, and the fantastically-shaped Langdale Pikes, the most bold and irregular in their forms of any mountains in Westmoreland or Cumberland. The Pikes have three summits, two of which rear their pointed shafts to the sky, whilst one, with a broader head, seems as though it had been pushed out of the perpendicular, and beetles awfully over its base. They are naked and dark, and their steep sides are furrowed by ravines. The craggy and stupendous hills of this district have received very appropriate names, which appear to have been conferred by a people of rude and homely imaginations: one is called Hardknot, another Wrynose, a third Rainsbarrow, a fourth Wetherlam, &c. South of this group is the regular and lofty mountain, called Coniston Old Man, with a pile of stones on the summit. This brings us round to Furness fell and the lake; the islands from hence

form a picture of inexpressible loveliness, and beyond which the lake with its wooded and waving
shores stretches for several miles in a narrowing vista,
till it is terminated by the hill above Newby bridge,
crowned with a monument.

We stood a long time surveying this splendid
view. Matilda's eye rested on the softer parts of the
scenery—Calgarth, Brathay, the islands, and the
white houses and meadows on the opposite shore.
But George gazed with insatiable delight on the wild
magnificence of the Pikes,—that kind of scenery
being quite new to him, and kindling all the enthusiasm of his nature.

Returning to our boat, we rowed directly across the
lake, intending to skirt the foot of Furness fell, for
the sake of varying the prospect, and to land upon
Belle Isle before returning to Bowness. When we
were gliding over the glassy water, the following
conversation arose :—*Matilda :* " Did not you say,
William, that Professor Wilson lived at Elleray ? Is
he the ' Isle of Palms' Wilson ?'" *William :* " The
same : he is Professor of Moral Philosophy in the
University of Edinburgh. He spends his time betwixt Edinburgh and Elleray : he is, as you may
infer from his poems, devotedly fond of the sublimities and beauties of nature, and especially of this
' loveliest of all earthly Lakes,' as he calls it."
George : (pointing to the Professor's cottage)—"Look,
Matilda ! look, aunt ! Does not Elleray answer well
to his description of it ?—

E

> And that sweet dwelling rests upon the brow
> (Beneath its sycamore) of Orest-hill,
> As if it smiled on Windermere below,
> Her green recesses and her islands still."

Mrs. Anabella : " The situation is truly delightful ; it would make a poet: I think the Lake Poets have all chosen their houses judiciously." *Matilda :* " How many are there of the Lake Poets, and where do they live ?" *W. :* " Five or six: Wordsworth, the father and king of the school, lives at Rydal Mount, a house charmingly situated at the extremity of the valley of Ambleside,—the front of it commanding a view of that valley and Windermere, whilst from his garden he looks down on the little lake of Rydal, which on the small scale is the loveliest landscape in nature. Southey lives at Greta-hall, near Keswick, with Skiddaw at his back, and Derwentwater spread out before him. Coleridge, who married a sister of Mrs. Southey, has abandoned the Lakes, and lives at Highgate ; but he has a son, Hartley Coleridge, whose verses you have seen in the Annuals and in Blackwood ; he lodged for some years at the inn in Grasmere, but has since been a poet-errant. De Quincy, the author of the ' Opium-Eater,' makes up the number ; he had a house in the vale of Grasmere, but he likewise has left Westmoreland, and lives in Scotland." *Matilda :* " What sort of a man is Professor Wilson ?" *W. :* " I have never seen him: he is still in the prime of life ; when a young man he was a noted athlete— an accomplished wrestler and a great leaper, being fitted for gymnastic exercises by his height, strength, and agility : he used to be fond of the chase, and was also the patron of the yearly wrestling matches that take place at Low Wood. If you have read his works, I dare say you will think that his bodily powers and personal accomplishments have not interfered with the cultivation of his genius."

We were now opposite Belle Grange, the house of Mr. Edwd. Curwen, at the foot of Furness fell, near its northern extremity; and we rowed down the lake towards Belle Isle, greatly admiring the shifting islands, and the reflection in the lake of the wooded steep which rose above us. George lavished the most enthusiastic eulogies on the scene, and quoted the lines of Wilson—

——————" All those sister-isles that sleep
. Together, like a happy family
Of beauty and of love"—

Matilda asked the names of the islands. " The island opposite to us—the larger of the two—is Lady Holm, so called from having formerly been the site of an Oratory dedicated to 'our Lady,' the Virgin Mary; the smaller island, nearer to us, is Hen Holm; that higher up the lake is Rough Holm; House Holm and Thompson's Holm are before us; and two little specks of islets beyond are called Lily of the Valley Holms." *Matilda :* " Wilson may well call them ' sister-isles,' for they seem all to have the same surname: the family of the Holms is a large one here, and I dare to say ancient. They seem also to be maiden isles." *George :*

"Then they are old maids; they are a thousand
times too pretty—(here the rude boy checked himself,
perceiving the colour come into Mrs. Anabella's face)
—I mean to say that the name is as old as the Saxon
times: *holme* signifies a river-island." *William*: "*Holme*
also signifies a hill.   That is a pretty idea of Matilda's,
that these are maiden isles—they are so bewitchingly
beautiful, and just as nature made them.   Belle Isle
is the eldest sister, and *her* name and appearance
bespeak the matron; yet, methinks, art has added to
her dignity without imparing her gracefulness."

We had now arrived at Belle Isle, and we landed
at the northern extremity, near some gigantic oaks.
The gardener, espying us, came up and offered to
accompany us round the island.   We accepted his offer
for the sake of the information he might give us, and
he described to us the various improvements effected
by his late master, who planted all the young trees on
the island, as well as a great many acres of larch on
Furness fell.   The larch woods had been planted thirty
years, and were now becoming valuable.   We admired
every thing on the island, except the house, which is
neither handsome nor in character.   The walk round
the island presents many delicious views; differing
greatly from each other.   The view on the west is
limited to the glassy lake, and the grand but sombre
forest which towers above it—

"Insuperable height of loftiest shade."

The east, on the contrary, is a bright, lively, and lumin-

ous prospect, embracing the village and bay of Bowness, green meadows and pastures, several pretty villas,
and the hill in the rear. From the north we saw the
fine expanse of the upper part of the lake, with the
high mountains around its head. And from the south
a more confined and sober, but still most lovely landscape,—the bays below the island,—the pretty islands
called Crow Holm and Berkshire Island,—the strait of
the Ferry, and the woody promontory on which stands
the neat, white Ferry-house,—beyond this, another expanse of the lake, smooth and translucent as a mirror,
on the further side of which the beautiful mansion of
Storrs rises out of its ornamental groves, with a point
of land running into the lake, at the extremity of
which is a little naval temple built by its former
proprietor (Sir John Legard, Bart.),*—and then,
stretching beyond for several miles, the lower part of
Windermere is seen, gradually dwindling to a point
betwixt its wooded shores.

Having nearly completed the circuit of the island,
we re-entered our boat at the landing-place, admiring
a majestic Spanish chesnut, fifteen feet in girth, which
overshadows the spot. We left the island with regret,
believing that we should see nothing more beautiful in
the course of our tour. George and I had enjoyed
the fine exercise of rowing during the whole of the

* Storrs-hall was partly built by Sir John Legard, and finished
by Col. Bolton, a Liverpool gentleman, and the electioneering
friend of Mr. Canning and Mr. Huskisson. The deceased
statesmen were frequent visiters at Storrs.

morning's excursion, and we availed ourselves of every
opportunity to take the same exercise whilst we were
at the Lakes.†

† The names of the gentlemen's seats near Bowness and on the
banks of Windermere will be found in the ITINERARY—See *Bowness, Newby Bridge,* the route *from Bowness to Ambleside,* and
Ambleside. The INDEX will enable the reader instantly to find all
the pages both of the Companion and Itinerary where any town,
village, gentleman's seat, or other place, is mentioned.

CHAPTER VII.

We left Bowness for Ambleside about two o'clock
in the afternoon. On the same day several different
parties had arrived at and quitted the White Lion, as
well as the Crown, a smaller, but even better situated
inn at Bowness. They came from all points of the
compass, and were of very different qualities and
characters. We had not much time to observe them,
but we learnt who they were from the book in which
travellers enter their names at the hotel.

The Ambleside road runs parallel with the lake,
but generally at the distance of a few hundred yards
from it. The greater part of the way it is shaded by
trees of luxuriant growth, amongst which the oak,
the sycamore, the beech, the chesnut, and the ash
are the most abundant. The plentifulness of the
wood, though in itself so ornamental, prevented u
from having frequent views of the lake; but as the
road ascends and descends with the very unequal

surface of the ground, we sometimes caught glimpses
of the lake from an elevated spot, and occasionally
obtained extensive prospects of the most striking
beauty.

As we proceeded Matilda made a very just observation concerning the scenery of Windermere : " It
seems," she said, " as if Furness fell were placed on
the other side of the lake as a side-screen, to vary
the scenery. At Bowness it shuts in the view with
its high and solemn forest—though I wish the trees
had been oak, instead of those formal larches—and
confines the eye to the lakes and the islands, which
are enough to fill the imagination, and which perhaps
would not look so delicious if the scenery were open
all around : and then, as you pass up the lake, it is
as if the screen were gradually removed, and this
magnificent view of the Langdale mountains is revealed." *George :* " Yes : the change is delightful,
and I scarcely know which to prefer—the secluded
beauty of Bowness, or this splendid amphitheatre of
mountains, with the noble expanse of water that floats
in its midst." *William :* " Both the views are grand
and both lovely ; but in the one the beautiful predominates, and in the other the sublime. I think
they have their best effect when taken in the order
in which they have presented themselves to us."

When we came near Troutbeck bridge, where the
rushing streamlet that gives its name to the valley
pours itself through the grounds of Calgarth into the
ake, Mrs. Anabella espied the old hall, which is in a

half ruinous state, and inquired to whom it belonged. " It was," I said, " the seat of the Philipsons, anciently a family of the first distinction in these parts, who possessed not only Calgarth, but the large island in Windermere which we visited this morning, where they had a house called the Holm-house. During the Civil Wars in the reign of Charles I. Mr. Robert Philipson sustained a siege of eight or ten days in the island, and was then relieved by his brother, Mr. Huddleston Philipson. The former obtained the nick-name of *Robin the Devil,* from an act of desperate enterprise which he performed, in riding with three or four companions into Kendal when it was in possession of the royalists, and entering the church on horseback, during service, to search for a special foe. He missed his man, but he himself escaped unhurt, after killing a sentinel. The old hall is said to be haunted: two human skulls for a long time occupied a place in the windows, and tradition says that when taken away, though they should be buried or burned, they invariably re-appeared in their place at the window; they were supposed to have belonged to two poor old people who were unjustly executed for a robbery. So says Mr. West; but Mr. Green* informs us

---

* Mr. Wm. Green, the late artist, and author of " *The Tourist's New Guide,*" in two octavo volumes, published in 1819. This gentleman resided at Ambleside, and for many years devoted all the powers of his pencil and his pen to illustrate the picturesque scenery of the Lakes. His water-colour Views of the Lakes may be seen in the Exhibition at Keswick, and will gratify the visiter. Mr. Green's " Guide" contains by far the most elaborate and

that Time has proved more than a match for the invisible agent that sought to perpetuate these monuments of wrong, and that one of the skulls has turned to dust, and the other is fast mouldering." *Matilda :* " I commend the taste of the ghost ; he has chosen a pleasant situation.   The architect of the new hall was no witch ; he has made a great staring house."

William.—" This is precisely the place for a ghost story, so rude and simple are the people.   If we had sufficient time, it would be worth our while to ascend the valley of Troutbeck to the village, which is in a secluded and beautiful situation, two or three miles hence.   The houses are very ancient, and if any genuine specimens remain of the old manners, customs, and superstitions of Westmoreland—any true descendants of ' the rude forefathers of the hamlet,'—it would be in Troutbeck.   Here you might hear of the pranks 'of the goblin, *Hobthurst ;* here you might see, in the houses of the statesmen, the ancient, substantial, oaken furniture, carved with quaint devices ; here you might eat the genuine *haver-bread* (oat-bread) ; and here probably courtships are still carried on in a style which would outrage the delicacy of modern

complete account of the Lake district ever published ; and its only fault is, that it is too minute in its descriptions, and therefore swells to too large a bulk to be convenient to travellers.   A visiter making a long stay at the Lakes will find a mass of interesting and useful information in these volumes, and directions for penetrating into every nook of the mountains and valleys, which the author discovered in his frequent rambles, and which he has described with taste and enthusiasm.

days." "Statesmen!" said George, "do any statesmen live in Troutbeck?" "A *statesman*," replied
Mrs. Anabella, "is the name given in these counties
to a landed proprietor who farms his own estate: I
remember to have heard the title applied to a dull-
looking, farmer-like man near Keswick, during my
last tour." *William:* "Yes, ma'am, and in some of
these valleys you may find lands which have descended for centuries in the same families; yet their
owners have no genealogical pride. They are men
who work like horses, who drive their own ploughs,
and look after their own sheep on the mountains."
Mrs. Anabella: "I should think that in such a situation you would find as much of health, happiness,
simplicity, and virtue, as is to be found any where in
the world." *William:* "I really cannot tell; the
inhabitants are almost necessarily ignorant, and I
question if ignorance was ever the parent either of
virtue or true simplicity. I apprehend you would find
the same evil passions and fraudulent purposes in
these retired valleys as in populous cities, though
differently manifested. As to health, formerly rheu-
matism and ague were very prevalent in these parts;
I believe they are less so now. Perhaps the husband-
man's limbs grow stark, and his frame wears out, from
the effects of toil and exposure to the weather, as
soon as the citizen sinks under his confinement and
commercial care. I have heard a medical man in these
parts say, that from the extensive intermarriages in
the small population of the villages and valleys, you

may know the diseases of the whole valley if you know those of a single family. You would perhaps not suspect, but it is perfectly true, that there is one town at the Lakes where there is an extensive taint of insanity."

We had now reached the summit of a hill between Troutbeck bridge and Low Wood, which commands one of the finest views of the head of Windermere, the valleys of Great and Little Langdale, and the mountains.* Loughrigg fell, at the head of the lake, now looked a very bold eminence; and Brathay park, which lies at its foot, and spreads its rich lawns and woods over a broken surface, had a beautiful effect. The lake, as seen from hence, is superlatively grand. Langdale Pikes now appeared more towering than they had done before, and their remarkable form became still more strikingly conspicuous.

We descended to Low Wood, a hamlet on the very brink of the lake at its widest part. There is here a spacious and handsome inn, which stands in a finer situation than perhaps any other in the district of the Lakes. It is much frequented by visiters, who find around the place many interesting walks, and have every facility for rowing on Windermere. The view is nearly the same as that just mentioned from the hill; but the mountains, and especially the Pikes, appear to have still greater elevation and grandeur

---

* The mountains are seen from this place in the same order in which they are mentioned in the stage from Kendal to Bowness, chap. v

from Low Wood, and the lake forms one of the loveliest mirrors ever spread out by Nature. If our time had allowed, we might have spent some days here very much to our satisfaction. There is an annual Regatta held on Windermere in the autumn, with boat-races and other amusements. On these occasions Low Wood, Bowness, and the Ferry-house are the head quarters of the company, which is very numerous and of the highest respectability.

As we were proceeding to Ambleside, I mentioned that the two principal feeders of the lake are the rivers Brathay and Rothay, the former of which flows through Great Langdale, and the latter through the lakes of Grasmere and Rydal. The rivers unite half a mile before they fall into Windermere. The trout and char of the lake go up these rivers, in the season, to spawn; and it is a remarkable fact that the trout always choose the Rothay, and the char the Brathay. The char is a delicate fish, resembling the trout: it will only live in deep lakes, and is most abundant in Windermere, some parts of which (opposite Low Wood) have a depth of two hundred feet. The angler has a great choice of fine trout streams at the Lakes, and he may pursue the streams up to the lonely tarns in the heart of the mountains, many of which abound with fish.

At the head of the lake is a spot which is indicated as the site of a Roman city and burial-place. Of this station there were considerable remains as late as the time of Sir Daniel Fleming, (at the beginning of the

last century) who says of them—" There is the
carcase as it were of an ancient city, with large
ruins of walls; and without the walls the rubbish of
old buildings in many places." The traces of the city
are now almost entirely obliterated, but its position is
indicated by the Rothay flowing on its western side,
and the lake washing its southern. Roman weapons,
armour, coins, and other antiquities found here, are
to be seen in the museums of Keswick and Kendal.

The small town of Ambleside* is a mile above the
head of the lake, in a superb valley; and, as we
approached it, we admired its picturesque situation.
It hangs on the side of a steep hill, which forms the
root of the mountain ridge called Scandale, and at
the mouth of a narrow glen down which rushes the
brook, or *gill*,† named Stockgill. This glen runs up
betwixt Scandale and Wansfell to the elevation of
twelve hundred feet, and then opens on to Kirkstone-
moor, over which lies the mountain pass to Patterdale
and Ullswater. Another lateral valley branches off
from the main valley on the same side as Stockgill;
and both of them are richly hung with wood. Opposite the town are the craggy heights of Loughrigg
fell, the lower parts of which are also begirt with
wood. The valley is nearly three miles in length,

---

* Ambleside was spelt Amelsate in 1273, and afterwards Hamel-
side, Amylside, and Amelside: the name has had its present form
since the reign of Elizabeth. This town is supposed by Horsley
to have been the Roman *Dictis*.

† *Gill*, or *ghyll*, is a mountain torrent with steep banks.

and at its upper extremity it seems to be blocked up by Fairfield, a huge mountain which rises to the height of 2,950 feet above the sea ;* but, though this is the appearance, the valley does not end there, but turns off abruptly to the left, between Fairfield and Loughrigg, and afterwards opens out so as to form the bed for the small lakes of Rydal and Grasmere.

The town is very ancient, and irregularly built; but at either extremity, and on points of the hill above it, there are several neat and handsome houses, surrounded by gardens well filled with fruit and flowers. Beneath the town is a valley, whose verdure is always kept fresh and brilliant by the streamlets which flow down the sides of the hills, and by the winding Rothay. The woods of Rydal hall, and of the different glens which diverge from the valley, adorn the prospect from Ambleside; whilst, in contrast to the towering and bulky form of Fairfield at one extremity of the valley, the sheet of Windermere opens out in sweet repose at the other.

We drove to the Salutation, an excellent inn, and found the house quite full of visiters. However, a party went away in the course of the same afternoon, which made room for us. Having ordered dinner, we

* That part of Fairfield which is seen from Ambleside is generally called Rydal head; yet this is more properly the head of the *valley* of Rydal than the mountain itself; but as the valley runs up in a wide ravine to the very summit of the mountain, that summit is generally called Rydal head. The upper part of most of the valleys, where they terminate among the mountains, is called the *dale head*.

walked up to Stockgill Force,* perhaps the most
beautiful waterfall amongst the Lakes, which is at
the distance of half a mile from the inn.   We climbed
a rugged foot-path, through a deep and narrow glen
choked with wood, in the bottom of which a streamlet
rushes over its rocky bed.   The waters are perfectly
limpid, and even after they have brawled down a
steep declivity, or tumbled in foam over a perpendicular rock, they are seen in the basin below transparent
to the depth of several feet, and gliding gently on, as
though, like the sleep of infancy, forgetful of the past
and careless of the future.   It was beautiful to see
the torrent, through the deep shade of the glen, and
at a considerable distance below us, wheeling from side
to side, leaping from rock to rock, or suddenly brought
to repose in basins set round with moss-covered
crags.

We had pursued our upward course for some time,
when, on climbing a sharp ascent, and going to the
edge of the chasm, the cascade burst upon us in all
its splendour.   It was immediately opposite to us,
and we were about midway between the top and
bottom, its height being one hundred and fifty feet.
The stream is divided into two portions by a huge
crag interposed just in the centre of the precipice over
which it flings itself, and covered with bushes and
trees; yet both branches of the fall are visible at once,
and the division heightens its beauty.   They do not

* The name of *Force* is common to nearly all the waterfalls at
the Lakes; its meaning is obvious.

reach the abyss at a single leap, but, after falling about half the depth in smooth lines of silver, they meet with a projecting rock, from which they rebound in larger volumes of flashing foam and spray,—uniting at the bottom in a very deep, but clear basin, darkened by the rocks, as well as by the numerous trees which have taken root in their crevices, and which throw out their tender foliage in search of light and moisture. This, like all the cascades at the Lakes, varies exceedingly with the wet or dry weather, being swelled to a thundering torrent by a heavy fall of rain, and dwindled to a mere trickling rill after drought. We saw it when it had about the average quantity of water, and we thought it highly picturesque.

From the hill-side just above the force there is a fine mountain view. On an autumn evening, soon after sunset, this view is peculiarly rich and grand. The rugged forms of Loughrigg fell and Silver How, and the bold summits of Bowfell and Langdale Pikes, all invested in a mantle of the deepest purple, stand in striking relief against the western horizon, which glows with a mellow and golden light. To a mind imbued with the love of nature, and apt to rise from her works up to their almighty and all-wise Creator, I know no scene more calculated to inspire lofty yet serene and delightful contemplation.

CHAPTER VIII.

LANGDALE EXCURSION—CHANGES IN THE WEATHER—GREAT LANGDALE—SKELWITH FORCE—LOUGHRIGG TARN—ELTER-WATER—LITTLE LANGDALE—COLWITH FORCE—BLEA TARN —HEAD OF GREAT LANGDALE—THE STICKLE PIKES—DUNGEON GILL—HIGH CLOSE.

Of the many excursions that may be made from Ambleside, the most interesting is that through Great and Little Langdale.*   We had therefore fixed to make this expedition, if the weather should be favour-able,—for, as it is necessary, on account of the roads, to go in an open car, or a cart, the weather may make all the difference between great enjoyment and posi-tive misery. By one of those sudden and seemingly capricious changes which are common in mountainous countries, a beautiful evening was succeeded by a dripping morning,—the sight of which drove George to bed again, when he had risen early with the view of scaling Loughrigg fell or Nab scar before the

---

* In the opinion of some, the excursion to Coniston Water Head may be more interesting than this. I acknowledge that it is ex-ceedingly beautiful, but we had not time for both, and I recom-mend the Langdale Excursion in preference. Coniston Water is best visited from Ulverston, as it was in the *Excursion on Horseback*, which see.

ladies had opened their eyes. Many a time did we rise from breakfast, to see if the clouds which hung upon the sides of Rydal head showed any disposition to ascend and disperse. Many a transient gleam of hope was dissipated by thicker volumes of cloud driven by the wind down the great ravine of the mountain. Many a consultation did we hold with the landlord, car-driver, hostler, and every person about the place who could have the least pretensions to meteorological skill. At length the clouds broke, and the sky became clear ; but, before the car was brought out, another shower passed over the town, which made us apprehensive that in the long ride we contemplated we might have a succession of such visitations. It was eleven o'clock before there was an appearance sufficiently settled to induce us to set out. We then entered the car, having provided ourselves with sandwiches, in the expectation (which proved to be well founded) that the excursion would occupy between six and seven hours. As we advanced, the weather became bright and beautiful, and we had to congratulate ourselves on enjoying that transparent state of the atmosphere so well described as " the clear shining after rain."

Having crossed the valley of Ambleside and the sparkling Rothay, we held along the foot of Loughrigg fell, having the craggy and wooded steep on one hand, and the undulating park of Brathay, with the sheet of Windermere, on the other. Passing the village of Clappersgate, we came to the banks of the river

Brathay, the water of which is of crystalline clearness, though frequently roughened by its rocky bed.

The entrance of Great Langdale* wants the soft beauty of the scenery we had already beheld, but it possesses what tends more to exalt the imagination, namely, a character of wildness and stern grandeur, mingled with beauties in which art has no share, but such as nature often scatters with a careless yet magnificent profusion in a mountainous country. The trees are plentiful, and mount high up the craggy hills, feathering the sides of rugged precipices; the verdure of the dale is of a living green; but no artificial grove, or shapely lawn, or handsome mansion offends the character of the place. The Brathay winds in the bottom—sometimes a huddling stream hemmed in by thickets, and sometimes spreading out in small sheets, which reflect the pastures, trees, and hills with the most brilliant clearness.

A little within the vale, we found ourselves surrounded by an amphitheatre of wooded hills, and in the midst of a scene which, of its own character, is perhaps not to be equalled at the lakes. The woods of Loughrigg rose behind us, and those of Skelwith mantled the opposite hill. Wansfell reared his pike beyond Windermere and Ambleside, and Wetherlam lifted his sublime mass over Little Langdale.

* *Langdale* sufficiently explains its own meaning—*long-dale*. Yet it is a modern corruption of *Langden; den* being the Saxon word for valley. In Yorkshire this termination is common, e. g. Todmorden, Ripponden, &c. The termination *dale,* however, prevails more in Westmoreland and Cumberland.

Amidst scenery such as this, varying its details at every turn of our winding and uneven road, we came down to Skelwith bridge, three miles from Ambleside, where we left the car, and proceeded a short distance up the river to Skelwith force. This waterfall is remarkable, not for its height, but for the body of water it contains, which is greater than in any other fall at the Lakes. Its height seemed to me not more than twenty feet, yet the scene is fine, and well worth visiting. The river Brathay is contracted, for some distance above the fall, within the space afforded by a chasm in an enormous bed of rocks. After rushing down this crooked trough, the waters are precipitated, with the noise of thunder, into a foaming abyss. The bold masses of rock, and the rush and fall of so great a body of water, make Skelwith force grand and interesting.

Our next object was Colwith force, which we might have reached in about two miles by crossing Skelwith bridge, and keeping along the hill-side into Little Langdale; but this is a very rugged road, and our driver wisely determined, as his car was heavily laden, to go round by Elterwater, which, though upwards of three miles, would be easier for his horse. I found, indeed, that he had a hankering after a route, which would greatly abridge our excursion. Though I had clearly explained the route we designed to take before we set out, he pretended to have understood that we only wished to go up Great Langdale as far as Dungeon Gill, and then return to Ambleside.

He also pleaded the difficulty of the road through Little Langdale and by Blea Tarn, and said that he had never taken a car by that route, but that parties always went in a cart. As, however, the plan he proposed would have cut off the finest part of the excursion, and as I was convinced that a car might pass those roads as well as a cart, I insisted on his proceeding according to the original plan, but offered that the party should walk at the steep hills and difficult places. Finding that he could neither cheat nor frighten us, he took our course ; and, as he had a strong horse, we got through with very little difficulty.

Ascending the hill on the north side of the valley, we passed Loughrigg tarn—a small lake in a woody hollow of the hill, over which towers, at a great perpendicular elevation, the head of Loughrigg fell. When I told our party the name of the lake, adding that *tarn* was the name given to a small lake found at a considerable elevation on the hills—" I like," said George, " these old-fashioned and rough-sounding names—Loughrigg, and Langdale, and the Pikes, with *force* and *fell, tarn* and *scar, gill, glen, holm,* and *mere :* there is an ancient Saxon simplicity about them ; they breathe a mountain air." " I should like to hear what you can make of Loughrigg ?"—said Matilda. " Oh !" replied he, " I could not make it out till we came to this little lake, but now I find it means *the hill of the lake—lough* or *loch* meaning *lake,* and *rigg* meaning *ridge* or *hill.*" " The name," I observed, " is no doubt derived either from the lake *upon* the hill, or from those by which it is surrounded: as we proceed we shall find many *riggs*." *Matilda*: "Well, brother, you are very clever, but I hope you will take care, in your rage for climbing, not to ' *run a rig*,' for riggs in these parts seem to be formidable things."

After having ascended a considerable hill, we came in view of the small and pleasing lake of Elterwater, lying in the bottom of the valley. From this elevation we also saw the grand valley of Langdale stretching before us for several miles, betwixt hills whose sides form a splendid concave sweep; and in the bottom the infant Brathay, wandering through the green pastures and meadows, with irregular dotted lines of trees and thickets marking its course, and little rustic arches here and there spanning the stream. At the head of the valley rises the frowning summit of Bowfell; on the right the Pikes lift their gigantic heads, and seem to nod over the chasm that intervenes between them and the rugged Lingmire. Harrison Stickle sits upon a throne of rocks piled up to the clouds, with an inferior Pike on one side, and the craggy brow of Pavey Ark on the other. Langdale makes a bend near the head, and is lost to the view among the mountains, whose rocky fastnesses have from this point an awful appearance. Hence must Wordsworth have drawn his sketch, when accompanying his friend, the Wanderer, in his *Excursion* up Langdale to Blea Tarn :—

———— " He led towards the hills ;
Up through an ample vale, with higher hills
Before us, mountains stern and desolate ;
But, in the majesty of distance, now
Set off, and to our ken appearing fair
Of aspect, with aërial softness clad,
And beautified with morning's purple beams."

Hence, too, Mr. Allom must have taken his lovely and striking view of Langdale, which does so much credit to his taste and the power of his pencil.*

We descended the hill to the village of Elterwater, situated at the head of the lake of that name, and, crossing the river, went through a considerable wood and over a hill into Little Langdale.

This valley branches from Great Langdale, and runs nearly parallel with it, but at a higher elevation : the two dales are separated by the high, black, heath-covered hill of Lingmire, at each end of which there is a communication between them.   The ancient road from Kendal to Whitehaven passes through Little Langdale : and the narrow valley of Tilberthwaite runs from it to the south, overlooked, like Little Langdale, by the huge, dark mountain of Wetherlam, also called Tilberthwaite fell.   There is in this valley an appearance of mountain wildness and seclusion more decided than any thing we had hitherto seen ; in many parts not a single human habitation is visible. At the entrance, which is narrow and crooked, there is a great deal of wood, consisting chiefly of birch and

* In Fisher's Picturesque Illustrations of Westmoreland, Cumberland, &c.

hazel bushes; and the river, which runs in a deep glen, is concealed by the wood that envelops its sides. The rugged hills by which we were surrounded are covered with heath and fern, which, as the sun shone upon them, seemed to clothe them in a rich and party-coloured mantle. The heath was now in full flower and in all its purple splendour, and the fern had been turned by the sun's rays into a lively red; so that, in the midst of desolation, we saw proofs of the exuberant bounty of Him, "whose paths drop fatness upon the pastures of the wilderness," and make "the little hills rejoice on every side."

Colwith Force is not far from the entrance of the valley. We left the car, and walked to it through a pathway walled on each side by hazel bushes, which hung their clusters of nuts temptingly before our faces. An opening in the copse reveals the force, which, both from its grandeur and the sublimity of the situation, excited our high admiration. A stupendous crag rises out of the river, so placed as if it had been flung in by some Titanian hand for the express purpose of blocking up its course. Below this crag the glen sinks at once to a depth of more than a hundred feet; the river, diverted from its course, rushes round the side of the rock, and at four several leaps plunges into the gulf below. Clouds of spray shoot up from the abyss, and the waters, after boiling in the whirlpool, dart forth down the glen, as if in mortal terror. The water here is not scanty, as in most of the other falls at the Lakes, but is a river scarcely inferior to the Brathay at Skelwith Force. The four falls are several yards apart, but the lowest is of greater depth than all the other three, and the whole are in view at once. In beholding the headlong rage, the flashing and boiling of the cascade, George was transported with delight, and exclaimed, in the words of Wilson— "Well done, Water!" He and I let ourselves cautiously down the steep side of the glen, by the aid of the trees, and obtained a view of the force from its foot, which was very striking; but we did not remain there long, as the clouds of spray which rise from the fall, and which are carried about by gusts, plentifully bedewed us.

From this place we proceeded about two miles up the valley, passing Little Langdale tarn and the peaceful hamlet of Fell-foot, sheltered by trees, and situated amidst a considerable tract of green pasture. We then quitted the old Whitehaven road, which crosses Wrynose, and turned to the right, in order to pass over a slack* into Great Langdale. In this slack, the general appearance of which is wild, barren, and desolate, lies a green hollow, and in the midst of it a little lake, named Blea tarn, overhung by the enormous and ragged precipices of Blakerigg, called Bessy Crag. So completely secluded from the world is this remarkable recess of the mountains, that it might be the chosen abode of a hermit. Wordsworth

* A *slack* is a dip in the hills, or a pass —itself elevated—between two higher elevations.

has made it the residence of his Solitary, and has painted the scene with such perfect fidelity, that I need only copy the passage—observing that he and his friend approached Blea tarn from Great Langdale—

" We scaled, without a track to ease our steps,
A steep ascent ; and reached a dreary plain,
With a tumultuous waste of huge hill tops
Before us ; savage region ! which I paced
Dispirited ; when, all at once, behold !
Beneath our feet, a little lowly vale,
A lowly vale, and yet uplifted high
Among the mountains : even as if the spot
Had been, from eldest time by wish of theirs
So placed,—to be shut out from all the world ;
Urn-like it was in shape, deep as an urn ;
With rocks encompass'd, save that to the south
Was one small opening, where a heath-clad ridge
Supplied a boundary less abrupt and close ;
A quiet treeless nook, with two green fields,
A liquid pool that glitter'd in the sun,
And one bare dwelling ; one abode, no more !
It seem'd the home of poverty and toil,
Though not of want; the little fields, made green
By husbandry of many thrifty years,
Paid cheerful tribute to the moorland house."

Excursion.

The grandest view we had this day was from the edge of the slack, looking down upon the head of Great Langdale, where the Pikes stood directly in front of us, and Bowfell on our left, all of them seen at one glance from the base to the summit. These mountains are only separated by a narrow dell, forming the head of Langdale, which runs up a mile or two further into the heart of the mountains, where cultivation ends, and the strip of verdure terminates

F 2

in a wilderness of heath and rock. All the features of this view are simple, but of the most striking sublimity. The Pikes tower aloft like pillars of the skies. The highest of them, called Harrison Stickle, has an elevation of 2400 feet above the sea; and the other, called Pike o' Stickle, of 2,000 feet. The latter is pointed by a shaft of naked rock, apparently slender, but in reality enormous, and which appears to be perpendicular towards the valley. Gimmer Crag, between the two Pikes, presents to the valley a lofty and prodigious mass of rock. Bowfell lifts his rugged peak to the height of 2,911 feet, and a long range of crags, called Crinkle crags, extends to the neighbouring heights. The sides of the mountains are furrowed with deep and awful ravines. Our whole party were lost in admiration of the stupendous scene; and I question if they afterwards saw any thing which impressed them so strongly, except, perhaps, the view from the top of Skiddaw. I was the object of envy to George, when I told him that I had sat on the point of the Stickle Pike, and on the loftier platform of Harrison Stickle, both of which on this side appear to be inaccessible.*

A steep and rugged descent brought us down to Wall End, the last house but one in the valley; from which we began our return down Great Langdale,

---

* An account of the ascent of Bowfell and Scawfell Pikes, from the head of Langdale, will be found in the *Excursion on Horseback*; and an account of the ascent of Langdale Pikes will be found in the Second *Excursion on Foot*.

and in two miles further we came to Mill-beck.
From this place we climbed the mountain-side for no
contemptible distance, to see the waterfall of Dungeon
Gill, which is a beautiful fall situated in a deep cleft
of the hill under Harrison Stickle. The profound
chasm in which it is situated is called, in the lan-
guage of the country, a *dungeon*, whence the name
of the fall. The quantity of water here is not considerable, but the fall is high and exceedingly picturesque. It descends in a fine sheet of foam betwixt
two walls of perpendicular rock, which I should judge
to be more than a hundred feet high. Two enormous
rocks have fallen into the top of the chasm, and
hang suspended in a way alarming to the spectator.
Trees have taken root in the sides of the cleft, and
hang out their branches to receive the perpetual rain
of spray from the waterfall. Wordsworth has a pretty
poem, founded on the fact of a lamb being carried
over the fall, and plunged into the basin below,
whence it was rescued unhurt. From Mill-beck
travellers not unfrequently climb to the Stickle tarn,
celebrated for its superior trout, and to the summit of
Harrison Stickle ; the ascent is steep, and requires a
great exertion, or rather great patience and perse-
verance.

The remainder of our journey presented no object
particularly worthy of notice, except the extensive
slate quarries with which Langdale abounds, one of
which, at Thrang Crag, we entered, and admired with
awe its enormous masses of slate-rock, threatening to

entomb the spectator by a hideous fall. At Elterwater
there is a manufactory of gunpowder. We returned
by the route of High Close, which crosses Loughrigg
fell, and passes through the beautiful vales of Grasmere and Rydal ; but as we saw these exquisite scenes
again on the following day, I shall leave my account of
them to the next chapter. The views from High
Close, both on the Windermere and Grasmere sides,
are of singular magnificence and beauty, and should
be seen, if possible, by every traveller.

CHAPTER IX.

AMBLESIDE TO KESWICK—RYDAL HALL—RYDAL MOUNT—MR. WORDSWORTH—THE FLEMING FAMILY—RYDAL WATER—VIEW FROM LOUGHRIGG FELL—GRASMERE LAKE AND VALE—HELM CRAG—DUNMAIL RAISE—AN ANTIQUARY—ANTIQUARIAN INFORMATION. .

We quitted Ambleside for Keswick between ten and eleven in the morning, as it had been agreed that we should take an early dinner at Keswick, and afterwards go on Derwentwater in a boat. The distance to that place is sixteen miles, and perhaps England does not afford a ride of equal length so abounding in romantic and magnificent scenery. The road passes nearly the whole distance through a valley, on one side of which towers the gigantic chain of Helvellyn and Fairfield, whose broad and rugged sides rise steeply from the vale; and, on the other, stand the lower, but more diversified, broken, and picturesque ridges of Loughrigg-fell, Silver How, Steel-fell, and the Thirlmere and Derwent fells. Three lakes, Rydal Water, Grasmere Water, and Thirlmere, two of them small but extremely beautiful, lie in the several divisions of the valley, and, by their soft repose, as well as by the luxuriance of their borders, afford a charming relief to the sternness and barrenness of the mountains.

For something more than a mile our road lay through the valley of Ambleside, and on the banks of the Rothay, when we came to Rydal Hall, the seat of Lady le Fleming. This mansion (which I cannot help calling a great, staring, yellow house) stands on a slight eminence, not far from the road, and is sheltered by fine old timber, of which there is an abundance in the grounds and on the hill side. Behind the house rises the steep and lofty Fairfield. A few minutes' walk in the ascent of the hill would have brought us to the residence of Mr. Wordsworth, named Rydal Mount. In this place, within view at once of Windermere and Rydal Water, the father of the Lake School of poetry has passed, I believe, the greater part of his life; and the scenery around him, scarcely equalled in beauty by any in Westmoreland or Cumberland, has probably tended to enrich his imagination, to refine the natural purity of his feelings, and to produce many of the noble and exquisite descriptions of nature which adorn his poems. We had the offer of being introduced to him by a friend on whom we called in Ambleside, but, though we should have appreciated highly the opportunity of conversing with such a man, we found that our time would not allow us to make any stay at Rydal Mount.* The same cause prevented us from leaving

* For an account of Mr. Wordsworth's residence, see the *Excursion on Horseback*, chap. iii.

the carriage to see two small, but highly picturesque
waterfalls in the grounds of Rydal-hall, which I
should recommend other tourists, who have more
leisure, to visit.

When I mentioned the name of the owner of
Rydal-hall, George observed that *Le* Fleming had an
ancient sound, and he inquired if the family was not
old and of foreign origin. " The family of the
Flemings," I replied, " is one of the most ancient
and honourable in these parts. Sir Michael le Fleming
was related to Baldwin, Earl of Flanders, brother-
in-law of the Conqueror, and was sent by him to assist
William in England. His services were repaid with
large grants of land in Furness. Rydal came into the
family in the reign of Henry VI. by marriage with
Isabel, a co-heiress of Sir John de Lancaster, of How-
gill castle; and it has been the principal seat of the
Flemings ever since. Sir Daniel Fleming, who was
created a baronet in 1705, made large collections of
materials for the history of his own family, and also
of the counties of Westmoreland, Cumberland, and
Lancaster, which are still in existence at Rydal-hall.
Like several other members of his family, he repre-
sented the county of Westmoreland in the House of
Commons. The present owner of the hall is the relict
of the late baronet.

Just beyond Rydal-hall, the valley contracts and
turns abruptly to the left, through a defile formed by
the northern point of Loughrigg-fell on one side, and
Nab-scar on the other. At the foot of the latter is

the extensive slate quarry of White Moss.   Here we
came upon Rydal Water, which is a gem amongst the
lakes.   It is not more than a mile long, and has little
depth, but the water is of a sparkling transparency,
and its surface is spotted with several woody islands,
on one of which is a heronry.   Hemmed close in by
the hills, it has an air of seclusion which very few of
the lakes possess.

As we were skirting Rydal Water, which lies under
the northern side of Loughrigg-fell, I mentioned that
some of the most extensive views of lake scenery are
obtained from the top of that hill, which, though only
of the height of 1050 feet, is so placed in the midst
of a wide circle of loftier mountains, and is so surrounded by lakes, that it commands a much finer
prospect than many hills of greater elevation.   From
it are seen Windermere, (in nearly its whole extent),
Esthwaite Water, Blelham-tarn, Elterwater, Loughrigg-tarn, Grasmere Water, and Rydal Water; the
mountains of Coniston and Furness, Bowfell, the
Langdale Pikes, the Langdale and Borrowdale fells,
Silver How, Helm Crag, Skiddaw, Helvellyn, Fairfield, Scandale, Kirkstone, Hill Bell, and Wansfell
Pike; and the towns and villages of Bowness, Hawkshead, Elterwater, Grasmere, Rydal, and Ambleside.
From Nab-scar, which is a salient point of Fairfield
overlooking Loughrigg-fell, a yet more extensive prospect is obtained; and from Helm Crag, in Grasmere,
nearly the same objects are seen, with some variety in
the details.

A little beyond Rydal Water, the valley opens out
into a small plain, and forms a bed for Grasmere
Water, which is a sweet lake about a mile in length.
The mountains here form an amphitheatre several
miles in circumference, yet they are so lofty that the
valley which they enclose appears of small dimensions.
Loughrigg forms the southern barrier, and the rugged
hills of Silver How the western: on the north are the
Carrs, Helm Crag and Steel-fell; and on the west
the long and lofty ridge of Fairfield from Nab-scar
to Seat Sandal. Being shut in on every side by
these hills, Grasmere appears to be perfectly secluded
from the world; and as the meadows and pastures are
luxuriantly fertile, and their green surface is agreeably sprinkled with wood, there is a tranquil beauty
in the vale, calculated to excite in the mind the most
peaceful and delightful emotions. The lake has one
considerable island in the centre, which rises into
an eminence, and, being covered with grass, forms an
agreeable bank of verdure. It has only a small clump
of trees at one end, and a mistal to shelter the cattle
and sheep which feed there: a sprinkling of wood
on the island would make it a much more interesting object. The small, scattered village of Grasmere at the head of the lake, with its whitened
and rural church, has a lively and pleasing appearance. The plain terminates in two upland valleys,
one of which, named Easdale, runs up into the
heart of the Langdale fells, and the other, lying
between the range of Fairfield and Steel-fell, rises

with a long ascent into a slack, that separates the
valleys of Grasmere and Wythburn.   Several pretty
houses, surrounded by trees, quite in character with
this rural scene, lie at the foot of the hills ; one of
which was formerly inhabited by Wordsworth, and
another belonged to De Quincy.   Gray came upon
this valley from the side of Keswick, and calls it "a
little unsuspected paradise."   Perhaps the finest view
of it is that which we obtained yesterday, in passing
over High Close, and down the northern side of
Loughrigg.   Butterlip-how, a grassy knoll in the
midst of the valley, affords a charming panorama.   In
the rear of the village, and in the gorge of Easdale,
is a waterfall of considerable elevation, which, after
rains, pours down a broad and ample stream.   It is
formed by the rivulet that flows out of Easdale-tarn,
and from its constant whiteness it has received the
name of Sour Milk Gill.

The most remarkable feature of the vale of Grasmere is Helm Crag, a lofty conical hill which stands
at its head, and whose summit is a huge mass of shattered rocks.   Fancy has discerned resemblances to
several animate objects in these jumbled and toppling
crags ; the most striking of which is to a lion and
lamb, both couched down, and facing each other.   It
is remarkable that there are two groups of rocks,
each of them bearing this resemblance—one seen from
the vale of Grasmere, and the other from the ascent
of the hill to Dunmail Raise : the latter group has
also been likened to an old woman cowering ; and

under it is a cavern—a retreat and breeding place for foxes. I have clambered up this hill, and sat upon the lion's head, enjoying the splendid view which it commands. Wilson has a sonnet written on Helm Crag in a storm at midnight. George declared that he envied him the sublimity of the situation, and he seemed very anxious to ascend the hill, which he thought might be done in a quarter of an hour or twenty minutes. I told him that the ascent had cost me an hour, and that the grand and simple forms of this and the surrounding hills deceived him as to the height of Helm Crag. With some difficulty we dissuaded him from attempting the ascent whilst we were walking up the long hill to Dunmail Raise.

The valley which lies between Helm Crag and Steel-fell on one side, and Seat Sandal on the other, appears at the first glance so narrow, that George thought a nimble giant might leap across it. When, however, at my suggestion, he fixed his eyes steadily on Steel-fell, he found some difficulty in distinguishing the sheep which hung browzing on its sides from the stones that lay scattered about upon it, and could only ascertain what they were by observing if they moved. This showed him the real dimensions of the scene, and proportionably exalted his ideas. Matilda was delighted with the lion and lamb on Helm Crag, and bid me notice how affectionately the lamb raised its mouth to the nose of its grim protector, and with what magnanimity the monarch bowed his awful head to the caress of his meek protegé.

The top of the pass which separates the valley of
Grasmere from that of Wythburn also divides the
counties of Westmoreland and Cumberland.   It is
720 feet above the level of the sea, and is the lowest
pass in the chain of mountains which forms the
southern boundary of Cumberland, from near the sea-
coast to the county of Durham.   On this spot, and
touching the boundary wall, is the ancient monument
of Dunmail Raise, a considerable heap of pebble stones,
said to have been raised on the defeat of Dunmail,
King of Cumbria, in this place, A.D. 945, by Edmund
I. King of England, who put to death the vanquished
monarch, with his four sons, and gave his dominions
to Malcolm, King of Scotland.   This cairn, therefore,
marked the frontier of the two kingdoms, as well as
commemorated the victory of Edmund and the extinction of the kingdom of Cumbria.   It is about
seven miles from Ambleside and nine from Keswick.
We had read a good deal concerning this monument
in our guide-book, and George had raised his expect-   .
ations very high.   Matilda also anticipated something
striking and stupendous.   When we came to it, we
found two carriages standing near, and the parties
who belonged to them gathered round the cairn,
listening to an elderly gentleman, who expounded the
antiquarian lore concerning it.   Matilda, however,
demanded in the first place where the monument was;
and, on being shown a heap of stones on the road-side,
only a few feet in height, and fifteen or twenty yards
over, (which certainly no unlearned passenger would

have taken for a monument, or for any thing more
than materials to repair the road with) she exclaimed,
in a tone of extreme disappointment, loud enough
to be heard by the old gentleman, " Is this all ?"

The antiquary no sooner heard this disparaging
observation than he raised his spectacled eyes from
the heap on which he stood, and looked at us with
ineffable contempt. He was a meagre, sallow, and
most slovenly sexagenarian, with a countenance
expressive of great acuteness, and eyes at this moment lighted up with fervour and indignation ; for he
was in the very midst of an oration in praise of this
inestimable specimen of antiquity, and was triumphantly displaying the stores of learning which he had
accumulated on the subject. " This all !" he exclaimed, " and pray what did you expect, Miss ?
Did you expect a heap as high as the moon ? Perhaps you thought it was a pyramid with hiero-
glyphics, or an obelisk, or a Doric column, like the
London monument ? When you leave school, Miss,
you will learn that this species of monument, simple,
unadorned, natural, and characteristic of the age
when it was reared, is more precious in the eyes of
the true lover of antiquity, than all the gaudy pillars
which please children. This *all !* indeed. The true
cairn or *raise* of British antiquity—more venerable in
my eyes than the tumuli on the shores of Ilium !"

Matilda was at first quite disconcerted, and her
cheek flushed, by this rude attack in the presence of
strangers ; but, recovering herself before the peevish

old man had ceased, she said with spirit—"I crave your pardon, learned Sir, for the display of my ignorance; it is true that I have not studied antiquities so long as to make little things appear great in my eyes; I did not indeed expect to see either a pyramid or a column, but, as you have reminded me of school, I must say that I expected to see a somewhat larger heap than a parcel of school-boys might throw up in a holiday afternoon."

"Bravo!" exclaimed two or three gentlemen of the company, who seemed struck with admiration at Matilda's beauty and wit; and one of them immediately insisted that the "old fellow" should apologize to the lady for his incivility. They declared that she had buried him under his own cairn, and they proceeded to demand his apology with a very determined air. This only put him in a towering passion, and unpleasant consequences might have ensued, if Matilda, with a generosity and discretion which surprised every one, had not gone up to her adversary, and given him her hand, saying that she had a great veneration for learning, and was extremely sorry that she had unwittingly offended one of its votaries, but she hoped they should forgive one another, and be good friends. This quite subdued the old gentleman, and he began to pour out a flood of apologies, oddly mixed up with assertions of the real dignity of the monument, and his duty, as an humble member of the Antiquarian Society, to maintain it against all disparagement. He then, at her request, though at greater length than she would have liked, narrated the history of the monument to her, and explained the controversies which had arisen upon it, proving that his own conjecture was in all respects indubitably true, and that every other was utterly contemptible.

He also enlightened us on several other points of antiquity, concerning which we were in danger of going astray. Some one having observed that he supposed Helm Crag was so called from its resembling a helmet, he said that that was altogether a mistake, as the real, ancient name was not Helm, but Holme Crag, which signified *hill-crag*. I also hazarded my conjecture that Grasmere derived its name from the verdure around it, and on the island in the lake, adding that none of the lakes had such a grassy margin. But this, too, was quite wide of the mark; for the old name, he said, was Gresmere, or Grismere, and that it signified the lake of *swine*, from the Saxon *grise*, which had that meaning. He added that this country was in former days famous for its wild swine, as was proved by the names of many places round, as Grisedale, Boredale (Borrowdale), Stybarrow, Styhead, &c. George asked if Rydal was not formerly Rydale, and if it was not so called from the growth of *rye* in the dale. "Such a derivation," replied our oracle, "has been assigned to it by illiterate persons; but I coincide with the erudite Sir Daniel Fleming, of Rydale, that the name is an abbreviation of Rowtha-dale, from the river Rowtha, in modern days corrupted to Rothay: the same senseless passion for

modernizing names has led to *Rowth Mere* being
turned into Rydal water." These explanations induced Matilda to say to him, that his learning had
as much lowered Grasmere in her esteem, as it had
elevated Dunmail Raise; and then, with a profusion
of courtesies on all sides, of which Matilda received
the greatest share, we parted company, and entered
our respective carriages.

CHAPTER X.

At Dunmail Raise we entered Cumberland, the
country of the ancient Cimbri, " the true and genuine
Britons," who long maintained themselves amongst
these mountains when the more level parts of the
country had become entirely Saxon. The names still
retained by several places indicate a British origin
—as Helvellyn, Glenridden, Glencoin, Penrith,
Penruddock, &c. Cumberland contains the highest
mountains and the most sublime scenery in England,
and the greater number of the lakes are also in this
county.

From Dunmail Raise we looked down upon the
valley of Wythburn and the lake of Thirlmere. Here
also we obtained the first view of Skiddaw, whose
double summit rose majestically beyond the valley
which stretched before us, at a distance of about sixteen
miles. His base was concealed by the Derwent-fells,
but we saw nearly the whole bulk of the mountain,

which, having great regularity of outline, and being clothed with grass to its summit, has a character of beautiful and simple grandeur. Immediately on our right hand, and forming the eastern side of the valley of Wythburn, arose the rugged and precipitous form of " the mighty Helvellyn," on which in many parts the naked crags spring up to a great perpendicular elevation, and below them lie strewn large quantities of stones and shingle, which are broken off by frosts, and slide down the steep declivity. His sides are furrowed by ravines, wrought by the perpetual descent of small torrents, which wet weather frequently converts into fine cascades. The top of Helvellyn is not visible from the valley until you come within three miles of Keswick,—the broad shoulders of the mountain projecting so far as to hide his head. The bulk of Helvellyn is much greater than that of Skiddaw, and he is somewhat higher,* but, being hemmed round by other lofty mountains, he is less frequently visible in a tour through the lakes, and has far less distinctness of form than his rival, who, standing apart and alone, may be seen nearly on every side in his entire elevation.†

Before us, and lying along the foot of the fells, which separate this valley from that of Watendlath,

---

* According to the trigonometrical survey, the height of Skiddaw above the sea is 3022 feet; and that of Helvellyn 3055 feet.

† Helvellyn may be ascended from the Horse Head, Wythburn, and also from the sixth mile-stone from Keswick : the ascent is steep and arduous—much more so than that of Skiddaw. An account of the ascent from Patterdale is given in a subsequent chapter.

stretched the dark, narrow lake of Thirlmere, which
bears also the names of Leathes Water and Wythburn Water.* It is nearly three miles in length, but
about the middle the shores approach each other so as
almost to divide it into two distinct lakes,—a bridge
being thrown over the strait. It is overhung and
shaded by crags, some of which are stupendous, and
all naked and gloomy. The most conspicuous is
Raven-crag, near the foot of the lake, which forms
a striking object for many miles,—resembling a
gigantic round tower, blackened and shattered by
the lapse of ages. Thirlmere has a higher elevation
than any other lake, being 500 feet above the level
of the sea : its greatest depth of water is eighteen
fathoms. Its borders are not adorned, like those of
the other lakes, by wood, with the exception of a
few fir plantations, (which rather increase the gloomi-
ness of the scene), and of a bold wooded eminence,
called the How, at the foot of the lake. This valley
has no luxuriance, and its general character is wild
magnificence. The road descends through it for
several miles with scarcely any change in the objects.
If the traveller, however, should be able to cross the
strait I have mentioned, and to pass down the other
side of the lake, he would see the house and grounds
of Dale-head, and some beautiful scenery, which are

---

* It is called Leathes Water, from having been for many
generations the property of the family of Leathes, or Laithes, at
Dale-head ; and the name of Wythburn Water is derived from the
village of Wythburn, the most considerable place on its borders.

hid from the passenger on the high road by an intervening elevation.

When we had passed down the valley four or five miles, we found it divided into two branches by Naddle fell—on the right of which is the interesting valley of St. John or Wanthwaite. This is a verdant and peaceful vale, lying betwixt enormous crags, and through its vista is seen the noble mountain of Saddleback, or Blencathara. This mountain derives the name by which it is commonly known from the peculiarity of its shape ; on the south-west side it rises with a regular convex swell from the base nearly to the summit, and being rounded off on each side, and covered with verdure, the whole side or *back* of the hill appears like a smooth, sloping *saddle* for some Brobdingnagian rider. The summit is craggy, and on the east and south-east the hill is scarred with awful ravines. The foot of Saddleback touches that of Skiddaw.

Leaving the vale of St. John on our right, we crossed the river Greta, which flows out of Thirlmere lake, at Smalthwaite-bridge, and passing betwixt the How and Naddle-fell, we came upon a desolate moor lying between the latter hill and the Derwent-fells. At length, about two miles from Keswick, we began to ascend Castlerigg, the hill which slopes down from the Derwent-fells to the valley of the Greta.

When we had passed along the top, and came to look down upon Keswick, a grand and extensive prospect, of which we had not yet had even a glimpse,

opened to our view. An amphitheatre twenty miles in
circumference lay before us, environed by a multitude
of bold and lofty mountains, and adorned by two fine
lakes. On the north rose the majestic form of Skiddaw, now revealed from the base to the summit, and
from the Dod on his western flank to Latrigg on the
eastern. At his foot lay the small town of Keswick,
and a valley branched off from the plain on either
side of him. In that which ran to the north-west,
lay the sheet of Bassenthwaite or Broad Water, a
lake about four miles in length, and at an equal distance from Castlerigg. To the south of Keswick, in
the bottom of the great mountain-basin, we saw the
beautiful and interesting lake of Derwentwater,
adorned with several woody islands. Its whole extent
was not visible from this place, but as we descended
the hill, we saw the head of the lake, and the jaws
of Borrowdale beyond. The mountains on each side
of Derwentwater are peculiarly bold in their forms,
and present several sharp ridges of great elevation
running off obliquely from the lake; at its head is
the wild valley just mentioned; and at its foot a considerable plain of great fertility and beauty, and
plentifully sprinkled with wood, extending to the base
of Skiddaw, and onwards to Bassenthwaite Water.

Our party gazed on the splendid prospect with eager
eyes, and, after they had perused its general features,
all my topographical knowledge was called forth to
satisfy their inquiries as to the details. " The bold,
steep hill," I said, " that overlooks the head of Bas-

senthwaite Water on the west, (beyond Skiddaw) is called Barf, and Lord's Seat is the neighbouring elevation.   Further to the left is Whinlatter, over which passes the road to Crummock Water. The high mountain that rises next, in tracing the hills on the horizon from north to south, is Grisedale Pike; then the still higher summit of Grassmoor; then the horned top of Causey Pike, to the left of which is the beautiful vale of Newlands. Beyond the extremity of this vale, you see the sharp point of Red Pike, and the higher elevation of High Stile, which rise above the further shore of the lake of Buttermere: then Robinson and Hindscarth, the latter of which has a pile of stones on the summit. The sharp ridge, with two hunches, whose grassy side slopes down to the head of Derwentwater, is Catbells: it is not unlike the back of a camel. Beyond are the crags of Borrowdale, and in the valley you perceive a conical hill clothed with dark firs, called Castle Crag. At the upper extremity of Borrowdale are Scawfell Pikes, and you may discern upon them the pile of stones which stands upon the highest point in England. The crags of Lowdore are at the head of the lake; and this broad and towering precipice, just on our left hand, with a fine wood spread at its base, is Wallow Crag. The conical hill that stands between us and the lake, so finely clothed with wood, is Castle-head." This magnificent assemblage of objects fully engaged our attention whilst we descended the steep hill that brought us into the town of Keswick.

We drove to the Royal Oak, and were speedily provided with apartments by the active and attentive
landlady, who told us that her house was now quite
full, and had been so for the last six weeks. The
Queen's Head also, another good inn, and all the
lodging-houses, had been filled, and they had had a
very busy season. Keswick, in fact, is the metropolis
of the Lakes, where tourists often take up their
head-quarters, and whence they visit all the surrounding lakes and mountains. It is the largest and most
central town of the district, has better sources of
amusement in unfavourable weather than any other,
and enjoys the most magnificent situation. Here
meet nobles and commoners, merchants and tradesmen,
students and idlers, artists, poets, mineralogists,
anglers, the valetudinarian in search of health, the
healthful in quest of pleasure, the man of pleasure
in pursuit of variety, foreigners, authors, lovers,—in
short, samples of every class of mankind, whose circumstances enable them to travel.

I have omitted to mention that at Ambleside we
fell in with, and were introduced to a very interesting party, with whom we have peculiar reasons for
hoping to be better acquainted. The party consisted of Col. H——n, his daughter and niece,—and
the daughter was the young lady who had so powerfully attracted the admiration of George in the court
at Lancaster. We found that Col. H——n was an
old friend of George's father; they had been schoolfellows, and the Colonel had visited at the house of

G

Mr. G., where he had seen Mrs. Anabella when in
her teens. He was a man of great talents and virtues ; had served many years with distinction in
India, where he lost an amiable wife; and had sent
his daughter to England, to be educated in the family
of his brother-in-law. Affliction had exercised a
softening and exalting influence on his mind. After
a long absence, he had returned over land to England
about two years ago, and he was now revisiting a scene
with which he had been familiar in his youth. It
would be superfluous to say that George was delighted
beyond measure with this happy rencontre : and after
the bashfulness he always manifested on a new introduction had subsided, he took an active part in the
conversation, and endeavoured, with a natural and
honest eagerness, to ingratiate himself both with
the father and the daughter. So well did he develop
his talents and information in this interview, that I
believe he succeeded in his object ; and, on the other
hand, we were all charmed with the Colonel and his
interesting daughter. We spent the evening with
them at Ambleside, and they had preceded us this
morning in the journey to Keswick, where it was
agreed that we were to dine together, and afterwards
to row round Derwentwater.

The Colonel having arrived nearly an hour before
us, dinner was ready quite as soon as the ladies of our
party were prepared for it ; and, though the hour was
early, the keen pure air of the Cumberland mountains
had so sharpened our appetites, that we did ample

justice to the viands. Rising soon after the cloth was drawn, we all set out, accompanied by a boatman, to make the circuit of Derwentwater.

We had to walk upwards of half a mile from the town to the lake, skirting the beautiful pasture of Crow Park, which swells gently above the foot of Derwentwater. When we got into the boat, the sun had made considerable progress on his downward march; but I think, on the whole, we were not losers by the circumstance, as he poured such a flood of glory on the woods and fells which tower over the eastern border of Derwentwater, that we were fascinated by the scene. We rowed up that side of the lake, and of course saw the shores and the islands to the utmost advantage, whilst the hills on the opposite shore were shaded, and their grand outline was relieved against a splendid evening sky.

Derwentwater and the lands around it were formerly in the possession of the unfortunate family of the Ratcliffes, who took their title of Earls of Derwentwater from the lake. They had anciently a castle on Castlerigg, and afterwards a house on one of the principal islands of the lake, which has since borne the name of Lord's Island. The family did not usually reside here, but at Dalston, in Northumberland. Whilst in their possession, Crow Park, at the northeast corner of the lake, and all the long slope of the hills on the eastern shore, were covered with noble forests of oak, which gave to the scene a character of grand solemnity. But when Lord Derwentwater

forfeited his head on Tower-hill for partaking in the
rebellion of 1715, his estates were confiscated, and
bestowed upon Greenwich Hospital, the trustees of
which charity, with the discretion that often charac-
terizes the management of distant property, especially
by public bodies, cleared away the forests at one fell
swoop, and stripped the hills of their majestic mantle !
Great and irreparable as is the injury, it must be
admitted that the knolls and lawns now seen on the
waving surface of the shore are highly beautiful:
several of the small hills and promontories are again
covered with trees, which enclose and enrich the
tracts of verdure ; and the steep sides of the fells are
feathered with natural wood, which, if a less rich and
ample, is perhaps a fresher and livelier covering than
the old forests. The trustees of the hospital also,
whilst the estate was in their possession, refused
to let the land on long leases, of which complaint has
been made, as it prevented individuals from building
mansions on the shore, which, in the opinion of the
complainants, would be a great ornament to the lake.
In my judgment, however, Derwentwater would be
spoiled by the erection of villas and mansions on its
borders. I like it now for its seclusion, and should
be sorry to see it environed by houses. Windermere,
the scenery of which is soft and beautiful, may have
its charms heightened by introducing the elegance of
art. But the character of Derwentwater is high sublimity: on every side the mountains lift their rocky
heads to heaven: and in expatiating over the vastness

of the scene, the mind rises far above the insignificant works of man, and delights to feel itself at liberty, unconstrained by the observation of others, to range and exult in the magnificent temple of nature.

The ancient demesne of the Derwentwater family is now in the possession of John Marshall, Jun., Esq., M.P. for Leeds, second son of John Marshall, Esq., of Hallsteads. The estate was bought by Mr. Marshall, when sold by the Trustees of Greenwich Hospital in 1832. This property includes one-third of Derwent lake, with the exclusive right of fishing, the manors and manorial rights connected with the township of Keswick, and a great extent of commons, besides the good land between Castlerigg, Keswick, and the lake, and a considerable part of the eastern border of the lake.

Another third of Derwent lake belongs to the Earl of Egremont, and the third at the head of the lake to the freeholders of Borrowdale.

CHAPTER XI.

Derwentwater is upwards of three miles in length, and somewhat more than a mile in breadth,—which is wider than any other of the lakes. It is adorned by several considerable islands, richly clothed with wood, of which the principal are Lord's Island, Vicar's Island, St. Herbert's Island, and Rampsholm. From the extent of the plain in which it lies, and the several valleys diverging from it, a much greater number of mountains is seen from its surface than from any other lake; and their rocky, irregular, and tumultuous character gives to the scenery of Derwentwater a wild sublimity, equally distinct from the solemn grandeur of Ullswater and the soft beauties of Windermere.

It was a bright and sunny afternoon, as I have already mentioned, when our combined parties embarked for the purpose of rowing round the lake. We took a boat at a small pier, in a bay formed by Crow Park, now the race-ground, on the north, and the promenade of Friar Crag on the east.   Vicar's Island is immediately opposite this spot, at the distance of a few hundred yards, and we rowed there for the purpose of seeing the beautiful pleasure-grounds of General Peachy, who has a house on the island. Having asked and obtained permission, we walked round the grounds, accompanied by the gardener. The island contains about five acres and a half, and this small space is laid out to the utmost advantage in lawns, shrubberies, and parterres.   A grove of beautiful trees encompasses the island, with only one opening to the south ; and the house, which stands on a rising ground, commands through this opening a splendid prospect of the lake and mountains.   The front of the house is covered with ivy, and it has not a disagreeable effect from that side on which alone it can be seen.   The island is sometimes called Pocklington's Island, from the name of its former proprietor, and General Peachy gives it the name of Derwent Isle ; but "every true lover of antiquity," as our friend of Dunmail Raise would have said, will continue to give it the old name of Vicar's Island, which it derived from having formerly belonged to Fountain's Abbey in Yorkshire.   Having hastily made the circuit of the island, and admired the taste with which it is laid out, we re-entered our boat.

Our course now lay between the island and the promenade, and past the rock at the extremity of the latter, which has obtained the name of Friar Crag, as is said, from the fact that St. Herbert, who lived on

the island in the centre of Derwentwater, used to
land there when he visited the shore. We then
entered a bay formed by Friar Crag on the north and
Lord's Island on the south, in which the one mighty
object is Wallow Crag, whose awful precipice towers
over the wood spread around its base, to the height of
a thousand feet above the lake. We landed on Lord's
Island, and saw the traces of the house built here by
the Derwentwater family : nothing remains except the
mere foundations, all the building-stone having been
removed to erect the town-hall of Keswick and other
houses. The whole island, of which the extent is six
acres, is now covered with wood. Again entering the
boat, we passed up the channel between Lord's Island
and the shore, from whence beautiful prospects are
obtained—on the one hand, of the majestic form of
Skiddaw, with the woods of Castlehead and Cockshot
Park in the foreground ; and on the other, of the
upper part of the lake, the beautiful islands of St.
Herbert's and Rampsholm, and the rugged crags and
mountains of Borrowdale. Col. H——n was the first
to point out to the ladies a deep cleft in the face
of Wallow Crag, wrought by the descent of a torrent
in wet weather, and choked with wood, which bears
the name of the *Lady's Rake,* from the circumstance
that the Countess of Derwentwater is said to have
made her escape by night up the ravine, when intelligence of her husband's arrest reached her. Col.
H——n took occasion to state, by way of bringing to
the recollection of the ladies a passage of history

which they might but faintly remember, the events of
the period as connected with the unfortunate family of
the Ratcliffes. He sketched the circumstances with
simplicity, and not without feeling.   The rebellions
of 1715 and 1745,—the active part taken by the Earl
of Derwentwater in the first, and by his son in the
second, on behalf of the Pretender,—the ruin of their
noble house, by clinging to the fortunes of an ill-
starred, despotic, and stubbornly unteachable race of
princes,—and the disasters of some other branches of
the family,—were briefly narrated, with a pathos
perhaps insensibly heightened from the scene of the
Countess's perilous flight being before our eyes.   The
romantic character of the incident itself, and of the
mountain-pass through which the lady fled, brought
vividly to our minds some of the descriptions in
Waverley, where highland glens and " hair-breadth
'scapes," unsuccessful rebellion and the ruin of ancient
families, are so graphically depicted.   Matilda, however, took the liberty to doubt whether any lady could
by possibility make her way up a place which seemed
nearly perpendicular.

Our boat glided softly down the eastern side of the
lake, and we sat for some time silently admiring the
noble crags and fells which rose above us, the unruffled surface of the water, the changing positions of
the islands, the beautiful vale of Newlands on the
opposite shore, the simple sublimity of Skiddaw at
the foot of the lake, and the picturesque horrors of
Borrowdale at its head.

When we had left Lord's Island behind us, and entered another bay overhung by Falcon Crag, our guide pointed to a boat-house at a considerable distance over the water, which seemed to us to be on the opposite shore of the lake; and we were surprised to learn that it was on St. Herbert's Island, which is nearly in the centre of Derwentwater. This was a remarkable proof how difficult it is for an inexperienced eye to judge of the distance of objects seen over a sheet of water.[*]

We landed near Barrow-house, the seat of Joseph Pocklington, Esq., and walked up to see a very pretty cascade in the rear of the house. The quantity of water is not great, but it falls in a picturesque manner down the face of a rock, at two distinct leaps,—the total depth being a hundred and twenty-two feet. The cascade is situated in a wood on the steep side of the hill, and a summer-house has been built on the rock above it, which commands a fine view of the lake.

When we approached the head of the lake, it was so remarkably clear and smooth, that we saw a reflection of the hill-side in the water, as distinct in the forms and as vivid in the colours as the original. This

* We had not time to call at St. Herbert's Island, which is usually visited on the return from Lowdore. I have landed there on another tour. That St. Herbert had his hermitage on this island is certain from the authority of the Venerable Bede, as well as from tradition. A chantry long stood here, where mass used to be sung. The island belonged to the late Sir Wilfrid Lawson, who built a grotto, called the new Hermitage, upon it. The island contains four acres, and is covered with wood.

effect may often be seen on a small scale, but it very
rarely happens that a hill several hundred feet high,
of much greater longitudinal extent, and covered with
trees, rocks, and other objects, is seen reflected in the
water with any thing like distinctness. Yet here the
hydrographic repetition was as faithful as if the scene
had been returned by a mirror without a flaw; and
the setting sun, illuminating the whole, made it a
lovely picture.* A range of lofty crags stretches beyond the head of the lake and round the fall of Lowdore; and, being nearly perpendicular and clothed
with natural wood, they form a splendid silvan theatre,
amongst which appear rocks of varied shape and hue.
These crags terminate in a grand pillar of rock, named
Gowder Crag.

At the south-east corner of the lake there is the
phenomenon of a Floating Island, which rises occasionally above the surface of the lake, but, being
attached to the bottom by its sides, does not change
its place except by rising and sinking. The extent
of this island is sometimes half an acre; it has risen
only seven times since the year 1808, and generally
appears in hot summers; it appeared in the successive
summers of 1824, 1825, and 1826. The most probable conjecture as to the cause of the phenomenon is,
that the vegetable substances upon it, in the process
of decomposition, form a large quantity of gas, which

* In a subsequent tour I saw a still more splendid reflection of
the whole of Catbells, Swinside, Skiddaw, and the islands, in the
lake, with a morning sun. See the second *Excursion on Foot.*

pervades the spongy substance of the island, and
makes it so light as to rise to the surface.   Heat pro-
motes the accumulation of gas, and when the gas is carried off by exposure to the atmosphere or is condensed
by cold, the island sinks. When the surface is pierced,
gas issues forth, which has been collected, and found
to consist of equal parts of carburetted hydrogen and
azotic gases, with about six per cent. of carbonic acid.
It has been supposed that the water of a small cascade,
named Cat-gill, which tumbles down the rocks near
this place, and which then finds a subterraneous passage into the lake, may have been the cause of buoying
up the Island : but this supposition is generally dis-
allowed by men of science.

The river Derwent, up which we rowed a short
distance, is perhaps the most limpid and colourless
stream in this country ; we saw the small gray
pebbles which form its bed at the depth of six or eight
feet, and should scarcely have known that any
medium denser than air was betwixt them and the
eye, but for a certain glassy smoothness which the
liquid necessarily gives them.

Landing on the eastern bank of the Derwent, we
walked a few hundred yards to the celebrated Fall of
Lowdore, situated in a chasm to the rear of a hamlet
of that name. This cascade has much grandeur of
effect when the stream is swelled by rains, but at this
time the quantity of water was small. Its height is
about a hundred and fifty feet, and the water tumbles
over and amongst a jumbled pile of rocks, dashing,

brawling, and foaming, and in no place (at this period) falling more than a few yards at once. The stream comes down a ravine of the hill, out of the valley of Watendlath, and, when sudden rains augment its quantity and force, it flings itself furiously over the precipice, and hides all the rocks which obstruct its descent, roaring with tremendous dissonance, and scattering the foam of its wrath far and wide. It is said that the noise of the cataract can at these periods be heard to a distance of ten or twelve miles; which, however, seems scarcely credible. The effect of the scene is greatly increased by the prodigious crags which rise on either side of the fall, one of them, called Gowder Crag, to the perpendicular height of five · hundred feet. The opposite mass of rock is called Shepherd's Crag. Numerous trees have taken root in the face of the cliffs, and throw out their branches into the air ; and, looking upwards from the chasm at the foot of the waterfall, you see the innumerable leaves and twigs, with their fine outlines printed on the clear blue vault of the sky. The wood is principally the mountain-ash and the birch, and a few elegant young trees stand perched on the very crest of the rocks, and waving in the wind, as graceful and well-balanced as birds upon a spray.

In the meadow where we landed on leaving our boat, an extremely fine Echo is to be heard. It proceeds from the side of the fells, which here rise so nearly perpendicular as to resemble a vast wall. The place where we stood being several hundred yards from the hill-side, it required rather a loud shout to obtain a response; but the number of syllables which might be uttered before the answer came, was of course proportioned to the distance. The Colonel, George, and myself hollaed loud and long; we invoked *Skiddaw, Helvellyn, Niagara, Himalaya, Glaramara,* and other magnificent and sounding names, all which the faithful reflector flung back upon our ears, as distinctly as if the words had been palpable and elastic objects, and had struck the rocks with the sharpness of a hammer. I believe a person of good lungs and nimble tongue, like Mathews, might obtain a perfect replication to the name of the race-horse, *Caifakarata-dadera*—a name given, I suppose, in the hope that the horse would run the faster from having so many *feet*. We endeavoured to prevail upon the ladies to try their voices, but they pleaded inability to produce an echo at such a distance. At length Matilda called out *Dunmail Raise* with a small shrill shout, which the cliffs returned in such a tone of scoffing mockery, that if our antiquarian friend had been present, I am persuaded he would have flown into a rage. The singularity of the sound, and the scene it recalled to our minds, produced a loud and general fit of laughter; at which the fells unexpectedly awoke their obsequious mirth, and shook their sides with laughter. Our experiments were terminated by the discharge of a cannon, which is placed there for the purpose, and fired by the people of Lowdore Inn for the amusement of those who will pay for it. Mrs. Anabella

and Matilda were so much alarmed by the preparations, that they ran to a distance of fifty or sixty
yards, whilst Miss H——n stood calmly near the
piece, like a soldier's daughter. The reverberation
was truly awful: from Borrowdale fells it was hurled
back to the opposite heights of Catbells and Causey
Pike, whence it roared round the whole amphitheatre
of mountains in a prolonged peal. Such is generally
the solemn stillness of this scene, that we felt a kind
of superstitious awe at having thus violently disturbed
it, by calling upon the spirits of the mountains to
answer us;—as some enchanters in Eastern tales are
alarmed when their invocations are obeyed by the
appearance of awful genii.

The effect was increased by the approach of evening;
for we had lingered so long at Lowdore, with the
cataract and the echo, that the sun had gone down
nearly an hour, and the twilight was rapidly deepening into dusk. We hastened therefore to the boat,
and directed the boatman to lose no time, but to take
us down the opposite side of the lake from that by
which we had ascended. He complied by pulling
vigorously across the southern extremity of the lake,
and along the western shore. We were now immediately opposite the jaws of Borrowdale, and could
just see the tall, shaggy forms of Grange Crag and
Castle Crag, which guard the entrance. The extreme
wildness and ruggedness of the cliffs on either side,
and the darkness which brooded over the valley beyond,
caused a shudder to come across the ladies as they

contemplated it.   The obscurity of the scene only
gave play to their imaginations, which probably
conjured up ideas of Borrowdale as not less horrible
than the valley of the shadow of death.   The mountains on the western side of the lake, which seemed
almost to overhang us, were a mighty shade : and the
rugged outlines of Catbells and Causey Pike were
traced in the strongest relief against the sky, still
illumined by the white light which lingers on the
horizon in an autumn evening.   On the north,
Skiddaw reigned in lonely majesty, his double summit resembling a crown ; he seemed to spring up
directly from the edge of Derwentwater, and his
broad base stretched across that end of the amphitheatre.   The white houses of Keswick had before
been visible at the foot of the lake, and we now
recognized the situation of the town by its lights.

The night was one of the most brilliant I ever
beheld, and long before we arrived at Keswick the
stars shone out with the purest lustre.   The crescent
of the new moon was divinely pencilled on the firmament.   In the lake the heavenly lights were reflected
with a tremulous movement, occasioned by an evening
zephyr which crept silently over the surface. Stillness
the most profound—a holy stillness—prevailed ; and it
was with serene solemnity that we looked up to the
gigantic features of earth which stood in shadow
around us, and the glorious canopy of heaven above
our heads.   The silence was broken by Colonel
H——n : " Can that man breathe," he said, " who

could view a scene like this, and doubt the existence
of an almighty and all-wise Creator? Who can
behold that moon, renewing her light without the
deviation of a second in time, or of a hair's breadth
in space—those constellations, beaming the same
'sweet influences' as at the hour 'when the morning
stars sang together,'—and dream that they are upheld
and guided by a hand less than infinite? Or who,
that reflects for a moment, can doubt, that the same
Power who sustains the whole frame-work of nature,
from its most sublime to its minutest forms, surveys
with omniscient eye the movements of all the intelligent spirits which animate it, and judges them by
rules of immutable righteousness? How high a
lesson does this scene convey! It solemnizes our
vain thoughts, and raises them from earth to heaven,
from time to eternity. In the contemplation of it,
man feels his immortality."

These remarks strengthened the impression which
the scene was calculated to make upon us, and turned
our conversation into a higher channel than that in
which it had hitherto flowed. Shortly afterwards we
landed, and, being chilled by the evening air, we
walked quickly to the inn, where a blazing fire and a
dish of fragrant tea soon restored us to comfort. Our
conversation turned principally on the interesting
objects we had witnessed, and I am sure none of us
will ever forget our evening sail on Derwentwater.

CHAPTER XII.

MORNING brought the lamented departure of Col.
H——n, his daughter and niece, who were on their
route to Scotland. In our conversation the preceding
evening, many had been the hints given by George
and Mrs. Anabella how charming it would be if the
threatened departure could be postponed, and how
interesting were the objects which we might all
see together. We meditated excursions to Skiddaw,
Borrowdale, and Buttermere, none of which had
Miss H——n or Miss Seymour yet visited; and
Mrs. Anabella, who was quite touched by the polite
attentions of the Colonel, bewailed the necessity we
should be under of foregoing the advantage of his
company and information in these expeditions. George
described to Miss H——n with great eloquence
all that he had heard or read about the objects still to
be seen; but there was a blushing eagerness about
his representations, which I think must have told a
tale to the Colonel. However, all this breath was

thrown away, except perhaps on the heart of the lady; for her father told us that, notwithstanding his great desire to enjoy the pleasure of our company some days longer, he was compelled to proceed northwards, by having previously engaged to dine with a friend of his, at his seat in Dumfriesshire, on the following day. This of course put an end to our dissuasive arguments, though not to our lamentations; and early the following morning, after receiving a pressing invitation to visit the Colonel on his return at his own house, we saw our friends drive off on the road to Penrith.

Scarcely had the carriage disappeared, when the waiter introduced a guide, who was to accompany us in the ascent of Skiddaw. The day was cloudy, but there was no reason to apprehend rain; and though the summit of Skiddaw was occasionally tipped with vapour, the atmosphere was clear, and our guide thought we should have a good view from the mountain. This expedition had been determined on without much previous consultation with the ladies: as soon as it was mentioned, Mrs. Anabella declared herself eager to achieve the ascent of so celebrated a mountain, and Matilda, who knew very little about the matter, offered no objections. The latter, however, began to suspect that she had engaged in no light, half-hour's trip, when I advised her to put on her plainest and warmest clothing, an old bonnet, and a pair of strong boots. And her suspicions were more powerfully excited by the preparations which our

guide recommended, who proposed to lay in an extensive stock of sandwiches and brandy. She demanded
how long we were to be absent, and, on hearing that we
must calculate on five or six hours, she put on a most
rueful, unromantic countenance, and exclaimed—" Oh
I am tired of seeing great stones !"   Mrs. Anabella and
George were highly indignant at a remark so derogatory to the sublime scenery we had witnessed, and
pronounced Matilda utterly destitute of taste: the
observation certainly showed that she was not troubled
with an excess of enthusiasm, and indeed she on all
occasions manifested a true English preference of
comfort over most other objects of ambition. She was
also dissatisfied with the appearance of the guide,
whom she pronounced to be not only mean-looking,
but so much in-kneed that she believed he would
never get up the hill. The waiter assured us, however, that he was a very experienced guide, and
had not unfrequently ascended Skiddaw twice in one
day ; and we afterwards found, that he could walk
up hill much quicker than either George or myself.

All Matilda's objections being over-ruled, two
ponies were ordered to the door for the ladies ; George
and I were to walk at their sides for their security.
We set out, therefore, on the Penrith road, and,
after going about half a mile, we crossed the Greta
by a narrow bridge. Turning to the left, we began to
ascend by a road which passes behind the house of Mr.
Calvert, of Greta-bank, and winds round the front of
Latrigg, a smooth and verdant hill at the foot of

Skiddaw, which has obtained the name of " Skiddaw's cub." It is deformed with one or two parallelograms of fir plantations.

Our guide and our horses were both of opinion that we should commence the ascent at a very slow and steady pace, which was not at all pleasing to George, he being confident in his strength, and eager to reach the summit. I told him that he would have need of his vigour before we had accomplished the ascent of five miles, and that if he did not begin calmly, he would both exhaust his strength, and, by heating himself, run some risk from the cold air on the top. With these representations he was hardly persuaded to keep by our sides.

Almost before we were aware, we found ourselves considerably elevated above the town, and commanding a splendid view of the plain of Keswick, the lakes of Derwent and Bassenthwaite, and the surrounding mountains. The beauty of this view in some degree reconciled Matilda to the expedition. We soon, however, found ourselves nearly shut out from this prospect, by passing round to the rear of Latrigg. We also lost all appearance of a road, and proceeded along a path which seemed to be merely a sheep-track. After passing for a short distance on level ground, and then descending into a little hollow, we began a very steep and long ascent up the eastern side of Skiddaw, with a deep ravine on our right hand. Here we were obliged frequently to halt, and when we advanced it was at a slower than funeral pace. We were now literally climbing, and in this part of the mountain it is scarcely possible for the pedestrian to be too deliberate.   The ponies toiled patiently up the steep, but often stopped and panted for breath.   The hill immediately on our right hand in this sharp pull, and only separated from us by the ravine, is Lonscale-fell ; its sides are covered with heath and fern, and a gleam of sunshine fell upon it just at this moment, as if for the purpose of lighting up the innumerable heath-bells, which clothed the hill with a robe of the richest purple.

After more than an hour and a half's labour, we came to a rounded, down-like part of the mountain, called Jenkin-hill, covered with a thick carpet of grass and moss, from which we looked down on Derwentwater. Stopping to survey the prospect below, we found that its features had most materially altered. We were already higher than several hills which appeared from the lake to be nearly as lofty as Skiddaw ; a much greater number of summits became visible ; and the lake shrunk in its dimensions, whilst the houses, fields, and woods on its margin seemed as if traced on a map, they lay so far beneath. We felt as if we had left the world and mankind below us, and were ascending towards the regions of eternal silence. The scene we had quitted formed a lovely picture, its beauties being heightened by contrast with the wild hills amongst which it lay embosomed, and which now opened very extensively to our view. On our right hand, as we pursued our march, was Saddleback, appearing as the rival of Skiddaw. There is great beauty in the flowing lines of these sublime mountains as seen from this place. Before us were the two summits of Skiddaw, on the highest of which is a pile of stones; but they were still far above us, and the ladies, who thought we must be near the top, heard with consternation that we were not much more than half way up the mountain. To travellers who ascend in warmer weather it may be interesting to know, that on Jenkin-hill, and near the foot of the first cone of Skiddaw, there is a spring of pure water, and that higher up no supply of this element can be obtained.

As we were proceeding, there opened upon us, to the great surprise and delight of most of our party, a view of the sea, at the distance of twenty miles, seen between Skiddaw and Grisedale Pike; and we even descried the hilly shores of the Isle of Man, at nearly three times that distance. Passing to the north of the first summit of Skiddaw, these interesting objects were concealed from us again by the mountain, but Solway Frith and the Scotch mountains then became visible on the north. After the long and steep ascent which I have described, the rest of the ascent is quite easy, at least under ordinary circumstances: there is no track over the grassy carpet of Jenkin-hill for some distance, but the path is found again very distinctly marked when the traveller comes to the north of the first summit of the mountain.

Here a great mountain basin, called Skiddaw forest, (though without a tree) several miles in diameter, lay below us on the right. There is no appearance of cultivation, and but a single house, in this vast hollow of the hills; which is enclosed by Skiddaw on the west, Saddleback on the east, and High Pike and Carrock Fell on the north. The river Caldew, which flows into the Eden, takes its rise here, and may be traced for some miles through " the forest :" the valley in the bottom of which it runs, looks as if it had formerly been the bed of a mighty river.

The greatest hardship of the journey now began to be felt. A bitter north-east wind, which became a stiff gale as we ascended towards the higher regions of the atmosphere, blew right upon us from the direction of Carrock Fell, and made it difficult for the ladies to sit upon their horses. I turned towards it, and felt the blast penetrate my clothes, which were open at the breast, and wrap round my body, as if a damp sheet were drawn about me. We made a pause, during which Matilda once mentioned the idea of returning; but, as she was unsupported in her pro- position, we armed ourselves for the worst, the ladies fastening their bonnets upon their heads with hand- kerchiefs, and George and myself putting on our great coats, which the guide had providently brought with him. We then resumed our march, the guide leading Mrs. Anabella's horse, and George walking by her side to support her in her seat, whilst I rendered the same service to his sister.

When we arrived at the foot of the steep and rugged ascent, which brings us to the summit of the mountain, we found the wind a hurricane. It would have been safer for Matilda to dismount; but as I had myself ascended this place on horseback, I urged on our sure-footed pony, and we struggled up the hill over the slippery shingle. When we had conquered this difficulty, we found ourselves on the ridge which forms the summit of the mountain, but still two or three hundred yards from the pile of stones which stands on the highest point; we therefore pushed on, though alarmed at the awful depth and steepness of the descent on either side of the ridge along which our road lay, and leaned with all our strength against the wind, to avoid being blown down the opposite side of the mountain.* The surface of this ridge is a mere bed of rough stones and shingle, which made our footing very uncertain. At length, to our infinite satisfaction, we reached the pile of stones on the summit, called Skiddaw Man. When I had helped Matilda off the animal, and seated her in a little stone-built hut close to the pile, she was nearly exhausted, and sobbed out—" O William, I would not do that again for the world!" It was nearly ten minutes before Mrs. Anabella and George joined us,

---

* I have been on Skiddaw when the wind was so tremendous, that a lady and gentleman who had ridden up the hill, but had dismounted, were blown down to the ground, or threw themselves down, three several times, and, being utterly unable to accomplish the short remaining distance, returned without attaining the summit. Their footman had been obliged to stop before they did, and was clinging to the stones on the hill-side: and the guide and horses appeared to be in danger of being blown down the hill, I was on horseback, and could give them no assistance.

H

as they had walked up the last ascent, and had with extreme difficulty kept their feet. The lady was obliged to rest some minutes before she recovered herself so as to enjoy the astonishing prospect beneath us.

Cumberland and Westmoreland, with all their mighty clusters of mountains, their lakes and rivers—Lancashire, Yorkshire, Northumberland, the Solway Frith and a range of Scottish hills beyond—the Irish sea, and on the far horizon the hills of the Isle of Man;—such was the range of this glorious and sublime prospect. Bassenthwaite Water lay so immediately beneath us, that it seemed as if we might easily be blown from our dizzy elevation into its bed. We looked down upon the town of Cockermouth, and beyond stretched the level part of Cumberland, three thousand feet below us, to the sea coast, and northward to the Solway Frith. The whole of that fine estuary lay under our view, and we traced the Scotch coast with perfect distinctness to Burrow-head, the promontory that separates Wigtown Bay and Luce Bay. I have no doubt that we saw the Mull of Galloway beyond, but our guide thought it was never to be seen from Skiddaw. I have not, however, found the guides infallible, especially as to distant objects. It is said that the city of Carlisle cannot be seen from Skiddaw, but the smoke of the city was very obvious, and I also saw the tower of the cathedral. The town of Penrith is hid, but some houses in the suburbs may be seen, and the beacon on a hill a mile from the town is a conspicuous object. To the south, Derwentwater was concealed by the second summit of Skiddaw, but beyond it a tumultuous sea of mountains, wild, dark, and rocky, stretched in magnificent confusion. Above them all towered Scawfell; and the nearer summit of Helvellyn appeared to rival him in dignity. Far away to the south-east, the broad head of Ingleborough was just visible over some of the Westmoreland fells, and, due east, on the distant horizon, rose the mountain of Cross-fell, rival to Skiddaw in elevation, and forming the highest point of "the British Appennines." The bold form of Saddleback seemed almost within arm's length, and, though we looked over his bluff summit, yet he stood like the twin-brother of Skiddaw.* None of the lakes, except Bassenthwaite, are visible.†

* The height of Skiddaw is 3022 feet, and that of Saddleback 2789.

† The following mountains are visible in the grand panoramic view from the summit of Skiddaw :—*Eastward*—Saddleback, and, to the north of that mountain, High Pike and Carrock Pike ; in the extreme distance, Cross-fell, Black-fell, and Stainmoor, beyond the vale of Penrith, forming part of " the British Appennines" or " the back-bone of England." Proceeding to the south-east, Swarth-fell, Hallen-fell, and Place-fell, all on the southern shore of Ullswater ; Kidsey Pike and High-street ; then the Helvellyn chain, including White Pike, Dod-fell, the Styx, Catchedecam, Helvellyn, and Seat Sandal ; the head of Ingleborough, at the distance of fifty miles ; Wansfell, seen over Dunmail Raise ; Steel-fell, and the Derwent and Borrowdale fells : *South*—(beyond the extremity of Borrowdale)—the parabolic summit of Pike o' Stickle (in Langdale), Eagle Crag, Coniston Old Man, Bowfell, Glaramara, Great End, Scawfell Pikes, (with the pile of stones on the top), Lingmell, Great Gavel ; proceeding westward, Dalehead,

Scarcely any thing is more inspiring to a person of susceptible imagination than to be thus placed as it were on a pinnacle of the world, and to look down upon a vast and varied territory, covered with human beings, who, with all their works, lie so far beneath him, that he feels as if he no longer partook their nature, and were rather a spectator than a tenant of this inferior globe. Whilst he pities the littleness of man, his mind exults in the sublimity of nature. Even the dullest mind is roused by such a situation, and the imaginative feel emotions of uncontrollable admiration and delight.

The circumference of this grand panoramic view can scarcely be less than three hundred miles. We continued gazing upon it for some time in high admiration, and listening to the explanations of our guide; and the ladies, though with disordered hair, blue noses, and chattering teeth, declared that they were amply repaid for their exertion. When the guide, however, produced the sandwiches and brandy, we all acknowledged their rival charms : the former were speedily demolished, and such was the effect of the thin, cold atmosphere, that even the ladies partook of the brandy without complaining of its strength. We remained on the summit, beneath the shelter of the

Hindscarth, Kirk-fell, the Screes, Robinson, Pillar, Steeple, High Stile, Red Pike, Causey Pike, Grassmoor, Grisedale Pike, Whiteside : *West*, Lord's Seat and Barf, (on the other side of Bassenthwaite water,) and North Barule in the Isle of Man : and *North*, a long and high range of Scotch mountains, extending across Kirkcudbrightshire, Dumfriesshire, and Roxburghshire, of which the most conspicuous is Criffel, near the Solway Frith.

pile of stones, or in the little stone hut, about half an hour, and then addressed ourselves to the task of descending the mountain. It is needless to particularize the hardships of the way: suffice it to say, we overcame them all, and had no more serious disaster than the temporary loss of my hat, which, as it was carried by the wind over the brow of the mountain, I had no doubt would be deposited in Bassenthwaite Water, but which our guide with better hope pursued, and found in a deep ravine. We did not wait for him, but, wrapping my head in a supplementary shawl of Matilda's, we hastened down the hill. He overtook us after we had gone a couple of miles, and in about six hours from our quitting Keswick we re-entered it, by no means ashamed of our disordered appearance, but only anxious to get to the fire-side. Dinner, the sofa, and a blazing hearth were to us luxuries, compared with which the epicure and the indolent never tasted luxury. The evening was not long enough to talk over our adventures, and Mrs. Anabella and Matilda have laid up a stock of glory which will last them their lives. A calmer day would have made their enterprise comparatively easy, but it would have deprived them of their after-enjoyment—the exquisite delight of remembered hardships.

I have ascended Skiddaw several times in more favourable weather than on this occasion; there was then little wind and bright sunshine, and the ascent was pleasant and easy, though still requiring patience—the grand requisite in such an expedition. I can never forget the view which burst upon us, seaward, on one of those expeditions, when we had reached the summit. It was a bright afternoon, and from the reflection of the sun's rays on the calm sea, the whole expanse of waters resembled a sheet of molten silver, out of which rose, with surprising distinctness, the rocky shores and hills of the Isle of Man, of a deep neutral tint, and with an aerial softening produced by distance. The effect was truly glorious. At the same time a single bright cloud hung over our heads, so near as to have a very unusual appearance; it glowed with deep amber, exquisitely melting off into a snowy white. The blending hues, the softness and effulgence of the cloud, sailing smoothly through the blue heaven, and brooding as it were over the mountain top, made it an object of awful beauty.

CHAPTER XIII.

EXCURSION TO BORROWDALE, WASDALE, ENNERDALE, AND BUT-
TERMERE—THE LADIES LEFT AT KESWICK WITH AN OLD
ACQUAINTANCE—STRAITS OF BORROWDALE—BOWDER STONE
—CASTLE CRAG—ROSTHWAITE—WAD MINES—SEATHWAITE—
ASCENT OF STY-HEAD—VIEW OF SCAWFELL PIKES—NEW
COMPANION——WASDALE HEAD——WAST WATER——CALDER
BRIDGE—CALDER ABBEY.

We spent a Sabbath at Keswick,—a day on which
we thought it not right to " seek our own pleasure,"
but repaired to the sanctuary, conceiving it more
agreeable to Christian duty to worship God in his
courts than even in the temple of his sublimest
works.

On Monday morning George and I quitted the
ladies, on an excursion to Wast Water. This step
may appear so ungallant as to require explanation.
The excursion to Wast Water, then, be it known,
comprehends some of the most sublime scenery
in Cumberland, and takes us over a hill which forms
part of Scawfell, the highest mountain in England.
This mountain is not to be seen, except distantly and
partially, without going to Wasdale. Very few
persons make the excursion, as it is long, and leads
over rugged tracks; but this only made us the more

desirous of accomplishing it. Not having seen that part of the Lakes before, I was anxious to add it to my stock of knowledge respecting them; and George was ready for any project, especially any which would take us into the wilder parts of the country. Nor was he at all sorry, as he uncivilly expressed it, to get rid of the incumbrance of his aunt and sister; for if we went into Wasdale, it was next to impossible that they should accompany us, owing to the length and difficulties of the road. How to effect our object, however, was a matter which perplexed us a good deal. To leave them alone at Keswick was out of the question, and we could devise no means of disposing of them for the two days that we should be absent.

We had almost abandoned the enterprise in despair, when we unexpectedly met on the Saturday evening an old friend of Mrs. Anabella's, who, having lately entered into the holy bands of matrimony, was on a wedding excursion to the Lakes. The bridegroom, I apprehend, will never again see his fiftieth year, nor the bride her fifty-fifth, yet they were dressed out in the latest Parisian *mode*, and looked as blithe as the youngest votaries of Hymen. He was a man of family, a beau, and dilettante, who, having spent his life in hovering round the ladies, and endlessly busying himself about trifles, had been too fastidious and fickle either to obtain a wife, or to answer any one useful end of existence; until the failure of a scheme in which he had invested his money had obliged him to

understand the significant commiseration of a wealthy
widow, and to plunge into the arms of matrimony.
The lady, though very far indeed from answering to
the picture which his youthful dreams had formed
of a bride, was a good-natured, comfortable dame, who
had a great admiration for her husband, and was cor-
diality itself to all his friends. When she was
introduced, therefore, to Mrs. Anabella and the rest
of our party—though at the moment of meeting a
slight blush of confusion appeared in the face of the
gentleman—a good understanding was immediately
established amongst us, and George and I saw the
means of accomplishing our projected trip to Wast
Water. Not to trouble my readers with the way in
which it was brought about, we settled it, to the satisfaction of all parties, that I and my cousin were to set
off on Monday morning, and were to take Crummock
Water and Buttermere in our return, where the three
ladies and the bridegroom would join us about noon
on Tuesday.

We set out, therefore, at half-past eight on Monday
morning, with a single horse, which we were to ride
alternately. This plan had been recommended to me
by a friend, and we found it far more agreeable than if
we had taken either two horses or none. The road
is of such a nature that you cannot in many places
safely go beyond a walking pace, and it is much less
fatiguing to walk and ride alternately than to ride the
whole distance. In a mountainous country particularly, it is very disagreeable to be tied to a horse,

and bound to preserve undeviatingly the beaten track.

We went along the whole length of Derwentwater, on its eastern side, and saw from the land the views which had charmed us so much when seen from the water. The morning was brilliant, with a cool breeze, which ruffled the surface of the lake, and gave a delightful freshness to the dark blue waters. Passing Barrow-house, which is advantageously situated, so as to command a fine view of the lake and islands, we came to the hamlet of Lowdore; but as there was no more water in the stream than when we were last there, we did not go to the Fall. Another mile, skirting the foot of grotesque and tremendous rocks, brought us to Grange,* a village on the Derwent, situated in the straits of Borrowdale. Here the mountains and crags on either side approach each other so closely, as to leave a very narrow entrance to the valley beyond. Borrowdale appears from this

---

* I cannot deny myself the satisfaction of mentioning the hospitality I once experienced at the house of Mr. Thomas Threlkeld, of Grange—a Borrowdale " statesman"—when driven by a storm of rain, along with a lady, to take refuge under his roof. We were received by his wife with a simple and hearty welcome, ensconced in huge upright arm-chairs by the fire-side, which was of antique dimensions; fresh wood was heaped upon the blazing hearth, and home-made cheese, butter, and bread brought forth, with rich milk, butter-milk, and oat-cake, for our refreshment. I was the more pleased when I found afterwards that Gray had been hospitably entertained at the same village. The hospitality of Borrowdale is proverbial, and I shall afterwards have to mention my kind reception by Mr. Fisher, of Seatoller, who has done as much as any other individual to gain for this valley the reputation of a hearty and generous treatment of strangers.—See the *Second Excursion on Foot.*

point to be choked up with immense rocks and fragments, which lie strewn in the wildest disorder, as if
they had been torn by some great convulsion of
nature from the neighbouring mountains, and tumbled
down into the valley.   A deep and narrow channel
is left in the bottom for the river, but all besides is
rock, either perfectly bare and formless, or slightly
covered with moss.   Rising just opposite Grange,
indeed, is a conical hill, which has in process of time
received a covering of earth sufficient to afford root to
trees, and it is now clothed with wood.   But, with
this exception, the first mile of Borrowdale is strewn
with the hideous *débris* of the mountains ; and in the
higher part of the hills slate-quarries are worked,
which add to the deformity of the scene.

The road here was formerly very rugged and winding, requiring care in the rider, and putting the
shoes of the pedestrian to the test ;* but it is now
greatly improved.   After passing for a mile through
this kind of scenery, with the vast precipice of Gate
Crag on our right, and the steep of Grange-fell on
our left, we came to Bowder Stone, a rock of enormous size, which appears to have been detached from

* As the result of considerable experience, I may say that shoes
are much preferable to boots for walking in mountainous countries, as leaving the ancles unconstrained, and being less liable to
chafe the feet.   The shoes should be very strong and roomy, and
gaiters should be worn, to keep out sand and small stones.   Too
much attention can scarcely be paid to these particulars in mountain excursions, as, when the foot is once hurt or inflamed, all
enjoyment is at an end, and the traveller is perhaps laid up for two
or three days.

the neighbouring height, and to have slidden or rolled
to its present situation.   From the position in which
it lies, it has been compared to a ship resting on its
keel ; and, though larger than an ordinary house, it is
so balanced on one of its edges, that two persons on
opposite sides may shake hands through a hole under-
neath it.   This mass of rock is sixty-two feet in
length, and thirty-six in perpendicular height ; it is
estimated to contain 23,000 solid feet, and to weigh
1,971 tons.   It stands on a platform of rock, at a
great elevation above the bed of the river, and near
the edge of a precipice.   A cottage has been erected
hard by, and is tenanted by an old woman, who gains
a subsistence by talking about the stone to travellers.

Opposite to Bowder Stone, and rising very precipitously from the river, is the noble height of Castle
Crag, so called from having anciently had a fortification on its summit, the vestiges of which were lately
to be seen, but have now been effaced by the working
of a slate quarry on the spot.   It was no doubt
erected to command the pass of Borrowdale, through
which the depredating inhabitants of the northern
parts of the island might have made their way southward, and more particularly into the fertile district of
Furness, in Lonsdale north of the Sands.   It has been
said that the castle was of Roman construction, and
that it was afterwards held by the monks of Furness
to guard their possessions ; but neither of these state-
ments rests on satisfactory evidence.   The Crag is
lofty and peaked ; and its sides are finely mantled in

wood. The summit commands a magnificent view of Derwentwater and Skiddaw, with all their beauties, on the one side, and of Borrowdale, with all its rugged grandeur, on the other.

The old road up Borrowdale led, by many ups and downs, immediately past Bowder Stone ; but the improvements in road-making have reached even these valleys, and a new and good road now runs nearly on a level with the river, and avoids the elevation on which the huge Stone is perched.

After passing Bowder Stone, the valley widens, and forms a small and fertile plain, which, consisting principally of meadows and pastures intersected by luxuriant hedges, and being watered by the beautiful and winding stream of the Derwent, contrasts very advantageously with the scenery in the straits of Borrowdale. The vale is blocked up at the extremity by lofty mountains of an imposing boldness of form, some of which have a considerable quantity of wood around their base. Rosthwaite Cam and Glaramara rise in front, as the spectator looks up the valley from Bowder Stone ; Eagle Crag (where the royal birds formerly built their aerie) towers above the valley of Stonethwaite on the left, and Scawfell Pikes, Great End, and the regular cone of Great Gavel (or Gable) over that of Seathwaite on the right. We descended the hill to the level of the river, and proceeded to Rosthwaite, a village in the middle of the valley, a mile beyond Bowder Stone. Here is the last public-house to be found on this route, and therefore we stopped to obtain the materials for a lunch, which we intended to enjoy on Sty-head, within sight of Scawfell Pikes.

The traveller might be much worse provided, either with bed or board, than at the Royal Oak, Rosthwaite, which I venture to pronounce a snug, comfortable, and respectable house of entertainment.*

* I cannot deny myself the pleasure of introducing here Mr. Wordsworth's account of the former state of society in the valleys of Cumberland and Westmoreland : it is contained in his "*Description of the Scenery of the Lakes*,"—a critical dissertation composed with the taste of a poet, the discrimination of a philosopher, and the heart of a philanthropist. He says—

" From the time of the erection of these houses, (after the wars of the Roses) till within the last sixty years, the state of society, though no doubt slowly and gradually improving, underwent no material change. Corn was grown in these vales (through which no carriage-road had been made) sufficient upon each estate to furnish bread for each family, and no more : notwithstanding the union of several tenements, the possessions of each inhabitant still being small, in the same field was seen an intermixture of different crops ; and the plough was interrupted by little rocks, mostly overgrown with wood, or by spongy places, which the tillers of the soil had neither leisure nor capital to convert into firm land. The storms and moisture of the climate induced them to sprinkle their upland property with outhouses of native stone, as places of shelter for their sheep, where, in tempestuous weather, food was distributed to them. Every family spun from its own flock the wool with which it was clothed ; a weaver was here and there found among them ; and the rest of their wants was supplied by the produce of the yarn, which they carded and spun in their own houses, and carried to market, either under their arms, or more frequently on pack-horses, a small train taking their way weekly down the valley or over the mountains to the most commodious town. They had, as I have said, their rural chapel, and of course their minister, in clothing or in manner of life, in no respect differing from themselves, except on the Sabbath-day ; this was the sole distinguished individual among them ; everything else,

Leaving this place, we approached Borrowdale chapel a little rural structure which no one can see without interest ; and leaving the chapel and Rosthwaite Cam on our left, and turning our backs on the village and valley of Stonethwaite, we followed the curve of Borrowdale to the right, and went to Seatoller, a mile and a half beyond Rosthwaite, where Mr. Fisher, the principal " statesman" of Borrowdale, lives in yeomanlike style. Here the road to Buttermere begins to ascend a long and steep hawse on the west side of the valley. Our road, however, lay due south, and therefore, turning to the left, we proceeded two miles further, through a hazel wood and over some boggy pastures, to Seathwaite, a wretched village situated nearly at the extremity of the valley, where cultivation terminates, and where the overhanging mountains in front and on both sides apprise the traveller that he must prepare for climbing. You are here in the very centre

person and possession, exhibited a perfect equality, a community of shepherds and agriculturists, proprietors, for the most part, of the lands which they occupied and cultivated."

Modern improvements, both agricultural and manufacturing, have introduced considerable modifications into this state of society ; and Mr. Wordsworth, with the fond partiality for ancient times and modes which forms a part of his character, deplores the change. A younger man, though with far less practical knowledge, yet having perhaps less prejudice, ventures to doubt if at any former period either the "statesmen" or the labourers enjoyed so much comfort as at present. The same hand cannot with advantage drive the plough and the shuttle ; the union of employments so different is sure to produce bad cloth and bad husbandry. The farmers of Borrowdale are likely to be better clothed and fed when they sell their wool and their cattle, and buy the cloths of Leeds and Manchester.

and citadel of the mountainous district, and you can only proceed by scaling its frowning ramparts.

On the hill to the right of Seathwaite are the celebrated Wad Mines, where the mineral called plumbago, or vulgarly black-lead, and on the spot denominated *wad*, is found. These are the only mines of the kind in England, and the mineral is very rarely discovered in other countries, and of a very inferior quality. The article is of course a monopoly, and for many years the market has been supplied with just that quantity which the owners thought most advantageous for themselves: by stinting the supply, they keep up the price, and as the market is very extensive—the English black-lead pencils being used in many foreign countries—the mines must be very profitable. We learnt, however, from Mr. Crosthwaite, the intelligent proprietor of the Museum at Keswick, that the workmen are often many months seeking the wad, without finding any. It does not lie in veins, but in masses, or sops, sometimes of a ramified form like the root of a tree, and its discovery is consequently accidental.*

Having carefully inquired at Seathwaite the path we were to keep in crossing Sty-head, and being informed that it was marked by a bed of stones so distinctly that we could not miss it, we addressed ourselves to the ascent of the mountain. Keeping by the rocky channel over which the Derwent, now a

* An account of a visit to the Wad Mines will be found in the *Second Excursion on Foot.*

small torrent, urges its rapid and turbulent course, we crossed a rude bridge (called Stockley-bridge) thrown over a tributary streamlet, nearly a mile beyond Seathwaite, and then began to ascend the hill on our right. The path is very steep and winding, and the stream of Taylor's Gill rushes down a ravine by the side of it in one almost continuous fall.

The hill of Sty-head forms a slack between the two mountains of Scawfell and Great Gavel; its elevation is 1,250 feet above the valley, and it is comparatively level for about a mile, so as to form a narrow plain or valley betwixt them. The brow of the hill on the side of Seathwaite commands a very fine view down the whole length of Borrowdale, and the vale of Keswick, which is terminated by Skiddaw. After a good breathing, we attained this point, and were much gratified by a retrospect of our journey since leaving Keswick, as well as exhilarated by the pure mountain air. We did not pause, however; for the great object of our curiosity, the view of Scawfell Pikes, was to be enjoyed from the opposite edge of the small elevated plain we had attained. The path is here at once rocky and boggy, and requires care in the rider to prevent bad consequences to his horse and himself. The Derwent is now reduced to a mere rill, and one of its sources is a small tarn, called Sty-head tarn, which lay to the left of our path. Above it, at a dread elevation, towers Great End, one of the summits of the vast mountain of Scawfell.

Arrived at the southern extremity of the pass, we
stood on the brink of a precipice, and as it were on a
platform raised opposite Scawfell Pikes, and midway
between the summit and the base.   Immediately in
front of us, that mountain "reared his mighty stature."
We saw him at a single glance, from the verdant tract
of Wasdale at his foot, to the overhanging precipices,
crowned by a conical pile of stones, which indicate the
head of the Pikes, and the highest summit in England.
The side forms one long concave sweep, becoming
gradually steeper as it ascends, till the highest part
rises in perpendicular crags, like a mountain battle-
ment.   This is the only object in view, except the
small valley of Wasdale-head, and the distant sea—
Wast Water and the country beyond being shut out
by Lingmell, and the monotonous, shale-covered sides
of Great Gavel and Kirkfell.   Yet there is a simple
grandeur in this mountain view, which deeply impressed us, and at the moment when it burst upon
us George raised his arms in astonishment and
exultation.   The top of the mountain is not conical,
but the precipices stand all round the head of a
ravine which runs up from Wasdale, and resemble
the sides of an enormous quarry.   George was eager
to climb the Pikes, which appeared to be close at
hand; but I had had too much experience of mountains to venture over the uncouth rocks which lay
between us and the summit, without a guide or some
very precise directions.   We should have been very
likely to get into the situation which the hunters here

call "crag-fast," where we could neither get on nor back. Our horse, too, could not have been disposed of. We were therefore obliged to content ourselves with sitting down to feast our eyes upon the view, and we found it no unwelcome accompaniment to treat our empty stomachs to a lunch.*

We were here joined by a young and stout pedestrian, whom we had before met, with two gaily-dressed maidens, on the Seathwaite side of the hill. He told us that they were his cousins, that he had come with them from Calder-bridge, and had been setting them on their way to Keswick, where they were going on a visit, to attend the races, which were to take place on the following Thursday. They had ridden on horseback as far as Wasdale-head, and had then climbed Great Gavel on foot to Sty-head,—a circumstance at which we marvelled, as the ascent is not only very steep and long, but the path is covered with sharp stones, which perpetually slide down the

---

* Let no untravelled enthusiast despise me for the zest with which I have more than once mentioned the amusement of eating and drinking on the top of a mountain. Romantic feelings are pleasant, but romance on an empty stomach is a "windy recreation." When he has toiled up an ascent of a few thousand feet, as I have done many a time and oft, and with weary limbs and flagging spirits has nothing to feed upon but the thin mountain air, he will find that a little "provant" would not be amiss, and will long for the commissariat of Major Dalgetty. In short, he will find that prudent foresight goes much farther than enthusiasm; and, though I would advise no young and healthy person to shrink from a little fatigue or hardship, yet I would suggest to all, that if their object is enjoyment, that cannot be secured without moderation in their efforts, and proper precautions against pain and hunger.

face of the mountain. Our new companion manifested a wish to travel with us through this lone and silent country, the sublimity of which had no charms for him, and he offered to lead our horse down the hill— a task of no small difficulty, as the animal slid amongst the loose stones at every step. We cheerfully accepted his proffered aid and company, and derived from him some information and a good deal of amusement. The descent of the mountain, from the circumstances I have mentioned, was painful and fatiguing, but we saw none of the danger which our guide-book had promised us.

A walk of a mile and a half from the bottom of the hill—through the green pastures of Wasdale-head, and by the hamlet of that name, with its diminutive chapel—brought us to the lake. The patriarchal family of this valley is that of Mr. Thomas Tyson, a " statesman," a bold fox-hunter, and a right hospitable man. A little below the hamlet of Wasdale-head, we had a peep up the side-valley of Mosedale on our right, lying between Kirkfell and Yewbarrow, at the head of which valley soars the almost inaccessible summit of the Pillar. Up Mosedale, but keeping to the right, so as to leave the Pillar always on the left hand, is the shepherd's track from Wasdale to Ennerdale and Buttermere,—a track by which a horse could not be prudently taken.

Wast Water is three miles in length and three quarters of a mile wide. It is the deepest of all the lakes, being forty-five fathoms, and is never frozen over. Its banks have very little variety, the southern shore being a long, monotonous, and nearly perpendicular ridge, called the Screes, the surface of which is constantly crumbling away, and increasing the beds of shale which hang upon its sides. Within the last twenty years, as I was informed, the appearance of the ridge has very materially changed. The soft red ore used for marking sheep is found in holes under the cliffs, and men are let down occasionally from the precipices by ropes, to obtain a quantity of this substance: when they have finished their labour, they slide down the beds of shale to the foot of the ridge. At the head of the lake on the north-western side, is Yewbarrow, next to which rises Middle-fell; and below this the mountains recede considerably from the lake, leaving a wide space, on which, towards the foot of Wast Water, there are some gentlemen's seats and handsome woods. The dark and majestic form of Seatallan is, however, long kept in view. Betwjxt Yewbarrow and Middle-fell runs the lateral valley of Bowderdale, at the head of which is seen the Hay Cock.

We perceived, as we turned our backs on Scawfell, Kirkfell, and Great Gavel, that we were emerging from the hill country, and should soon be on comparatively level ground. Scawfell now presented to us another and more gracious aspect. Towards West Water the slope is more gradual, and the surface of the hill is covered with verdure; on this side the mountain bears the name of Lingmell, but it is in

fact the base of the Pikes.   As we stood upon the
banks of the lake, we saw a heron fishing in the
water : he watched us suspiciously, as if little accustomed to be disturbed by man ; and when our companion shouted to alarm him, he sprung up, and,
throwing out his long legs behind him so as to resemble a tail, winged his way heavily towards the upper
part of the valley.

Our original intention was to take up our quarters
for the night at Strands, in Nether Wasdale, a village
a mile beyond the foot of the lake, where there are
two small but neat-looking inns, and then to retrace
our steps on the following day to Wasdale-head,
whence we might go by the shepherd's track between
Kirkfell and Yewbarrow, over Black Sale, across the
narrow valley of Ennerdale, and over the pass of
Scarf-gap, between the Haystacks and High Crag,
into the vale of Buttermere.   But our companion,
who joined in our consultations, recommended us
rather to go on to Calder-bridge, seven miles beyond
Strands, where there was a much better inn than at
the latter place, and where the ruins of an abbey
were also to be seen.   He said that we might proceed
to Crummock Water and Buttermere on the following
day, taking the lakes of Ennerdale Water and Lowes
Water in our route.   It was a great recommendation
in his eyes that we should thus avoid the two mountain passes between Wasdale and Buttermere, and
should have a good carriage-road all the way ; and
the greater number of objects which this route would

include, added to the doubtful practicability of the
other route, for a horse, decided us to adopt his suggestion. At Wasdale-head our companion had picked
up two excellent horses, which he had borrowed from
a farmer at Calder-bridge, to convey his fair cousins
in the morning; and when we had determined to
proceed to that place, he urged the expediency of one
of us mounting the horse which he led, so that we
might get over the ground at a better speed. We had
now come to plain high road, and there was nothing
to be gained by walking: the afternoon, too, was
waning away, and we did not like the appearance of
the sky—a halo having encircled the sun, and a few
straggling and ragged clouds, which portended rain,
approaching from the north-east. We, therefore,
without hesitation accepted his offer, and, George
having mounted on a lady's saddle, we set off at a
round pace towards Calder-bridge.

We soon found ourselves nearly upon the sea-coast,
which is here very open. The mountain of Black
Comb, which we had not seen since we quitted Lancashire, now appeared in the south; and the hilly
shores of the Isle of Man were perceived with the
utmost distinctness, stretching out to a great length,
at the distance of forty miles. The country through
which we passed was rather pretty, but of course it
appeared tame to us, who had just issued from the
region of the sublime and picturesque. We reached
Calder-bridge at five o'clock, when we parted from
our new acquaintance, whom we could hardly persuade

to accept any remuneration for the services he had rendered us. Our day's journey had not exceeded twenty-seven miles, and we felt but slightly fatigued. Having ordered dinner, we walked to Calder Abbey, at the distance of a mile from the inn. It is a small and beautiful ruin, whose Gothic arches, mantled with ivy, and shaded by a row of stately elms, stand in the grounds and close to the mansion of the Senhouses, occupied by Captain Irwin. The ruin forms a boundary to his lawn, and the Captain, whom we found on the spot, told us that he had done a good deal to improve its effect, by taking down some modern encumbrances. The Abbey is seven centuries old,* and the central part is still entire. Some of the outbuildings have long been used as stables; we entered one of them under a venerable Gothic archway, and found that the cows ruminate now where the monks ruminated in former days. The grounds are pretty, and the woods, together with the woods of Ponsonby-hall, the seat of Edwd. Stanley, Esq., M.P. for the western division of Cumberland, give considerable beauty to the village. We had scarcely returned to the inn when a storm of rain came on, which might have excited our apprehensions for the following day; but we left the morrow to care for itself, and abandoned ourselves to the luxury of repose.

* It was founded in 1134 by the second Ranulph de Meschines, for Cistercian monks, and was dependant on Furness Abbey.

CHAPTER XIV.

MORNING WALK OVER COPELAND FOREST—LAKE AND VALLEY
OF ENNERDALE—LOWES WATER—CRUMMOCK WATER—SCALE
FORCE—BUTTERMERE—MARY OF BUTTERMERE—VALE OF
NEWLANDS—RETURN TO KESWICK.

We set out from Calder-bridge about seven o'clock
on Tuesday morning, having to go more than twenty
miles before arriving at the place which we had
appointed as a rendezvous with the ladies. We
intended to breakfast at Ennerdale-bridge, but
thought it not inexpedient to take a little bread and
milk before starting, as eight miles of dreary fells
intervened between us and the expected ham-rasher.
A good deal of rain had fallen in the night, and had
swollen the mountain streams, whose waters were
now as turbid as at other times they are clear. The
roads, of course, were not improved, and the air was
cold and raw. It may be supposed that this morning
stage was any thing but agreeable. After a considerable though gradual ascent from Calder-bridge,
we came upon the bleak downs or fells of Copeland
Forest, covered with scanty herbage, from which a
few black-faced sheep pick up a subsistence: we
wended our way across them with a north-east wind

I

in our teeth, and, though we had no rain, the clouds
were so low as to sweep the heads of the fells in
their passage.   Cold-fell on our right—a name we
felt to be extremely appropriate—and Dent-hill on
our left, were thus capped with vapour ; and as we
travelled along on no better pabulum than a basin of
cold milk, and with no better entertainment than
watching the shifts and openings in the clouds to
form a guess as to the weather for the day, the reader
will hardly be surprised to learn that we were not in
the highest spirits.

Happily, when we came to the brow of the hill
which looks down upon Ennerdale, our gloom passed
away like a summer's cloud.   Whether this was to be
ascribed mainly to the lively prospect which there
opened upon us, or to a sudden brightening in the sky,
which let in the sunshine upon the valley, or to the
sight of the village smoke, which, by irresistible
association, brought to the mind's eye, or, so to speak,
to the stomach's eye, the beatific vision of coffee, ham,
and toast,—I shall not particularly inquire.   Suffice
it to say, that each witnessed the brightening of the
other's countenance, and we began to extol, with the
usual interjections and notes of admiration, the lake
and vale of Ennerdale.   The vale, being at some
distance from the high mountains, is wide and fertile ;
green fields and hedges, a village and winding stream,
give it a character of lively beauty.   The lake, which
lay to our right, is two miles and a half long, and
three quarters of a mile wide.   It runs up towards

the heart of the mountains, and is skirted on each
side by stern and precipitous hills. Near its foot
are the woods of How Hall, but above this the scenery
becomes barren and sublime ; and beyond the head of
the lake is the narrow valley of Gillerthwaite, with
Great Gavel at its head, and ranges of stern mountains on each side, of which the most conspicuous is
the Pillar, rising to the elevation of 2893 feet.

The public-house of Ennerdale is of a very humble
character, and unluckily, when we arrived, there was
no fire in the principal room, whilst the kitchen was
small, dirty, and filled with roaring tipplers. However, by vigorous application to the old landlady, we
soon had a fire lighted, and a plentiful though homely
breakfast spread out before us. We resumed our
journey at half-past ten o'clock, keeping the road to
Lamplugh Cross, and through that place to Lowes
Water. The distance is six miles, and there is
nothing in the country we passed over worth noticing :
it is open, and rather elevated, but with no prominent object in view.

After winding round the lower part of Blake-fell,
we turned to the south, and there found ourselves
re-entering the mountainous country as suddenly as
we had quitted it at Wast Water. Below us, in a
deep valley, lay the small lake of Lowes Water, about
a mile in length, surrounded by mountains of great
elevation and bold forms. Blake-fell, which on its
western side has a very gradual slope, so that we
were not aware of its elevation as we approached it

in that direction, rises abruptly from Lowes Water
to a commanding height.   On the opposite side of the
lake is another hill of inferior magnitude, Low-fell,
and in front of us, as we descended into the valley
to the borders of the lake, stood the fine conical
mountain of Melbreak.   We afterwards found that
this mountain forms a long ridge running along the
western side of Crummock Water, and that its
extremity only, like the gable-end of a pointed roof,
is presented to Lowes Water.   The same conforma-
tion may be remarked in numerous instances amongst
the hills of Westmoreland and Cumberland.   The
mountains are principally composed of schist, and the
softness of this material, yielding to the gradual
influence of the elements, naturally produces an equal
slope on both sides of a ridge of hills, which causes
the extremity of the ridge to form a regular and beautiful cone.   There is scarcely any mountain or chain
of mountains in this district, which does not present
a conical shape on one of its sides.   When the
surface is covered with grass, as is very often the
case, the smoothness and regularity, the verdancy and
the great altitude, combine to give the mountain a
character of " gigantic elegance."   At the same time,
there are not wanting, as we have already seen, the
sterner features of a mountainous region, where the
hard rock predominates, and stands out in lofty peaks
and terrific precipices.

Lowes Water has an air of great seclusion, there
being few houses near it.   The bright verdure of its

margin, and the beauty of the woods on the mountain sides, were quite refreshing to our eyes. Pastoral interest is added to the scene, by the sheep browzing on Melbreak and Blake-fell, from the bottom to the top. Great numbers of sheep are bred in these and the other Cumberland mountains, and the task of the farmer, who has to watch them over such an extensive tract of unenclosed and uneven ground, must often be arduous; in winter it is even attended with considerable danger, from the sheep being sometimes buried in the snow, or having their retreat cut off by its accumulation.

The stream which runs through Lowes Water flows from north to south, and empties itself into Crummock Water; which is an exception to the general rule,—all the other lakes and valleys to the north of Scawfell (which is the central and highest part of the mountainous country) running from south to north.

When we had passed Lowes Water about a mile, we came in view of Crummock Water, which lies in one of the great valleys that descend from the heart of the mountains to the plain. This valley, which in its upper part contains also the lake of Buttermere, is joined by the valley of Lowes Water at the foot of Crummock lake, and stretches in a direction due north to Cockermouth. The valley of Crummock Water and Buttermere is separated from Borrowdale and the plain of the Derwent by a vast group of lofty and barren hills, the principal of which are

Grasmoor, Grisedale Pike, Hindscarth, and Robinson. The regular high road from Keswick to Crummock Water winds round the base of Grisedale Pike; and from the head of Buttermere there is also a horse road, through Gatesgarth-dale and over Borrowdale-hawse to the upper part of Borrowdale. But there is a much shorter route than either of these from Keswick, namely, up the vale of Newlands, which runs directly through the midst of these wild mountains, from the plain of the Derwent to the valley of Buttermere.

When we came within view of Crummock Water, where, as I have said, two valleys meet, we were charmed by the luxuriant profusion of wood which covers the whole space below the foot of the lake, especially as contrasted with the barren sternness of the two mountain ridges betwixt which Crummock Water lies—Grasmoor and Melbreak. The former is an immense mountain, whose barren sides are streaked with beds of shale. The monotony of these ridges is somewhat broken by a comparatively low but abrupt hill, called Randon Knot, which stands out into the valley at the foot of Grasmoor, and pushes a bold promontory into the lake. The lake is three miles in length and three quarters of a mile in breadth. It contains three small islands, one a naked rock, and the other two covered with wood. There is, however, a great deficiency of wood on the borders of Crummock Water, except just at the head and foot, and the general character of the scene is bold and naked grandeur.

Near the foot of the lake, at Scale-hill, is a commodious inn, where parties from Keswick often make a short stay, and where a boat may be had to go to Scale Force or Buttermere. Scale-hill, the land around Lowes Water, and the mountainous ranges on the western side of Crummock Water and Buttermere, are the property of John Marshall, Esq. of Hallsteads and of Leeds.

When we approached Crummock Water from Lowes Water, we found that we were already beyond the time appointed for meeting our party from Keswick; and, on looking at the map, it appeared that the high road would take us a round of several miles. The principal object worth seeing at Crummock Water is Scale-force, which is on the same side of the lake as we were now upon, namely, the western, but about three miles higher up. The road takes a sweep round the foot of the lake by Scale-hill, and up its eastern side: and if we had gone by the road, we must have returned, after reaching the head of the lake, a mile or two down again, on the western side, to see the cascade. Thus we must have gone at least seven miles to attain a point, which, if we could only find a road on the western side of the lake, at the foot of Melbreak, we might reach in three miles. We were not long in determining that, if the nearer route were at all practicable, we would pursue it; and as a countryman told us that there was a path for cattle at the base of the mountain, we forthwith proceeded along it. But I advise no person to follow our example:

rock and bog combine to render this track not only difficult, but really dangerous. Our horse sank so deep in some of the bogs, that we were apprehensive he would either stick fast, or break his leg in endeavouring to get out: and the rocks shelve so rapidly to the edge of the lake in one or two parts, that the animal would not pass along the track, and we were obliged to ride him into the water to get round the base of the rocks. We saved time, however, by taking this route, and arrived at the foot of the glen in which Scale-force lies, betwixt Melbreak and Blea Crag, at about two o'clock.

But here not a creature was to be seen. We looked in vain for our party, or for any one to hold our horse whilst we ascended to the cascade; and for a long time we were apprehensive that there was no opening in a high stone wall, which runs from the lake up to the mountain. We succeeded at length in finding a gate-way, to which we fastened the animal, and then we trudged up a rugged path by the side of a streamlet, which we concluded must come from Scale-force. The cascade is nearly a mile from the lake, and is hidden from distant view by being situated in a deep and narrow cleft of the hill. When we came close upon it, to our unspeakable satisfaction we beheld our whole party, the bridegroom, Mrs. Anabella, and all, sitting on a rock near the foot of the cascade. The salutations on all sides were very warm and hearty, for the ladies, after waiting more than an hour for us at the inn, had begun to be alarmed for our safety. They had come by way of Scale-hill to Buttermere; and at the instance of the bridegroom, they had at length taken a boat, crossed the lake, and come to see the force.

Scale-force has a considerably higher fall than any other cascade in Cumberland or Westmoreland. It makes one clear leap of a hundred and fifty-six feet, and there is a smaller fall below. The quantity of water is not great, except after heavy rains, and it did not appear that so much rain had fallen here last night as on the sea-coast. The stream was large enough, however, to raise a cloud of spray from the basin into which it plunges, and in climbing up the rocky chasm to within a few yards of the force, we were plentifully baptized. The rocks are vast walls of sienite, and numerous small trees have taken root in the crevices, being constantly sprinkled by the fall. There is little here of the picturesque beauty of Stock-gill-force; all is harsh and wild: yet the perpendicular rocks on each side of the chasm, the flashing cascade, the boiling abyss, and the cloud of spray, produce a very fine effect.

In descending to the boat, the guide who had accompanied the ladies told us that we should find some difficulty in getting our horse along the boggy pasture which lay between us and the inn. We thought it could not be so bad as the track we had already come by, but we found it worse, at least as to the swampiness of the ground. Having lost the narrow and faintly-marked track for the cattle, we

found ourselves in a savanna of soft peat, intersected
with numerous rills. George, who was riding, made
the horse pass a few of them, but the animal sank so
deep that it became alarmed, and at length positively
objected to cross one somewhat broader than the rest.
George, seeing no other mode of getting to Buttermere,
was resolved to make the horse pass the quagmire;
but hereupon the animal and he " joined issue ;" and
as a horse has great powers of passive resistance,
George urged and whipped in vain. At length, after
he had himself got mid-leg deep in the peat, whilst
trying to pull the animal over by the bridle, he gave
up the point; and, riding back again, he succeeded
in finding the path we had quitted. After fording
the river Cocker, (which flows out of Buttermere lake
into Crummock Water,) and making ourselves a road
through the fields, where there was neither high-way
nor bye-way, we arrived, wet and weary, at the hamlet
and inn of Buttermere.

The lake of Buttermere is about a mile higher up
the valley than Crummock Water, and is a small sheet
a mile and a quarter long, and nearly half a mile wide,
environed by superb mountain scenery. The eastern
margin of Buttermere is richly adorned with a large
quantity of wood ; and on the west the mountains of
Red Pike, High Stile, and High Crag rise precipitously to a sublime elevation. The rocky head of
High Crag seems to nod over the lake. Honister
Crag rears its noble conical form at the head of
Buttermere, and the valley to the west of that moun-

tain carries back the eye to the lofty summits of Great Gavel and Green Gavel. Buttermere Moss, backed and overtopped by Robinson, rises on the east side of the lake. Seen from an elevation above the inn, the two lakes, the valley, and the surrounding hills, form a grand and lovely prospect.

There is an air of sweet seclusion in this vale, which well fits it to be the scene of a romantic and pathetic story. The incidents of the life of *Mary of Buttermere* form an interesting, though a short and simple narrative, which it has become so much the practice to tell in the vale, and which has obtained so fixed a place in the guide-books, that it will probably be repeated to the traveller for ages yet to come. Mary Robinson, the daughter of the innkeeper at Buttermere, was seen by a gentleman who rambled over this country in the year 1792, (Capt. Budworth) and who, in publishing his " Ramble," described her as an eminently beautiful yet simple and artless girl of fifteen, whose manner and appearance, so unexpected in such a spot, had charmed him. This panegyric drew many travellers to Buttermere, and directed all eyes on the beautiful peasant. Flattery enough was addressed to her to corrupt her simplicity ; but she preserved her virtue unsullied and unsuspected. At length, in the year 1802, she was deceived into marriage by an outlawed criminal of the name of Hatfield, who had for some time before figured in this part of the country under the name of the Honourable Colonel Hope. He had the address and

talent to support his assumed character, but, being
discovered, he was apprehended, tried at Carlisle on a
charge of forgery, and hanged, within a year after
his marriage.* The young widow acted in the most
becoming manner under her misfortunes, and after
some years married again. This match was happier
than the former; she and her husband for a considerable period kept the inn which had been her father's,
and lived in much comfort. When I inquired about
her of the present landlady of this inn, I was told
that she had quitted Buttermere, and now lived in
a village near Bassenthwaite Water; it was added
that she had seven children, and was in comfortable
circumstances.

On leaving Buttermere, we had to mount a very steep
and long hill, or hawse, which interposes between Buttermere and the Vale of Newlands. It was with considerable difficulty, and taking many rests, that the
horses dragged up our carriage whilst we walked. The
road skirts the edge of a precipitous ravine, which
separates Buttermere Moss from Whiteless, and, as

---

* I have seen a letter from Hatfield whilst under sentence of
death, which, unless he remained a consummate hypocrite to the
last, shows that he was penitent for his crimes, and resigned to
death. Birkett, an ex-guide at Keswick, eighty-six years of age,
(1834) has related to me the excursions which he made with this
man, and his eccentric movements when attempting to escape the
pursuit of the officers of justice. The old guide had been
fascinated with the agreeable manners and generosity of the
adventurer, and could scarcely credit the fact of his being an
impostor. Birkett visited Hatfield in prison after his condemna-
tion.

there is no fence on the side of the precipice, we all felt it to be very dangerous.* The views, however, are truly magnificent. When we had reached the top of the pass, we looked down upon the vale of Newlands. The upper part of this valley, called Keskadale, lies under the side of Robinson: it presents nothing but bare mountain-sides, meeting at the bases in a narrow dell, down whose steep slope a torrent urges its course, and forms a considerable cascade. Two or three miles further, the valley is deeper, and the ground is much broken ; wood begins to beautify the landscape, and the pastures on the banks of the stream become green and fertile.

That which is properly called the Vale of New-lands is a wide and beautiful valley, plentifully adorned with wood, and winding like a majestic river, till it falls into the great valley or plain of the Derwent. An isolated ridge of considerable elevation, called Swinside, stands like an island at the mouth of the estuary, which sweeps round it on each side, one arm falling down directly upon Derwentwater, and the other stretching northward towards Bassenthwaite Water. This approach to the plain of the Derwent

---

* On another occasion, in passing down this hawse, I saw the hair-breadth escape of a gentleman in a phaeton. The vehicle, being too slightly built for so rugged a country, broke down in the steepest part of the descent; the gentleman, who had imprudently continued in the carriage, was thrown out, and the wheels passed over him, but happily without doing him any injury : the horse was seized on the instant by another of the party, or he would doubtless have galloped off in his fright, and been dashed down the precipice with the phaeton.

presented it in so different a view from any in which
we had before seen it, that we should scarcely have
recognized the spot, but for the well-known form of
Skiddaw, who rose in his majestic breadth and altitude
as the back-ground of the landscape. The fore-ground
and centre were rich and diversified almost beyond any
thing we had seen. A profusion of wood in the
valleys, on the plain, and on the islands,—the calm
expanse of Derwentwater, fringed with groves and
meadows,—and hills on every side and of every shape,
made a rare and splendid combination of natural
beauties. We reached Keswick as it became dusk,
considerably fatigued, but exceedingly gratified by our
two days' expedition.

CHAPTER XV.

ON the evening of our return to Keswick, we
mutually rendered an account of our proceedings
during the Monday, and up to the happy reunion of
our two parties at Scale-force. The story of the
ladies was shortly told: they had accomplished the
circuit of Derwentwater by land in the carriage, penetrated into Borrowdale as far as Bowder Stone, and
strolled into Hutton's Museum. The object which
had most struck them in the Museum was the model
of a slave-ship with all the slaves on board, packed
in a lying posture, tier above tier, almost as close as
herrings in a barrel. This was the identical model
exhibited by Mr. Wilberforce in the House of Commons during the discussions on the slave-trade, and
which produced a powerful impression on the House;
it was afterwards presented by that gentleman, who
was an old friend and patron of Hutton, to his Museum.

Hutton is an old guide, and has made a large and valuable collection of minerals and botanical specimens, all belonging to Cumberland and Westmoreland. He has also received numerous presents, and his Museum is curious and interesting.

On Wednesday morning, before setting out for Penrith, we visited the Museum of Mr. Crosthwaite. This collection was principally made by the late Mr. Peter Crosthwaite, the father of the present proprietor, and was first opened about half a century ago. It is well worth visiting on many accounts,—from its specimens illustrative of the mineralogy, geology, and zoology of Cumberland and Westmoreland,—from the very respectable assemblage of antiquities and curiosities belonging to every quarter of the globe,— and from the intelligence of the proprietor himself, who cheerfully imparts his information to the curious traveller. His book of visiters is very well filled, and on referring to a former volume, I found that I had been in the Museum that very day five years. After purchasing some minerals and lead-pencils, we returned to the inn.

I must not forget to mention, before quitting Keswick, that we saw Dr. Southey at the church on Sunday. This gentleman bears the character, among his neighbours, of a domestic, kind-hearted, and excellent man. He resides almost constantly at his house, Greta-hall, in the immediate vicinity of Keswick, where during the winter months he can command abundant time for his numerous literary pursuits, but where he must receive many interruptions during the summer and autumn.   Connected as he is by his writings with active politics, with ecclesiastical affairs, and with nearly every department of literature, he has a prodigious number and diversity of visiters, and may be considered one of the chief *lions* of the Lakes. The Earl of Lonsdale called upon him whilst we were at Keswick.

On leaving Keswick for Penrith, we took the old road, though it is very rough and passes over a steep hill, which the new road avoids,—our object being to visit the interesting Druidical temple on Castlerigg. The temple is in a field on the right of the road, and just on the crown of the hill.   It consists of forty-eight rude unhewn blocks of granite, placed upright in an oval figure, of which the diameters are thirty-four yards from north to south, and nearly thirty from east to west.   Ten of these stones are disposed in an oblong square on the eastern side of the oval, and this recess, which is seven yards by three, is supposed to have been the sacred place, exclusively appropriated to the Druids.   The largest of the stones is not more than seven feet high, and the greater number of them are only three or four feet high.   The situation of this ancient place of superstitious worship was skilfully chosen: Skiddaw, Saddleback, Helvellyn, and many other of the highest mountains in Cumberland, are visible from it ; and in the gloom of midnight, when the most solemn rites of the Druids were performed, the huge, shadowy forms of these

mountains, often wrapped in cloud and tempest, must
have impressed the minds of the credulous barbarians
with a weight of awe favourable to the effect of mys-
teries and' pretended magic.   There is a common
notion that no person can count the stones twice to
the same number ; but we certainly performed this
feat, and found their number to be forty-eight.

Soon after leaving the Druidical temple, we saw St.
John's Vale in the opposite direction to that in which
we had seen it in our journey from Ambleside, and
we were much pleased with its interesting scenery.
The Castle Rock of St. John's is a massive crag on
the eastern side of the vale, thus called from its
striking resemblance to the walls and towers of a
ruined fortress.   This is the principal scene of Sir
Walter Scott's romance, *The Bridal of Triermain,*
and he makes the castle open its portals to King
Arthur and de Vaux.

> " With toil the King his way pursued,
> By lonely Threlkeld's waste and wood,
> Till on his course obliquely shone
> The narrow valley of St. John.
> Piled in by many a lofty hill,
> The narrow dell lay smooth and still,
> And, down its verdant bosom led,
> A winding brooklet found its bed.
> But, midmost of the Vale, a mound
> Arose, with airy turrets crown'd,
> Buttress and rampire's circling bound,
>   And mighty keep and tower ;
> Seem'd some primeval giant's hand
> The castle's massive walls had plann'd,
> A ponderous bulwark to withstand
>   Ambitious Nimrod's power."

After passing the village of Threlkeld, from which the vale is seen, the journey was dreary and tedious. Saddleback continued for a long time in view on our left hand, and now looked as gloomy and dismal as, seen from the side of Skiddaw, he had appeared to us beautiful. The south side of the mountain is furrowed with deep and horrible ravines, and the eastern side is fronted with towering crags and fearful precipices. On our right was a monotonous hill, the commencement of the Helvellyn range. The dome-like hill of Mell-fell, which stands alone on the skirts of Hutton Moor, and which is of a peculiar geological structure, continued in view for many miles. We crossed a wearisome expanse of heath, after which we came to the village of Penruddock. Leaving Greystock castle, an ancient seat of the Howards, now belonging to Henry Howard, Esq. on our left, we descended into the delightful vale and pleasing town of Penrith.*

Our stay in Penrith was short, owing to the necessity we were under, if we would not lose a day, of hastening on to Lowther Castle and Pooley-bridge. After ordering a lunch at the New Crown, we walked up to the church, attracted principally by the account of *the Giant's Grave* in our guide-book. The church is a plain and good structure, but built of red stone, which, having a dingy and bricky hue, is not very agreeable to the eye. It was re-built in 1722, on a site which has probably been as long consecrated to

---

* *Pen-rith* signifies *red hill*, from a hill of red rock near the town.

religious purposes as any in the country. The interior is handsome, and it contains some curious monuments and inscriptions, amongst which are the inscriptions on a pair of brass chandeliers, which " were purchased with the fifty guns given by the Duke of Portland to the tenants of the honour of Penrith, who under his gracious encouragement associated in defence of the government and town of Penrith against the rebels in 1745."

Penrith and the neighbourhood are remarkably rich in monuments of British antiquity. *The Giant's Grave,* in the church-yard, is a rude monument, on which the speculations of antiquarians have been exhausted without any satisfactory result. It consists of two stone pillars, ten feet in height, and about thirteen feet apart from each other, in the direction of east and west, with four large stones of a semicircular form planted in the ground, two on each side of the grave. Tradition says that this is the tomb of an ancient British chief, Sir Ewan or Hugh Cæsarius, who attained his reputation, like Hercules and Theseus of old, by clearing the neighbouring forests of wild boars, which were a terror and scourge to the country. Our British hero, however, surpassed the stature even of a demi-god, if, as the vulgar believe, his body extended from one of these pillars to the other. But even this gives a Lilliputian idea of his size, compared with that you receive from another pillar at some distance from the tomb, about six feet in height, which is called *the giant's thumb.*

Leaving this *beau morceau* of antiquity, we proceeded to the Castle, which stands on the hill to the west of the town. We found that it looked much better from a distance than close at hand. The walls are high, but not strong ; and it is spoiled as a ruin by the area being filled with mistals for cattle. The castle is believed to have been built about the reign of Edward IV. and it was dismantled in the wars of the Commonwealth. From the time of Richard III. to the Revolution it was the property of the crown, when William III. granted it, together with the honour of Penrith and other extensive possessions in Cumberland, to his follower, William Bentinck, Duke of Portland. From this family it was transferred, with all their Cumberland possessions, to the Duke of Devonshire, in the year 1783, and it still continues in the possession of that distinguished house.

Had our time permitted, we should have visited the Beacon, which is a lofty tower on a hill about a mile from the town, commanding a most extensive and delightful prospect. We found it necessary, however, to return to the inn, where we lunched, and were then ready to proceed on our journey.

Penrith is a neat town, chiefly built of red free-stone, and the principal street contains several lofty and handsome houses. Being situated so near the Lakes, and on the great road from London to Carlisle and Glasgow, the inns are exceedingly good. It is about a mile from the confluence of the Eamont and the Lowther, the former of which streams flows out of

Ullswater, and the latter has one of its sources in Hawes Water. Near their junction, and on the Westmoreland side of the river, stands the fine ruin of Brougham Castle, which was anciently the seat of the Veteriponts, and from them descended to the Cliffords and Tuftons. It is still in the possession of the Earl Thanet, who is also the proprietor of the castles of Appleby and Brough, and of extensive estates in Westmoreland, of which county he is hereditary high-sheriff.* Brougham Castle is situated on the north side of the Roman station of *Brovoniacum ;* the vallum and the usual traces of a Roman encampment are still visible, and the present high road takes the line of the ancient Roman road.† We regretted that we were not able to visit this interesting spot.

* The castle was built for the greatest part by Roger de Clifford in the thirteenth century; it was restored, as well as several other castles, by the celebrated Countess of Pembroke, as the following inscription on a stone tablet in the castle testifies :—" This castle " of Brougham was repaired by the Ladie Anne Clifford, Countess " Dowager of Pembrooke, Dorsett, and Montgomery, Baronesse " Clifford, Westmorland, and Vescie, Ladie of the Honour of " Skipton in Craven, and High Sherifesse, by inheritance, of the " countie of Westmorland, in the years 1651 and 1652, after it " had layen ruinous ever since about August, 1617, when King " James lay in it for a time in his journey out of Scotland towards " London, untill this time."

† The etymology of *Brougham* has been much disputed, some antiquarians tracing it to the Saxon *Burg-ham* (in which way it was anciently spelt) signifying *Castle-town ;* and others believing it to be a corruption of the ancient Roman name of the station, *Brovoniacum.* The latter is preferred by Hutchinson, in his *History of Cumberland,* vol. 1, p. 297, and the former by Nicholson and Burn, in their *History and Antiquities of Westmorland and Cumberland,* vol. 1, p. 389.

On quitting Penrith for Lowther Castle, Carleton
Hall, the seat of John Cowper, Esq. lay upon our
left hand.　Our road crossed the Eamont and the
Lowther a little above their junction, and betwixt
the two bridges the postillion stopped for a few
minutes, to allow us to see a curious relic of British
antiquity, which immediately adjoins the high road,
on the right-hand side.　It is a circular grass-grown
area, twenty-nine yards in diameter, surrounded by a
broad ditch and an elevated mound, and bears the
name of *Arthur's Round Table*.　This is believed to
have been the scene of tournaments in the days of
chivalry, but whether the knights of King Arthur
were the first to joust in it must be left to the imaginations of antiquarians to decide.　Some have
believed that this was a castrensian amphitheatre, of
Roman construction; if this were the case, the mound
would serve for the spectators, and there are two
entrances cut through it, opposite to each other, by
which the combatants would enter the arena.

A few hundred yards to the west of Arthur's Round
Table there is an elevation called Mayburg, or Maybrough, on which is a large circular inclosure, a
hundred yards in diameter, the circumference of which
is a broad ridge of pebble stones heaped up to the height
of twelve or fifteen feet, and having in the centre a
massive pillar of unhewn stone, eleven feet high, and
in one part twenty-two feet in circumference.　It has
been disputed whether this is of Roman or British
origin, but it seems to be more probably the latter---

the upright stone bearing a great resemblance to several undoubted monuments of Druidical times.

About two miles below this place, in the rocky and perpendicular bank of the Eamont, is a huge cave, called *the Giant's Cave,* or *Isis Parlis.* This den can only be approached by climbing carefully along narrow ledges of stone on the side of the precipice, and supporting yourself by roots of trees : it is then found to be a deep hollow in the solid rock, though with no marks of having been artificially excavated. At the mouth a pillar of stone has been erected, and the marks of hinges remain, which prove that gates have formerly been placed at the entrance. According to tradition, it was the abode of a giant called Isir, who led the life of a Cacus, and it has at all events been used as a strong-hold.

Six miles north of Penrith, at Little Salkeld, is a very large and complete specimen of a Druidical temple. It consists of sixty-seven upright blocks of unhewn granite, disposed in a circle three hundred and fifty yards in circumference ; and near the entrance is a stone not less than eighteen feet high. The monument has obtained the familiar name of *Long Meg and her Daughters.*

On crossing the Eamont, we re-entered Westmoreland. When we had passed the Lowther, we found ourselves immediately in view of Brougham Hall, the seat of Lord Brougham and Vaux, the Lord High Chancellor of England. It is a plain but lofty and venerable pile, with an embrasured parapet, and has been erected at different periods.   Its situation being elevated, the terrace in front of the house commands an extensive and diversified prospect, including the fertile vales of the Eamont and the Lowther, the town of Penrith, and the rich country around it, the fine groves and lawns of many a noble park, and especially the woods of Lowther Park, which rise in a long ascent to the south.   Saddleback and the mountains round Ullswater, on the one hand, and the range of Cross-fell, on the other, form the back ground of this splendid view.   From the situation and the prospect, and especially from the fineness of its terrace, Brougham Hall has been styled *the Windsor of the North*.   It belonged for some time to the family of the Birds, one of whom gave it the name of *Bird Nest*, which it still retains in the neighbourhood.

The family of Brougham, or Burgham, is one of the most ancient in Westmoreland, and its members have for centuries held honourable offices in the country.   But they will derive their chief glory from the genius and patriotism of Henry Brougham, for so many years the terror of Tory Administrations, and the favourite of the people, as leader of the Opposition in the House of Commons ; and whose lofty ambition has led him, since his elevation to the Chancellorship, to effect larger reforms in his own court than all his predecessors together—cleansing that Augæan stable from the accumulated abuses of centuries. His country owes him a large debt of gratitude for the varied good effected by his wonderful energies.   The spread and

K

improvement of education, the reform of the law, and the extinction of West India slavery, owe more to him than to any other man,—not to mention that measure of unprecedented boldness and grandeur, the Reform Act, of which the chief glory belongs to his colleague, Earl Grey. Lord Brougham will not be recorded in history either as the soundest of lawyers or as the most prudent of statesmen; but he will have earned the praise of a champion of freedom, a reformer on the most enlarged principles, a Minister disdaining pelf and slighting patronage, an ardent friend of education, and a benefactor of the human race. Thrice rejected by his native county, Westmoreland, when he offered himself as a candidate to break the monopoly of the Lowthers, he was freely and as it were by acclamation elected member for the great county of York in the year 1830,—an event not without its bearing on the great political changes which followed, as well as on his own elevation to the chancellorship.

In the mansions and parks of her nobility and gentry England stands without a competitor among all the countries of the world; and one of the most princely of these residences, as well as one of the most admirable in point of natural situation, is the castle of the Earl of Lonsdale. *Lowther Castle is

* This powerful and wealthy family traces its genealogy to Sir Hugh de Lowther, who was attorney-general in 1292, knight of the shire in 1300 and 1305, and one of the Justices of the Court of King's Bench in 1330. Sir John Lowther was created Baron Lowther, Viscount Lonsdale, in 1696; he was appointed Lord Privy Seal, and was the great adorner and improver of the grounds

at the distance of five miles from Penrith. The park forms a long and gradual ascent from north to south, and the castle rises magnificently at the head of the slope, looking down upon spacious lawns and spreading woods, with the vale of Penrith, and, in the distance, Cross-fell, and some of the Scotch mountains. The noble growth of the timber in the park shows how much nature may be assisted by the cultivating hand of man. We had been accustomed, amongst the wild scenery of the Lakes, to trees of a rather feeble growth, though in some places plentiful, and disposed in picturesque beauty. It was, therefore, with pleasure and surprise that we saw the venerable oaks, elms, and beeches of Lowther Park, with their gigantic trunks and rich masses of foliage, either standing in solitary stateliness upon the lawns, and affording a shelter for the deer and cattle, or gathered together in solemn woods, whose shade gratefully invites to meditation.

The castle is quite modern, having been erected by the present Earl on the site of Lowther Hall, which had been partly consumed by fire a century ago. The castle was begun in the year 1808; the architect was

and neighbourhood of Lowther. The peerage became extinct in 1750, in the third lord (Henry), but the baronetage descended to James Lowther, descended from the Sir John Lowther who died in 1675. He was created Baron Lowther, Earl of Lonsdale, in 1784, and died childless in 1802. The title of Viscount Lowther descended to his cousin, Sir William Lowther, of Swillington, Bart. who was created Earl of Lonsdale April 4, 1807, and made a knight of the garter.

Smirke. It combines the majestic effect of a fortification with the splendour of a palace. The north
front is four hundred and twenty feet in length, and
is in the style of the thirteenth or fourteenth century. Its numerous towers, of different shapes and
elevations, are crested with battlements, and pierced
with slit windows : and the fresh colour of the stone
gives great richness to all these harmonious masses of
architecture. A high embattled wall surrounds the
entrance-court, and the entrance is through an arched
gateway. The terrace is five hundred feet long, and
one hundred wide. The southern front forms a remarkable contrast with the northern, being built in
the Gothic cathedral style, with pointed and mullioned
windows, delicate pinnacles, niches, and cloisters :
and the scene from this front accords well with the
solemn character of the edifice, being a lawn of emerald
green and velvet smoothness, shut in by ornamental
trees and shrubs and by timber of stately growth.
The interior of the castle is fitted up with corresponding taste and splendour. There is a plentiful use of
British oak, carved with Gothic ornaments, in the
furniture and wainscoting of the rooms.

The central tower, which is seen by the visiter
immediately on entering the castle, is supported by
massive clustered columns like those of a cathedral,
and the arches and columns in the upper part of the
tower are in the same rich and grand style. The
staircase passes round this tower ; it is of a solid
and costly construction, answering to the character of

the whole edifice.   In a corridor at the top of the
staircase are several fine pictures by Guercino, Guido,
Titian, and Tintoretto, and there are a few other good
pictures in an adjoining room.   After having gone
over the castle, we went with the gardener into the
gardens and on to the terrace which overlooks the
valley of the Lowther.   Every thing is laid out on a
scale becoming the grounds of a palace, and the pines
and cedars have attained a truly aristocratic elevation.

It was with reluctance we quitted this splendid
abode.   We crossed the river Lowther, which runs
through a most picturesque valley, and, after passing
for four miles through narrow and winding lanes, we
came to Pooley-bridge, where we took up our abode
for the night at a small but comfortable inn.

CHAPTER XVI.

ULLSWATER——POOLEY BRIDGE—DUNMALLET—SAIL UP THE LAKE—SWARTH-FELL—HALLEN-FELL—HALLSTEADS—GOWBARROW PARKS—AIREY FORCE—STYBARROW CRAG—UPPER REACH OF THE LAKE—PATTERDALE—SUBLIME SCENERY—PATTERDALE HALL—ECHOES ON DISCHARGE OF A CANNON.

WE were now at the foot of Ullswater, which is generally allowed to be the finest of all the Lakes. The morning being very fine, we anticipated with pleasure a sail up the lake to Patterdale, and we intended to send the carriage to the same place.

Our parlour, which was at the rear of the house, looked upon a pleasant pasture, on the further side of which rolled the clear and rapid Eamont, just after issuing out of the lake; and immediately beyond, as the principal feature of the view, rose the conical hill of Dunmallet, clothed with a mantle of the richest foliage, now beginning to assume the mellow tints of autumn. Thirty years ago this hill, then recently planted by Mr. Hasell, the proprietor of the neighbouring estate and mansion of Dalemain, was pronounced by more than one writer of taste to be too formal in the disposition of the trees to constitute an ornament to the landscape. This defect has been remedied by the subsequent growth of the wood, and the mount is now encircled by a grove of the highest luxuriance. Dunmallet was anciently crowned by a Roman fort, the vestiges of which are still visible. George and I climbed the hill in the hope of obtaining a good view of Ullswater from it; but the trees on the summit are so high and thick that we could see nothing beyond them. The wood is plentifully stocked with hares. On descending, we went with our host to see a preserve of eels belonging to him in a cage in the river : the cage was full of eels, some of them enormously large, but the slippery tenants glided about amongst each other's folds more smoothly and featly than ever belles and beaux swum through the mazes of the most " mystic dance." Some of them, alas! the unpitying net captured, in spite of all their attempts to slide out of it; and they were conveyed to the cook, to make such pasties as we had been pampered withal yesterday, and as constitute a favourite dish at the Sun, Pooley-bridge.

Ullswater is the largest of the Lakes, after Windermere. It is said to combine the beauties of all the other lakes, and in a certain degree it does so; but there is no part of it to be compared, for soft and Elysian beauty, with the central parts of Windermere. On the other hand, it runs up much nearer to the heart of the mountains, and therefore still more excels its rival in grandeur than it falls below it in beauty. Ullswater is nine miles in length, and, being forced by the bold hills which environ it to assume a

zigzag direction, its form is nearly that of a Z. The
lake is in many parts very deep, especially towards
the head, where the mountains descend in precipices
to the very brink of the water. "The mighty Helvellyn" lifts his manifold crags and summits in stern
magnificence over the head; and on the south and
east sides of the lake he is fronted by fells of great
elevation and boldness, not unworthy such neighbourhood.

The lower *reach* of the lake, about three miles in
length, is tame, when compared with the middle and
upper reaches; yet it is a fine sheet of water, and
its borders afford scenes of varied and lively beauty.
On the north the hills are not particularly bold, and
they rise gently from the lake, leaving a margin of
fertile ground, which has been improved and adorned
by art. There are several mansions and cottages
both on the Westmoreland and Cumberland sides,
which presented themselves to us advantageously as
we rowed up the lake. Some of the houses stand in
elevated situations, commanding an extensive prospect
over the surrounding country; whilst others are built
near the edge of the lake, under the shelter of the
rising ground and of encircling groves, betwixt which
ornamental lawns slope down to the water's brink.
Amongst the houses in the latter situation is Rampe-
beck-lodge, the beautiful residence of Mr. Stagg,
about the middle of the first reach, on the Cumberland side. Beau Thorn, so called from a plantation
of white thorns which surrounds it, and Lemon-house,

are also delightfully situated. Watermillock, the seat of the late Colonel Robinson, now occupied by the Rev. Mr. Tinkler, has long been celebrated by travellers; it stands on an elevated point on the same side of Ullswater, looking down the lower reach of the lake. The back-ground of the view from these houses is formed by Swarth-fell, a bold ridge which skirts the southern border of the reach, and runs up towards the Martindale fells. Our boatman pointed out a part of the fell, so steep as to seem to us nearly perpendicular, down which the late Mr. Hasell, of Dalemain, descended with his horse, having, in the heat of the chase, passed over the brow of the hill into a situation from which it was impossible to re-ascend. He dismounted from his hunter, and the sagacious and experienced animal, making common cause with him, slid down the long and perilous descent on his haunches, at once supporting and being supported by his master, till they arrived safely at the bottom. Under this ridge, near Pooley, is Eusemere-lodge, the seat of Mr. Bristow, formerly the residence of that distinguished philanthropist, whose name is identified with the abolition of the slave-trade— Thomas Clarkson.

A bluff mountain, called Hallen-fell, rises at the head of the first reach of Ullswater, and forces the lake out of a southerly into a westerly direction. Between Hallen-fell and Swarth-fell, the green vale of Martindale, (so named from having formerly abounded in the little animal called the *martin*,) runs up into the heart of barren hills. When we had doubled the promontory which separates the two reaches, a new and far more interesting prospect opened upon us. The middle reach of the lake is about four miles in length, and lies between the lofty and precipitous hills of Hallen-fell, Birk-fell, and Place-fell on the south, and the long sweep of Gowbarrow Parks on the north; whilst Helvellyn and the rocky mountains which stand around him like sentries form a magnificent termination to the view in front. His roots, pushed to the water's edge, compel the lake to assume its original southerly direction; and thus the middle reach, separated by sudden bends from the first and third reaches, appears like a distinct lake. From the same cause, the variety and picturesqueness of the views on Ullswater are much greater than on any of the other lakes, and would be so even independent of the greater boldness of the hills which are piled around it.

On our right as we entered this division of the lake, and just on the promontory which divides the first and second reaches, was Hallsteads, the seat of Mr. Marshall, lately high-sheriff of Cumberland, and for some years member for the county of York. His house commands one of the finest views of the lake, looking up the whole length of this reach, with Helvellyn in front, and having Hallen-fell, Swarthfell, and the beautiful recess of Martindale immediately opposite.

Gowbarrow Parks, formerly the property of the Duke of Norfolk, and bequeathed by the late Duke to Henry Howard, Esq. of Greystoke Castle, are ancient deer-parks, stretching along a concave bend of the mountain to the distance of four miles, and terminating in the wild, picturesque, and beautiful recess of Glencoin. They are not trimly kept or adorned by walks or buildings, but left nearly in the natural state, and covered in the lower part with woods, and in the more elevated parts with grass and fern. Their extent is eighteen hundred acres, but they are divided into three parks, Glencoin Park, Gowbarrow Park, and the Low Park; the first and last of which are farmed off, and the second, which contains eight hundred acres, is stocked with four hundred head of deer. Between Gowbarrow Park and Low Park there is a projection of the mountain, fronted with a towering mass of shattered rock, called Yew Crag. Gowbarrow Park is far more interesting and more accordant to the rest of the scenery, with its neglected woods, its aged oaks and thorns, and its rough carpet of grass and fern, than if all the elegance of art had been lavished upon it. Nature, and —what is almost as good as nature—antiquity, are the ideas it impresses on the mind; in beholding it, you think of ancient baronial times, and a pleasing melancholy, mingled with reverence, comes over you. This impression is heightened by the plain gray building, called *Lyulph's Tower*, standing on the edge of a wood, whose battlements lead you to suppose it a fortification.* It is, however, merely a hunting-box, erected in imitation of an old mansion, and decorated with those old-fashioned ornaments—tokens of the exploits of our British Nimrods—enormous antlers, and heads of deer and other animals. A fine cream-coloured bloodhound, kenneled near the door of the tower, is another characteristic appendage to the residence of a feudal baron.

We landed at the boat-house near Lyulph's Tower, and walked up to the house, the upper windows of which command a view of almost unrivalled grandeur, richness, and beauty. An ample expanse of the lake is spread out below, bordered by all that is stupendous and sublime in mountain scenery, with all that is rich and picturesque in woods and vales. Stybarrow Crag, a lofty promontory terminating one of the ridges that descend from Helvellyn, presents its oak-crowned front at the head of this division of the lake: Birk-fell and Place fell rear their vast mountain bulwarks on the southern shore, the former sloping down at one end into a gracious vale, which forms part of Martindale, and the latter swelling his giant bulk to an enormous elevation. On the northern shore is the wooded and uneven slope

---

* Lyulph's Tower has been so called after Lyulph, the first baron of Greystock, who received the grant soon after the Conquest, and who was the proprietor of Ullswater. The lake itself is said to derive its name from this ancient baron, the root of whose name is Ulf, whence L'Ulf, Lyulph. The estate of Greystock, in which this is included, came into the family of the Howards in the time of Elizabeth.

of Gowbarrow Park, terminating in the recess of Glencoin. And the sublime back-ground of the whole is Helvellyn, frowning, as it were, in collected might, with all his terrible array of crags surrounding him.

After gazing for some time upon this matchless view, we proceeded through the park and a deep winding glen choked with trees, to Airey-force—a cascade about a quarter of a mile distant. A pretty girl was our guide, and she tripped along the rough and stony path at a pace not quite convenient to some of our party. At length, after making a sudden turn so as to come into a nook of the glen, we arrived in front of the force, which is an extremely fine and picturesque object, rivalling Stockgill-force in beauty, though not so high. The water falls about eighty feet perpendicularly through a chasm of the rocks: at the top it is divided by a narrow ledge into two streams, which unite before they have fallen half-way down, and are dashed against a projecting part of the rock, from which they rebound in expanding sheets of foam. Amidst clouds of spray the waters plunge into a deep basin, and soon issue forth from the gulph in a rapid stream, as transparent as before their fall. The rocks and trees stand all round this cascade, so as to make it perfectly secluded; the oak and the ash bend their branches over the fall, and involve it in a cool shade. We ascended by a circuitous path to the top; and when we saw the fall from above, it struck us even more than the view from below. As the sun's rays fell upon the clouds of spray, an iris flung its lovely arch over the chasm —its splendour alternately brightening and fading with the greater or less density of the spray. We returned to Lyulph's Tower by a different path from that by which we had approached the cascade.

Re-entering our boat, I resumed the oar which I had held since we left Pooley-bridge, and we rowed up the lake, following for some time the indentations of the shore. This gave a remarkable variety to the scenes, by changing the fore-ground, and presenting the features of the landscape in different directions and combinations. At my instance, we rowed over nearly to the southern shore, which gave us a better view than we had yet had of the northern. Then, at the desire of the boatman, we crossed again to the side of Gowbarrow Park, just where it terminates in the deep and secluded valley of Glencoin,* which contributes its streamlet to the waters of the lake. He contrived that we should creep along the shore till we came close under a lofty crag, enveloped from the base to the summit in natural wood. Then, turning the head of the boat from the land, and desiring me to pull as strongly as I could, whilst he directed us all to keep our eyes on the crag, we shot out towards the middle of the lake. The effect was magical. The naked peak of a mountain, before concealed, seemed to rise up swiftly out of the woody eminence from which we

---

* Glencoin, or Glencune, signifies a *glen* in a *corner* of the mountains.

were receding, till it stood in its just proportions before us, and appeared many hundred feet above our heads, leaving at its base the bold crag from under which we had darted. The eye can scarcely persuade itself that the effect is simply produced by our own motion—the gray and shivered pinnacle of the mountain rises so unexpectedly from behind the wood which had overhung us, and so entirely changes the character of the view.

We were now within view of the last and finest reach of the lake, which is about two miles in length. Immediately before us was Stybarrow Crag—the noble promontory and hill which we had seen from Lyulph's Tower. The lower part of the Crag is precipitous, yet the oak has struck his roots into the interstices of the rocks, and grows up the steep, so that the Crag is hid in a grove of fine oak-trees. Just at the bend of the lake is House-holm, a small island of rock, covered with shrubs, and constituting an ornament to the view, but misnomered, as it bears no trace of a habitation; there are also three other diminutive islands in the upper reach. At this point, on the southern side, Place-fell " pushes its craggy foot into the lake like a lion's claw."[*]

When we had passed House-holm, the fertile vales of Patterdale and Glenridden, the former of which branches off into three at the head of Ullswater, lay before us. There is a peacefulness, a soft and exquisite beauty, in these vales, lying embosomed amongst the

* Mrs. Radcliffe.

high and sterile mountains, which cannot fail deeply
to impress a mind of the least susceptibility. Their
verdure is always of the brightest green, being watered
by innumerable springs and streamlets. Trees are
scattered in splendid profusion on the banks of the
streams, and on the sides of the green hills; and a
simple white house, appearing scarcely bigger than a
dove-cote, is planted here and there, beneath the
shelter of a hill or wood. The village church rises
not in vain in this sequestered but majestic temple of
nature, and suggests how comely it is for man to
worship the divine Architect. A few mansions,
elegantly but not ostentatiously built, adorn some of
the recesses of the shore, but do not obtrude themselves on the eye, or violate the character of the scene.
Some of the mountains which environ us have a noble
simplicity of form, and others a sublime ruggedness
and barrenness. Behind Patterdale, at a little distance, rises a regular conical mountain, called Dod
Hill, clothed with verdure to the summit. To our
right is an extremely bold hill, called St. Sunday
Crag, the round head of which is covered with herbage.
Behind it is the range of Fairfield; and the opposite
side of the lake is overhung by the dark and precipitous ridge of Place-fell.

To the whole of our party except myself this scene
was new, and their admiration of it was unbounded.
We had so arranged our tour, that what I considered
the noblest part of the Lake scenery might come last;
and I was gratified to find that the head of Ullswater

was unanimously acknowledged to surpass in combined grandeur and beauty all we had hitherto seen.

We now approached the head of the lake, where we saw Patterdale-hall, the house of Wm. Marshall, Esq., (the eldest son of John Marshall, Esq., of Hallsteads,) which stands on the level shore, and presents its front to the lake. This was formerly the seat of Mr. Mounsey, whose ancestors have for many ages borne the title of *kings of Patterdale,* said to have been given to them on account of a gallant exploit performed by one of the family, who, at the head of a few peasants, met a band of Scottish marauders at the pass of Stybarrow Crag, and defeated them. Mr. Mounsey sold the hall a few years ago to Mr. Marshall, and has built himself a house, called Deepdale Cottage, two miles further up the valley.

The landing-place is on the banks of a small stream which flows through Patterdale* into the lake. After leaving the boat, we had to walk a quarter of a mile to Mrs. Dobson's, the homely but comfortable inn of this delightfully-situated village. Here we took up our quarters for the night; and, after ordering dinner, we climbed a rock at the back of the house, where a small cannon is planted, which is fired for the sake of the echoes. As the mountains rise steeply on every side, the peal is flung from one to another, so as to be heard several times with as much distinctness as if each

* *Patterdale* is a corruption of *Patrick's-dale,* so called from *St. Patrick's Well* in the valley, near the hall. In the churchyard there is one of the finest yew-trees in the kingdom.

repetition was a fresh discharge. When the ladies had placed themselves at such a distance that they thought they were out of danger, the piece was fired. At first the peal roared along the hills behind us: anon, it appeared to rend the bowels of Place-fell, which rose immediately in front: then, when it had subsided, the thunder returned upon us from the higher part of the Helvellyn range: again it died away, but again revived along the distant hills of Gowbarrow Park. A fifth and fainter repetition of the peal was heard; but we did not catch the sixth and seventh echo, which are said frequently to be distinguished. There is something deeply impressive in the reverberation of such a burst of sound through a mighty theatre of mountains. It enlarges the conception of the mind with regard to the vastness of the surrounding objects: the ear supplies the deficiencies of the eye, and informs us of the loftier and more distant ranges which are shut out from our view. In these vales, so far from the busy hum of men, scarcely any sounds are ever heard but of the winds and waters; and in a serene autumn evening, stillness the most profound reigned over them, till our curiosity occasioned this awful uproar to be awakened, which startled Ullswater " from its propriety." We listened with wonder to the responsive tumult, and were glad when the scene was again hushed into its natural silence and repose.

CHAPTER XVII.

IT was our intention to go on Friday from Patterdale to Ambleside. The distance is only ten miles by Brotherswater and Kirkstone; and the road, though rough and mountainous, may be passed by a carriage with safety. But George and I had a strong inclination to ascend Helvellyn, which, being somewhat higher than Skiddaw, and more difficult of ascent, is much less frequently climbed by travellers. Neither for the ladies' sake nor for our own, did we wish them to accompany us; and they were themselves of opinion that they had done enough for glory in the ascent of Skiddaw, without tempting the more perilous heights of Helvellyn. We determined to set out on this expedition not later than eight in the morning, in which case we might get back to Patterdale between twelve and one, and afterwards proceed with the ladies to Ambleside.

We had arranged all our plans overnight, but in the morning the weather threatened to mar them, and to prevent us from ascending the mountain. The

waiter, in calling us, made the dismal announcement
—"Six o'clock, Sir—a very wet morning."   I got out
of bed, and, going to the window, found that it had
been raining heavily : the rain had somewhat abated,
but the clouds covered the tops of all the hills, and
hung gloomily about their sides.   The dense masses of
vapour rolled through the valley like volumes of
smoke from some huge furnace, and I observed with
despondency that the wind by which they were carried
along was from a rainy quarter—the south-west.
This prospect drove me to bed for comfort, and I lay
snugly till seven—George having very naturally sought
consolation in the same way.   At that hour we rose
and dressed.   The clouds were then higher than when
I first looked out, and light appeared round the edges
of the horizon, though the hill-tops were not yet
uncovered.   At eight our prospects were again darkened, and we found the barometer down at *rain*.   But
in about half an hour, just as the ladies made their
appearance for breakfast, we observed that the clouds
were rising and breaking, and that the wind had gone
about to the north.   The change of wind, and the
cessation of rain, gave us lively hopes that the day
would, after all, take up, but still it was doubtful
whether this would be in sufficient time to enable us
to ascend Helvellyn.   We calculated distances, and,
as the morning advanced, we kept abridging the time
necessary for ascending the mountain, and putting off
the hour at which we ought to leave Patterdale for
Ambleside.

At length the blue sky appeared in two or three places at once ; first, the hill above Stybarrow Crag became clear ; then Place-fell doffed his night-cap, and put on a " shining morning face."* We were now so confident that the day would prove fine, that we laid in our usual stock of sandwiches and brandy, and at half-past nine o'clock set out on our expedition in

* Our experience was like that of Cumberland, when, after a series of gloomy weather, the sun broke forth in Patterdale, and he composed the following beautiful ode :—

" Me, turbid skies and threatening clouds await,
Emblems, alas ! of my ignoble fate.
But see the embattled vapours break,
Disperse and fly,
Posting like couriers down the sky ;
The grey rock glitters in the glassy lake ;
And now the mountain tops are seen,
Frowning amidst the blue serene ;
The variegated groves appear,
Deckt in the colours of the waning year ;
And as new beauties they unfold,
Dip their skirts in beaming gold.
Thee, savage *Wyburn*, now I hail ;
Delicious *Grasmere's* calm retreat,
And stately *Windermere* I greet,
And *Keswick's* sweet fantastic vale ;
But let her naiads yield to thee,
And lowly bend the subject knee,
Imperial lake of *Patrick's* dale ;
For neither Scottish *Lomond's* pride,
Nor smooth *Killarney's* silver tide,
Nor aught that learned *Poussin* drew,
Or dashing *Rosa* flung upon my view,
Shall shake thy sovereign undisturbed right,
Great scene of wonder and sublime delight !
Hail to thy beams, O sun ! for this display,
What, glorious orb, can I repay ?
The thanks of an unprostituted muse."

the highest spirits. We had determined not to take
a guide with us, thinking ourselves superior to any
such aid, and disliking the restraint which the presence
of a guide would put on our motions and conversation. The latter, indeed, was rather a fanciful reason,
as the guides are usually very accommodating and
unobtrusive. I had taken the precaution to make
diligent inquiry of the boatman who came with us
from Pooley-bridge, and who knew the mountain
well, as to the path we should follow in order to reach
the top. He pointed out a faintly-traced pathway
about half the distance, as far as the summit of a
ridge which runs up on the north side of Grisedale-
beck, and conducts to the head of the mountain. He
then told us, that when we had got upon that ridge
we should see the top of Helvellyn, and, immediately
beneath it, a tarn; that there were two ways of proceeding thence to the summit,—the shortest, by
keeping along the top of the ridge, which was called
Striding-edge,—and the other, which was longer but
much safer, by descending a little on the opposite side
of the ridge, and re-ascending by Swirrel-edge, which
would leave the tarn on our left hand. He said that
the passage of Striding-edge, though frequently
accomplished, was attended with some danger, as it
was like walking along the narrow ridge of a steep
roof; and he intimated that we should probably find
that part of the mountain very different from what
we expected. Having made up our minds to over-
come by our own sagacity and exertions the difficulties

we might encounter, and supposing that the boatman somewhat exaggerated the perils of the ascent for the purpose of being engaged to accompany us, we made light of his warnings, but carefully treasured up his instructions in our memories.

For about half a mile we pursued the high road to Pooley-bridge, till we had crossed the bridge over Grisedale-beck, near Patterdale-hall, when we turned immediately to the left, and began to ascend the mountain at a very deliberate pace. Passing through a wood, we came shortly to the last cottage on the hill-side. The proprietor, of whom we asked the way, said that there was no road without trespassing over his ground. Of course we solicited a passport, and he then graciously took us through his fold, and pointed out the path we should follow. Keeping our eye on the part of the ridge which we had been directed to aim at, and which appears somewhat hollow, we slowly wound along the hill-side, reserving our strength for the more difficult parts of the mountain.

The views which we enjoyed in our progress were interesting and splendid. Immediately beneath us was the beautiful vale of Grisedale, which runs from Ullswater up to the heart of Helvellyn, and separates the hill we were ascending from the bold heights of St. Sunday Crag and Fairfield. In the bottom of the valley flows the beck, or streamlet, which forms the common channel for innumerable rills that trickle down the sides of the mountain, and, after watering the valley, empty themselves by this mouth into

Ullswater.   Cattle and horses graze the fertile pastures; and the hills which tower above them are nibbled by sheep.   The upper part of the valley becomes a mere ravine of the mountain, down which we saw many rills tumbling in different directions, and appearing, as the sun shone directly upon them, like waving lines of silver.   The lower part is beautified with wood, as is the delicious vale of Patterdale, now far beneath and behind us.   We could still see the inn, and thought it not unlikely that the ladies might discern us.   The dark blue sheet of Ullswater lay like a mirror of steel in the depth of the valley, margined with the most brilliant verdure. The mountain view expanded to the south and east, and we found ourselves approaching to the elevation of some of the bold hills, which appeared from the lake to be nearly as high as Helvellyn himself.

When we had reached the brow of the ridge, a new prospect to the north and east opened upon us.   The lower reach of Ullswater, the vale and town of Penrith, and all the surrounding country to a vast extent, as well as the numerous inferior hills which form the group of Helvellyn, were exposed to our view.   The head of the mountain itself, also, was now seen, crowned with a conical pile of stones, called Helvellyn Man; and immediately beneath it, at the foot of a precipice upwards of six hundred feet in depth, a small dark tarn, called Red-tarn, lay in a hollow of the mountain.   We now saw before us the two ways by which we might prosecute the ascent.

Two ridges, Striding-edge and Swirrel-edge, run down from the top of the mountain, enclosing betwixt them a considerable valley, in which lies the tarn just mentioned. Swirrel-edge is crested by a summit of the mountain, called Catchedecam, and is also connected with the summit of Helvellyn. The ridge we were upon, Striding-edge, was the shorter but more rugged path; and, in spite of the warnings of our boatman, we chose it, being incited by curiosity, and perhaps quite as much by the motive which actuates most men in fighting duels—a *fear* lest our *courage* should be called in question if we declined the danger.

We therefore addressed ourselves to the passage of Striding-edge; but if we had seen the most dangerous part much before we came to it, we should have been content to take the safer though more cowardly branch of the alternative offered to us. As we ascended, the hill became more steep and rugged, till at length the ridge presented nothing but rocks, the narrow edges of which lay upwards in the direction of the sky. Their sides became steeper and steeper, and it was with difficulty that we crept along paths not wider than a goat-track, to avoid clambering among the crags which formed the very ridge of the hill. At length it became impossible to find footing on the side, and we betook ourselves of necessity to the ridge itself. We now came in view of the most formidable part of Striding-edge, and found that it rather deserved to be compared to a narrow wall, several hundred feet in height, connecting the hill which we

L

had been ascending with the head of the mountain, than to the steep roof of a house. It appeared to us to be absolutely precipitous on each side, and the top of the rocky wall was not more than from one to two yards wide, whilst in some places we could not see, before we came to it, as much ground as would serve to plant a foot upon—the rocks presenting their sharp and rugged edges upwards, like slates or tiles standing on end. If we had had a guide, all this would have been much less terrific, because he would have led the way, and shown us where to place every footstep. The possibility that we might, after all, have taken a wrong direction, or that in some part of the pass we should find ourselves in a situation where we could neither advance nor retreat, gave us considerable alarm. Neither of us, however, expressed our fears at the time, and I felt myself bound to keep up both my own spirits and George's, as the blame would have been chiefly mine if any accident had happened. I therefore talked loudly and confidently as we scrambled along, keeping all my eyes about me, and giving him such instructions as his want of experience in climbing rendered necessary. He said little or nothing, and never ventured to cast a look either to the tarn which lay several hundred feet below us on one side, or to the equally awful depth on the other; but, fixing his eyes on the ridge itself as if he were fascinated, he crept on after me as cautiously and yet as fast as he could. In this way we crossed the long and dangerous pass of Striding-

edge, till we came to the last ascent of the mountain.
This part is exceedingly steep, but still there is ample
room for the foot, and, without waiting a moment,
we began to ascend as quickly as possible.   A vigorous
push for a few minutes placed us out of all danger,
and, to our unspeakable satisfaction, we found ourselves on the pinnacle of " the mighty Helvellyn."
 How sublime an elevation !   How glorious a panorama !   What a mighty assemblage of mountains !
What an infinite diversity of landscape !   *Water*—in
all its varieties, from the little tarn collected in the
hollows of mountains and the streamlet which trickles
down their sides, to the spreading lake, the far-
winding river, the broad estuary, and the unlimited
sea !   *Land*—in every form and dress,—the huge-
swelling, dark, and rugged mountain,—the inferior
hill, whose coat of fern is browned by the summer's
sun,—the deep, secluded valley, clothed in living
green, hung with woods which are putting on the
tints of autumn, pastured by flocks and herds, and
spotted with rural habitations,—and the wide-extended
plain, where the smoke of towns, and the inclosures
of parks and fields, bespeak the busy hand of man !
And all this magnificent scene illuminated by a mid-
day sun, and canopied with a cloudless sky !
 Well might we stand gazing with unsated admiration on this prospect ; and it was long before the
high and keen wind drove us to take shelter beneath
the pile of stones which stands on the summit.   We
felt more than recompensed for the toil and danger of

the ascent. Having emerged from the depth of Patterdale, we found it most interesting to behold again Skiddaw and Saddleback, Scawfell, and Langdale Pikes, and to trace with the eye, as on a map, all the journeys we had been making since we entered Westmoreland. This view, though similar to that we had had from Skiddaw in its general features and in its extent, presented many of the objects in such different positions as to give it the interest of a new prospect. The boundaries of the vast panorama were, the Scotch mountains on the north, the range of Cross-fell on the east, the hills of Yorkshire and Lancashire on the south, and the Irish sea on the west. Immediately beneath us, to the west, lay the rugged and savage scenery of the Borrowdale and Langdale fells, and beyond these appeared successively the ridges which separate Borrowdale from Buttermere, Buttermere from Ennerdale, and Ennerdale from Wasdale. Scawfell Pikes, Great End, Great Gavel, and the Pillar, stood " proudly eminent ;" Bowfell and Coniston Old Man were also very conspicuous ; Langdale Pikes, which appeared so lofty from the valley below them, now looked very humble. Southward were the summits of Fairfield, which hid from us nearly the whole of Windermere; but two small portions of that lake were visible, and, beyond the mountains, Morecambe Bay, and the large estuaries of the Leven, the Duddon, and the Esk, were seen with the utmost distinctness. High Street, Hill Bell, Kidsey Pike, and the whole range of the Martindale fells, with the dark broad breast of Place-fell in front, appeared in the south-east and east ; and still further south Ingleborough was distinctly visible. The lower part of Ullswater was seen ; Bassenthwaite Water in the north, and Coniston and Esthwaite lakes in the south : Derwentwater lay hid behind the Derwent fells, and the lakes of Thirlmere and Grassmere were concealed by the swelling sides of Helvellyn himself.

It was exactly noon when we reached the summit of the mountain, and we remained there twenty minutes. I scarcely need say that we did not return by way of Striding-edge. The other route, though steep, is safe and easy in comparison. As we descended, we cast many a glance at Striding-edge, and it then came into our minds that that must be the very place, from which the young man fell whose death has been commemorated by Wordsworth and Sir Walter Scott. The name of the unfortunate traveller was Charles Gough, and in the spring of 1805, on a day in which snow had fallen, attempting to cross the mountain from Patterdale to Wythburn, with no companion but his dog, he perished by falling down those precipices. His body was not found till three months afterwards, when the faithful dog was discovered still watching over the lifeless remains of his master. I cannot resist the temptation of copying Wordsworth's lines commemorative of this affecting instance of brute " Fidelity :" their simple pathos is beyond praise :—

" But hear a wonder, for whose sake
This lamentable tale I tell !
A lasting monument of words
This wonder merits well.
The dog, which still was hovering nigh,
Repeating the same timid cry,—
This dog had been through three months' space
A dweller in that savage place.
Yes, proof was plain that since the day
On which the traveller thus had died,
The dog had watched about the spot,
Or by his master's side :
How nourished there through such long time
He knows who gave that love sublime,
And gave that strength of feeling great
Above all human estimate."

On reaching Patterdale we ascertained that this was the very spot where the traveller perished, and we congratulated ourselves that we had not recollected the fact whilst we were crossing the ridge. It inspired us with a feeling of gratitude for our own preservation. The descent of the mountain was accomplished in little more than an hour, and we set out before two o'clock for Ambleside.

CHAPTER XVIII.

FROM PATTERDALE TO AMBLESIDE—UPPER PART OF PATTERDALE
—DEEPDALE—BROTHERSWATER—KIRKSTONE—AMBLESIDE—
RETROSPECT OF THE TOUR—ULLSWATER AND WINDERMERE
COMPARED—CONCLUSION.

I have now come to the last scene of our Tour
amongst the Lakes.

We quitted Patterdale with lingering looks at Ullswater and Helvellyn.   Our road lay for three or four
miles through the upper part of the valley, which
branches off at the head into three minor vales—that
of Deepdale on the right,—that of Hartshope, in
which lies the lake of Brotherswater, forming a con-
tinuation of Patterdale,—and a smaller vale to the left,
containing the hamlet of Low Hartshope, separated
from Hartshope by Dod Hill.   On the hills to the left
are two tarns, Angle-tarn, at the southern extremity
of Place-fell, and Hays Water-tarn, under the north
side of High Street, both of which contain delicious
trout, and are much frequented by anglers.

The first part of our journey was through shady
lanes, with luxuriant meadows and pastures on either
hand, watered by Coldrill-beck and several subsidiary
streamlets, and retaining, though at this advanced
period of autumn, their vernal green.   The valley is

deep and secluded, and even where it opens out near
the head into three branches, the very few human
habitations which are to be seen, and the immediate
vicinity of the mountains, to the heart of which each
valley conducts the eye, do not diminish the sense
of seclusion from the world.   Deepdale forms a beautiful upland recess, the whole extent of which is at
once visible: it is plentifully besprinkled with trees,
which rise high up the sides of the hills, and it conducts a tributary brook from the sides of Fairfield
into Coldrill-beck.   The vale of Hartshope is terminated at the distance of three miles further by the
rocky heights of Dove Crag.

The small lake of Brotherswater is pretty, and
looks much more so when approached from the side of
Kirkstone than from that of Ullswater.   In the former
case, it is the beginning of beauties; in the latter, it
is the termination of them.   Yet I do not recommend
visiting Ullswater from Ambleside; for then not only
is the finest part of the lake seen first, and the view
as you sail down it gradually deteriorates, but the
splendid effect of the upper reach, and of the branching valleys of Patterdale, Grisedale, Glenridden, and
Glencoin, with the noble mountains in their rear,
which open so delightfully upon you in sailing up the
lake, is in a great measure lost.   It may seem in
speculation to be a matter of indifference at which
end you begin, as, going over the same ground, you
will have all the beauties, first or last; but it is
found by actual observation that a great difference is

produced by the way in which objects present themselves; much depends on the first impression, and much on the order of improvement or of deterioration in which the views are seen.

Brotherswater is scarcely larger than a mountain-tarn. It is said to have received its present name from the fact of two brothers having been drowned there. Such an event occurred in the year 1785, and tradition also tells of a similar tragical event having happened there at a much earlier period. The ancient name of the lake, however, is Broaderwater, and it may be doubted whether the name has been suddenly changed or gradually corrupted. The meadows which extend to a considerable distance beyond it are as level as the surface of the pool itself, and we conjectured that they had once been covered with water, and that an alluvial deposit, or the accumulation of vegetable matter at the shallow bottom of the lake, or the widening of the passage by which the water flows out of it, had converted this considerable extent from a pool into a meadow.

Soon after passing Brotherswater, the valley rises rapidly, loses its verdure, and becomes a steep, contracted, and barren dell, just affording room for a road and a torrent, which descend from the height of Kirkstone-moor. The ascent is very long and arduous, and the road much worse than any our carriage had yet passed over. The ladies walked the greater part of the way up the hill; which the ruggedness of the track, and the power of the sun's rays, reflected from the shale-covered sides of the mountains, made a very fatiguing task. From the loftiness and steepness of the hills on each side, there is a simple grandeur in this pass; and its very barrenness prepares the traveller to enjoy more highly the diversified and charming prospect which opens upon him from the top. In ascending, a large stone is seen at the brow of the hill, on the right of the road, which, from its shape, has obtained the name of Kirkstone. It resembles a house seen at the gable-end, and may be equally like a spireless church.*

From the higher part of the pass, which is a small moor at an elevation of twelve hundred feet above Ambleside, lying betwixt two higher mountains, Colddale-fell on the left, and Scandale-fell on the right, we suddenly obtained a view of the head of Windermere far beneath us, and of the beautiful country beyond it, with the bold mountains of the Coniston and Langdale districts in the back-ground. As we descended, the groves and lawns of Brathay Park, disposed over a surface most picturesquely broken and irregular, came into view, and formed a delicious foreground to the landscape. The valley

---

* On the name of Kirkstone, as on every subject of antiquaquarian lore, there are divers opinions; some think that it has arisen from the resemblance of the large stone mentioned above to a church or *kirk;* others say that it is an abbreviation of *kirock-stone*—*kirock* signifying a heap of stones formerly used as boundary-marks or guides for travellers, and that such heaps of stones are found on the hill.

of Ambleside, the woods and crags of Loughrigg, and the winding streams of the Rothay and the Brathay, which join their waters before they fall into Windermere, add to the beauty of the prospect. Of the town of Ambleside, which lies under the hill, nothing is seen except a few chimneys amongst the trees, from which ascend wreaths of blue smoke. On our left as we descended, was the gill in which Stockgill Force is situated. These various objects beguiled the long and steep descent from Kirkstone to Ambleside.

It was our original intention to remain for the night at Ambleside, but, being on many accounts desirous of reaching home, we determined to go forward to Kendal. We accordingly proceeded to that place, and on the following day a long journey brought us in safety to our own homes.

I scarcely need say, that the splendid scenery we had beheld, the favourable weather we had enjoyed, and the friends we had unexpectedly met with, made us all look back upon our tour with feelings of high gratification. We had experienced just enough of fatigue and danger to give a relish to enjoyments, which, if they had been unvaried, might have been cloying. We had the grateful consciousness of having in some degree earned our pleasures by our own exertions, and felt a little of the self-importance of those who have to boast of dangers passed and difficulties conquered. To some of our party nearly every thing we had seen possessed the charm of novelty; the others had the pleasure of imparting information, and revived their own past feelings by exciting and directing the admiration of their companions. Sympathy constitutes no small part of the gratification of fellow-travellers. On the other hand, a difference of tastes, such as naturally existed amongst persons of different ages, sexes, and temperaments, does not detract from the general enjoyment, unless when it is too decided, or when accompanied with selfishness or ill temper. It enlivens and diversifies conversation, forms a check upon error, and brings a greater number of objects under particular notice. The grave enthusiasm of one of my cousins was agreeably relieved by the wit and sprightliness of the other: and when conversation flagged in our own company, it was revived and animated by the acquaintances we met with in various stages of our journey.

A party will not often be so much favoured by the weather as we were. A great quantity of rain falls in the mountainous country, and the changes of weather are very sudden. Passing showers often add to the interest of a landscape, by the effect of the contrast between storm and sunshine among the mountains; but settled wet weather defies all hope of enjoyment, except such as the tourist may find when thrown upon his own resources.

When our party came to compare opinions, on a retrospect of the whole tour, I found that the ladies dwelt with the most entire complacency on the

scenery of Windermere. They admitted the superior
grandeur of Ullswater, but it seemed to me that the
loneliness and solemnity of that lake had insensibly
weighed upon their spirits, whilst in the soft charms
of Windermere, and its cultivated and peopled borders,
they found something more congenial to their tastes.
George spoke with rapture of the stupendous scenery
of Scawfell Pikes and Wast Water, and of the views
from Skiddaw and Helvellyn. He preferred Ullswater to Windermere. I am disposed to believe that
the general opinion will coincide with that of the
ladies,—that, though Ullswater may be more admired,
Windermere will be thought more pleasing,—that the
former will produce a higher excitement, but that
something like awe will mingle with the astonishment
and admiration, whilst the latter will infuse into the
mind a calm and delicious enjoyment, more grateful
in a composed state of the feelings. Ullswater might
be preferred as a scene, but Windermere would be
chosen for a residence.

We all felt that our imaginations were enriched
by the glorious works of nature we had beheld, and no
doubt they will often arise to the mind, to cheer it
amidst the duller scenes of existence and the cares
and business of active life.

It will afford me great satisfaction if, in the description of scenes which early charmed and delighted
myself, and with which frequent visits have since
rendered me familiar, I shall have contributed to the
enjoyment and information of other tourists.

AN

EXCURSION ON HORSEBACK.

CHAPTER I.

COMMENCEMENT OF THE JOURNEY—LANCASTER SANDS—THE
CARTER — HOLKER-HALL — LEVEN SANDS — ULVERSTON——
SWARTH-MOOR HALL, THE HOUSE OF GEORGE FOX——
FURNESS ABBEY—CONISHEAD PRIORY—CONISTON WATER—
WATERHEAD INN.

In the tour which I have already described, one
interesting district of the English Lakes was wholly
omitted, namely the Lancashire portion, consisting of
Furness, Coniston, and Hawkshead. We left it out
not so much from want of time, as because we thought
it inexpedient to exhaust the beauties of the Lakes
at one visit,—having all of us the full intention of
revisiting scenes which had yielded us so much delight.
At the commencement of the summer of 1828, I
resolved to escape from the din and smoke of a
populous town, and to indulge in a ramble amongst
my favourite lakes and mountains. I had hitherto
seen them only in the autumn, and I was desirous of

seeing them in the garb of early summer.   My former visits had been in company ; and though far from insensible to the pleasure of sympathy in the admiration of a fine prospect, I wished for once to be alone amidst these sublime works of nature, and at liberty to range where my inclination might lead me.

As the most easy and agreeable way of accomplishing my purpose, I took a horse from Lancaster, and directed my course first to those parts which I had not previously seen.   Setting out at the same hour as the "over-Sands" coach to Ulverston, I arrived at Hestbank, on the shores of Morecambe-bay, three miles and a half from Lancaster, about five in the afternoon.   Here a little caravan was collected, waiting the proper time to cross the trackless sands left bare by the receding tide.   I soon saw two persons set out in a gig, and, following them, I found that one of them was the Guide appointed to conduct travellers, and the other a servant, who was driving his master's gig to the Cartmel shore, and was to return with the horse the same evening.   He had of course no time to lose, and had begun his journey at the earliest possible hour.   We found the Sands firm and level, except the slight wrinkles produced by the ripple of the waves, but they were still wet, having only just been left by the sea. The Guide appeared to drive with caution, and in no place went further than a mile from land. We had a good deal of conversation, and I found him intelligent and communicative.   His name is Thomas Wilkinson.   He is a tall, athletic man, past the

middle age, and bears marks of the rough weather he
has been exposed to in discharging the duties of his
post during the winter months. In stormy, and more
especially in foggy weather, those duties must be
arduous and anxious. It is his business to station
himself at the place where the river Keer runs over
the Sands to the sea, which is about three miles from
Hest-bank, and to show travellers where they may
pass with safety. The bed of the river is liable to
frequent changes, and a fresh of water after rain may
in a very short time convert a fordable place into a
quicksand. When we came to the river, he got out
of the gig, and waded over to ascertain the firmness
of the bottom, the water being about knee-deep.
Having escorted us a little further, till we saw the
Guide for the Kent at a distance, and having pointed
out the line we should keep, he left us to return to
his proper post. We gave him, as is usual, a few
pence; for though he is appointed by government, his
salary is only £10 a year, and he is of course chiefly
dependant on what he receives from travellers.

These sands are called the Lancaster Sands, and
the guide said that they were at present eleven miles
over, from Hest-bank to Kent's-bank, but that he had
known them when he could pass directly over in not
more than seven miles. The tide forms a channel in
the sand, where the water remains at the ebb; and
this channel has been gradually coming nearer the
shore for some years past, and has obliged persons
crossing to take a longer circuit. It was now the

spring-tide, and the sands we were travelling upon would at high water be seventeen feet below the surface of the sea.

The day was exceedingly fine, and the prospects in crossing over the sands were splendid. The whole coast of the bay, from Pile Castle round to the shore beyond Lancaster,—the stern crags of Warton and Arnside-fells on the right,—further eastward, the well-known form of Ingleborough, whose broad head is visible from every considerable hill in Lancashire, Westmoreland, and Cumberland, and seems to lift itself in serene and unchanging majesty over the neighbouring heights,—the broken and picturesque shores of the Kent, beautifully wooded, and forming a vista to the eye,—the fells of Cartmel rising in the mid-distance, their sides hung with forests, and several ornamental parks lying round their base,— and above and far beyond them, the noble chain of the Westmoreland and Cumberland mountains, whose lofty summits, clothed with light, formed a sublime barrier stretching along the northern horizon ;— such are the principal features of a prospect, which is not the less beautiful because it rises from the level expanse of the sands, and which was to me the more interesting from the novelty of my own situation.

The Ulverston coach, several gigs, and some persons on horseback, had followed us at a little distance, keeping the track left by the wheels of the vehicle which conveyed the Guide. When Wilkinson left us,

we rode on two or three miles before we came to the
channel of the Kent, and there we found a Guide on
horseback, who had just forded the river from the
opposite side. The Guide stationed here has long
gone by the name of *the Carter*, and it is difficult to
say whether the office has been so called from the
family in which it has been vested, or the family
have assumed their official title as a cognomen; but
it is certain that for many ages the duties of guide
over the Lancaster Sands have been performed by a
family named Carter, descending from father to son.
The present possessor of the office is named James
Carter, who has lately succeeded his father. He
told me that some persons said the office of guide had
been in his family five hundred years, but he did not
know how any body could tell that, and all he could
say was, that they had held it " for many grand-
fathers back, longer than any one knew." The salary
was only £10 a year till his father's time, when it was
raised to £20; yet I should suppose that the office is
a rather productive one, as the family have accumulated some property.

The Carter seems a cheerful and pleasant fellow.
He wore a rough great-coat and a pair of jack-boots,
and was mounted on a good horse, which appeared to
have been up to the ribs in the water. When we
came to him, he recommended us to wait till the
arrival of the coach, which was nearly a mile distant,
as the tide would then be gone further out. I asked
if there had been any accidents in this place lately,

to which he replied that some boys were drowned two
years ago, having attempted to pass when the tide was
up, in defiance of warnings ; but that, with that
exception, there had not been any accidents for a considerable time.*   When the coach came up, we took
the water in procession, and crossed two channels, in
one of which the water was up to the horses' bellies.
The coach passed over without the least difficulty,
being drawn by fine tall horses.   Arrived at the other
side, the man of high genealogy received our gratuities,
and we rode on, keeping close to a line of rods which
have been planted in the sand to indicate the track,
and which have remained there for many months.
We shortly afterwards met the coach *from* Ulverston
and several other vehicles, and, as we proceeded, the
views of the estuary and the distant mountains became
still more beautiful and interesting.   Three or four
miles brought us to Kent's Bank on the Cartmel shore.
I infer that the river is not fordable for any long
period, as the guide told the servant whom I have
mentioned that he must return in an hour if he wished
to pass over again that evening.

   The peninsula formed by the Kent and the Leven
is three miles over, and, after passing it, I came to the
latter river, the Sands of which are of the same
breadth, and must be crossed to reach Ulverston.   On
the right, approaching the Leven, is the beautiful seat

---

   * Since that time there have been several alarming accidents,
and more than once the coach has sunk in the sands, and the passengers have narrowly escaped.

of the Earl of Burlington (formerly Lord George
Cavendish), Holker-hall. It lies at the foot of the
Cartmel-fells, and looks upon the river and the opposite shore. The house itself is not remarkable, being
a plain building in the old English style, but it
contains a valuable collection of paintings, which I
should have turned aside to see if my time had
permitted. The park and grounds are strikingly fine.
Behind the house is a grove of lofty forest-trees,
whose heads form a dense and almost level mass of
the richest foliage. The fells immediately in the rear
are covered with fir and larch, which, though not very
ornamental, always bring to my mind, when seen on
the side of a steep hill, pleasing recollections of
Alpine scenery. In front of the house, the verdant
park slopes gently to the borders of the estuary, and is
cropped by herds of deer.

I here overtook a well-mounted farmer, who was
returning from Appleby fair to Ulverston, and we
crossed the Sands together. He told me that it is
safest to cross the Sands at the spring-tides, as the
water is then more completely out, and the force of
the tide sweeps the bottom clean from the mud and
sediment. The views up the river are fully as picturesque and grand, though not quite so extensive, as
those at the mouth of the Kent. A bold woody
promontory, projecting into the river above the ford,
and narrowing it to less than half the breadth, constitutes the foreground; the two ridges of the Cartmel
and Ulverston fells, the former clothed with wood

and the latter with verdure, run up inland, and carry the eye back to the mountains round the head of Coniston Water and Windermere; on the Ulverston shore, below the town, are the grounds of Conishead Priory, which adorn with their rich woods and lawns the gently waving side of the hill; and the mouth of the Leven opens out to the bay of Morecambe, the shores of which are visible to a great extent.

At the channel of the Leven we found a guide on horseback, who escorted us over; the water was scarcely so deep as at the Kent, though this might be owing to the tide being further out. The carriers had just passed over with their carts. As we rode on to Ulverston, my companion told me that he lived in the house formerly occupied by George Fox, the celebrated founder of the Society of Friends, or Quakers. The house is called Swarth-moor-hall, and the meeting-house built by Fox himself for the use of the Friends is near it. The farmer invited me to call upon him, as I expressed a curiosity to see the habitation and relics of so original and excellent a character; and I promised to take Swarth-moor-hall in my way to Furness Abbey the following morning. At the entrance of Ulverston I took leave of my companion, and reached the Sun Inn about eight o'clock.

Ulverston, popularly pronounced Owston, is a neat, cheerful-looking town, standing upon uneven ground, and not very regularly built, but bearing marks of prosperity, which it enjoys from the combined fruits of commerce, manufactures, mines, and agriculture.

It. may be considered as the capital of Furness—a
district which comprehends the whole of Lancashire
north of the Sands, except the parish of Cartmel; or
rather Ulverston is the capital of Low Furness, and
Hawkshead of High Furness. The country round
Ulverston has little beauty, except on the side of
Conishead Priory; the fells which rise above the town
are verdant, but have scarcely any wood and no gracefulness of outline. The want of wood may indeed
be generally alleged against the scenery of Furness,
though the soil is very fertile. The fells produce
great quantities of blue slate; the lower parts abound
in the richest iron ore found in Great Britain, and the
mineral treasures of the earth do not here, as in many
places, detract from the fertility of the surface.

In the morning I set out, after breakfast, to see
Swarth-moor-hall, Furness Abbey, and Conishead
Priory. The first of these places is at the distance
of a mile from Ulverston. In approaching it I crossed
a narrow dell, shaded by a grove of fine beech-trees,
and watered by a murmuring brook. The old hall is
overshadowed by two sycamores of large growth; but
its dilapidated condition, the barns and stables by
which it is surrounded, and the litter of a farm-yard,
give it no very classical air. My friend the farmer
welcomed my arrival, and, after he had put up my
horse, showed me over every room in the house, from
the venerable lumber-room and garret down to the
subterranean dairy. His wife was thriftily employed
in whitewashing the hall, which is a spacious apart-

ment, with oaken wainscoting, that had once been
handsome. I was taken into the study of George
Fox, where he reposed and meditated in the intervals
of those laborious missions which he undertook to
persuade men to make the gospel, in all its simplicity,
the standard of their conduct, in opposition to human
customs and inventions. The bed-rooms are spacious
apartments, and have in former-days been ornamented
with carved work, (which George doubtless found
there when he succeeded to the wife and mansion of
Judge Fell) now so damaged as to be no longer a deco-
ration. In one of them is a substantial old bedstead,
with carved posts, on which, as I was assured by the
farmer, the proto-quaker used to repose, and which
any of his followers is permitted to occupy for a
night; but he said not a single Friend had availed
himself of the privilege during the four years that he
had resided there,—a circumstance the less to be
wondered at, as the bed is now customarily tenanted
by the servants. On one side of the house is an
orchard, which appears at least as old as the building.
The hall stands high, and its upper windows, overlooking the trees of the orchard, command an
extensive and beautiful prospect. Fox did not reside
here more than four years, though he married the
widow of Judge Fell in 1669, and lived till 1690.
The lady and her daughters were amongst his early
converts, during the life-time of the Judge, who
himself protected the persecuted quakers. From the
hall we went to the meeting-house, which is about a

quarter of a mile distant. It is a neat, plain building, in perfect repair, and is still used by the Friends of Ulverston and the neighbourhood for their religious meetings. Over the door is carved in stone—"*Ex dono G. F.* 1688." A burial-place, surrounded with trees, is attached to the meeting-house.

Having taken leave of the obliging farmer, I rode on to Dalton, a small, neat, old-fashioned town, with a church of corresponding appearance, and a square tower, the remnant of an ancient castle. This was the capital of Furness when the neighbouring Abbey was in its splendour, but now appears as if not a house had been added to it for centuries. It is surrounded by undulating grassy hills, and has a single plantation just in its rear. A mile beyond the town, I turned from the high road into a lane shaded with oaks, running down a narrow valley or glen, called the "*glen of deadly nightshade;*" and at the bottom of this glen, under the solemn shade of majestic forest-trees, I came upon the ruins of the famous Abbey of Furness. The first effect would be much more imposing, if you did not approach through a farm-yard, and by a small manor-house; but beyond them you obtain a full view of the venerable ruin itself, with a grassy area in front, and enclosed on each side by noble groves of the plane, the ash, and the oak. The Abbey, though much shattered and having lost the central tower, is still extensive and magnificent. Lofty walls and arches, clustered columns, and long-drawn aisles, remain; and the fine symmetry and

noble proportions of the arches contrast most picturesquely with the rents and fractures of the pile.
The former extent of the building may in some degree
be judged of when I state that what remains measures
five hundred feet from north to south, and three
hundred from east to west. A man whom I found
digging for stone in the hill-side, became my cicerone,
and took me round first to the southern extremity of
the Abbey. Here I saw that the glen made a very
sudden bend just below the ruin, which gave it the
appearance of a *cul de sac*, terminating in a concave
sweep of the hill, which might have served for the
seats of an ancient theatre. I fancied that the situation
reconciled opposite advantages, and therein resembled
the monastic institution itself. The Abbey lies in a
nook apparently so secluded that it might be deemed
the utmost corner of the earth; yet you have only to
ascend the hills on either side, which is the work
of a few minutes, and you look abroad on the wide
world, embracing all the extent of sea and land prospect which I have described as visible from the shores
of the bay of Morecambe. So the monks came hither
professedly to withdraw themselves from worldly
vanities, and in solitude, mortification, and austere
simplicity to devote themselves to penitence and
prayer; yet they threw up for these purposes a structure whose splendour and vastness mocked the abodes
of princes, and where there was every provision for
the pleasures of sense. Thus, under the semblance of
extreme humility, may pride construct for itself the

M

haughtiest dwelling-place in the recesses of the human heart; thus, when men would withdraw farthest from the world, do they often deceitfully leave themselves the opportunity of peeping abroad on the fields of created good.

"This Abbey," says Mr. West, "was founded by Stephen Earl of Mortaign and Boulogne, afterwards King of England, A. D. 1127, and was endowed with the lordship of Furness and many royal privileges. It was peopled from the monastery of Savigny in Normandy, and dedicated to St. Mary. In ancient writings it is styled *St. Mary's of Furness*. The monks were of the order of Savigny, and their dress was gray cloth, but on receiving St. Bernard's form, they changed from gray to white, and became Cistercians; and such they remained till the dissolution of the monasteries." The Abbey flourished during four centuries, and held almost entire and unlimited possession of this rich and extensive district. In magnitude it was the second Abbey in England belonging to the Cistercians, and next to Fountain's Abbey in opulence. When the funds for its maintenance were withdrawn on the dissolution of monasteries, not only the monks were dispersed, but the Abbey itself soon became ruinous. It is now the property of the Earl of Burlington, who has recently improved the effect of the ruin by clearing away a great accumulation of rubbish.

As we entered the Abbey, my cicerone pointed to a plant of the deadly nightshade, from the abundance

of which the valley derives its name. The college and
the school-house are the most complete apartments
remaining: the former has an arched roof still quite
perfect: its tall narrow windows have no arch, but
terminate upwards in the shape of a pediment. The
school-house is equally perfect, but is smaller and less
ornamental. From these apartments we proceeded
over a space where scarcely a fragment remains, to
the kitchens, and thence to the refectorium, which
has been a very spacious hall, with a row of columns
in the centre supporting the vaulted roof, and the
walls counterarched. A few years since this hall was
filled with earth and fragments as high as the capitals
of the pillars on the walls; of course the pillars were
concealed, the arches lost their effect, the walls
appeared comparatively low, and nothing was known
of the row of columns in the centre. The removal of
the rubbish has shown what the design and appearance
of the hall have been. The proportions of the walls
and arches are restored, and the bases of the central
row of columns are all found, with considerable fragments of the columns themselves, which are placed in
their proper situations. The chapter-house, the most
sumptuous apartment of the building, is equally
a gainer by the operations. The fretted roof, which
fell in about the middle of the last century, was
supported by six deeply-channeled columns in two
rows, considerable fragments of which have been
rescued, and piled up in their places. The capitals
and key-stones are richly carved, and the arches in the

M 2

walls are beautifully proportioned. The porch of the
chapter-house has been adorned with small marble
columns, and at the entrance are Saxon arches with
very deep cornices. Two similar arches, but of smaller
dimensions, lead from the cloisters to the refectorium.
Passing through the cloisters, of which only the skele-
ton remains, we entered the church under the great
central tower, the lofty arches of which are yet
standing. The eastern window is of vast dimensions,
and its ornamented frame was anciently filled with
painted glass, some of which still exists in the church
of Bowness. In the wall at the right of the window
are four stalls, with a fretted canopy, where the
priests sat at intervals during the service of mass.
The church forms the northern side of the building,
but one of its walls, and both its rows of pillars, are
gone. Their bases, which remain, show that the
pillars were alternately round and clustered. Four
statues of admirable workmanship, two of marble and
two of stone, are shown to the visiter; one is in chain-
armour, two others also in armour, and the fourth is
a lady; they are in the recumbent posture, and have
lain upon sepulchral monuments. Near the central
tower are three chapels, with pavements of ornamented
brick-work, and traces of altars. At the western end
of the church is a winding staircase, still perfect, by
which I ascended to the top of the building, whence
there is an interesting view of the ruin. The best
view of the Abbey is from the hill-side opposite the
great eastern window, where you see the interior of

the church, (through that window), the chapter-house,
and indeed the whole pile from north to south, as well
as from east to west. The head of Stephen, the
founder of the Abbey, and that of Maud his queen,
both crowned, are seen on the outside of the eastern
window. As I was leaving the Abbey, a party of two
ladies and a gentleman arrived for the purpose of
sketching, and they could not have had a finer day
for the purpose. I could have lingered for hours, had
my time permitted, amongst these relics of departed
grandeur.

From the Abbey I returned to Dalton, and, half a
mile beyond that place, quitted the Ulverston road,
and took the road through Urswick and Bardsea to
Conishead Priory. Passing over Birkrigg, an elevated
common, I ascended to the top of it, and enjoyed one
of the most extensive prospects to be had in this part
of the country. The hill looks down upon the Priory
Park, and fully commands the grounds of Holker-
hall, on the opposite side of the Leven; indeed, every
object which I have mentioned as within my view
since leaving Lancaster is here seen in one grand
panorama. Not merely is the whole circuit of Morecambe Bay visible, but also the coast of Lancashire as
far south as Liverpool, and that of Wales beyond,
stretching out into the Irish sea, with the mountain
of Snowdon very conspicuous. The Isle of Man is
also seen to the west. It was high water, and the
bay was brimful, the spring-tide being carried up by a
brisk wind; the estuaries which I had crossed the

evening before, when the stream was shrunk to a thread amongst the sands, now seemed fit to float a navy. On the land-side, the heath-covered dome of Black Comb was very conspicuous to the west; and stretching eastward, Scawfell Pikes, Coniston Old Man, Helvellyn, Fairfield, Hill Bell, and a long range of mountains quite round to Ingleborough.

Descending from this elevation, I came down to Bardsea on the coast of the bay, passed the old hall, and went through the beautiful park to Conishead Priory. Major Braddyll has been seven years rebuilding his mansion (1828), and it is yet little more than half finished. If completed in the same style, it will be an elegant and splendid residence. It is in the style called the English Gothic, and is built entirely of Bath stone. The gardens are extensive and beautiful, and the conservatory of plants is tastefully constructed; its rich Gothic windows, with stained glass, and the ivy which covers the front, give it the appearance of a chapel. About half a mile from the house, and hid amongst the woods, is a hermitage, consisting of a " mossy cell" and a chapel: it is considerably more elegant than hermits are wont to construct for themselves. The walks through the grounds are extensive; and, both from their own beauty and the noble prospects they afford of the bay and the mountains, well deserve to be perambulated by the traveller.

From these delicious grounds, which West has not improperly designated as " the paradise of Furness,"

I returned to Ulverston. The round I had taken was about eighteen miles, and it gave me and my horse a good relish for dinner. Between five and six I left Ulverston, and had a delightful evening ride of sixteen miles to Coniston Water Head. On the high ground four miles from the former place, just where the Hawkshead and Broughton roads separate, the lake and vale of Coniston open to the view in their whole extent, forming a noble landscape. The lake is six miles long, and its foot is four miles distant. The ground below the foot of the lake is much broken and diversified: the shores of Coniston Water are enriched with wood, and the fells which rise above them are bold without sublimity: but the mountains at the head now stand before you in all their stern grandeur. On the western side of the valley, near its head, the Old Man is seen from the base to the summit; and, being flanked by Walna Scar on the left, and Wetherlam on the right, he is a not less magnificent object from Coniston Water than Skiddaw is when seen from Derwentwater. Scawfell Pikes, with their cloven summit, are also seen on one side of the Coniston mountains, and Helvellyn and Fairfield on the other, but all considerably in the rear.

From this place, and descending the hill, I saw some curious effects of cloud and sunshine on the mountains. At first the whole scene was overshadowed; then I saw a patch of sunshine on the broad and verdant top of Helvellyn: gradually the sphere of light was enlarged, and the whole of that distant range was illuminated, whilst the Old Man and his hard-favoured neighbours stood in the shade. In process of time, a few pencils of rays shot over the side of the Old Man, and gilded one of the highest ridges of Wetherlam. As the clouds gave way before the luminary, his rays, now almost level, streamed over the mountain-top, and wrapped the most prominent ridges in an atmosphere of gold and purple, which at once enriched and obscured them. Still further prevailing, the fervid orb at length chased all the clouds from the face of heaven, and looked down in parting splendour upon the lake. Finally, he himself disappeared. Thus—thought I, as I rode up the side of Coniston Water, in the serene stillness and solitude of the hour and place—thus have we seen great men struggling with the clouds of adverse fortune to the last act of life, and only dissipating them to fix the eyes of the world on their glorious exit! Thus triumphed and died Rockingham, Fox, and Canning!

One of the most admirable views of Coniston Water and the surrounding scenery is from its own borders, near the foot, on a hill a quarter of a mile beyond Nibthwaite. The house of Mr. Harrison, Waterpark, stands on the left hand, and a wooded promontory runs out beyond it into the lake. The meadows round the foot of the lake are of a rich green, and slope down to the brink of the water. The fells on the western side have a waving outline; they are in part verdant and wooded; other parts are dark and rocky, yet even those are rendered picturesque by the stripes of green which intersect the shelving rocks and black patches of heath. The road runs along the eastern side of the lake; and the views continue to improve as you approach the fertile and park-like tract which sweeps round the head of the valley, backed by the savage crags of Yewdale, and the loftier mountains of Coniston. About half-past eight I arrived at Water Head Inn, which is charmingly situated at the edge of the lake, looking down its whole extent.*

The head of Coniston Water deserves to rank with the finest scenes amongst the Lakes, both in point of beauty and of grandeur. Its broad margin of sloping fields and hanging woods, interspersed with villas and cottages, may vie with the borders of Windermere in richness; and the noble group of mountains which rise behind them, with their awful precipices, give to the scene all the advantage of the most striking relief and contrast. I should, however, strongly recommend a visiter to approach this lake from Ulverston, and not from Ambleside, if that be in his power, as the scenery increases in grandeur all the way from the foot to the head; but if he can only visit it from the direction of Ambleside, it would scarcely be worth his while to go more than a mile or two down the lake. Lower than that, he would turn his back upon the most sublime features of the landscape, and have before him what was comparatively tame.

* Near the head of the lake is Tent-lodge, the house of Mrs. Smith. The daughter of this lady, Miss Elizabeth Smith, was a young lady of the most extraordinary talents and attainments, and of exalted piety, who died at an early age: her merit has been recorded in an interesting Memoir, and Wilson has embalmed her memory in his verse.

M 3

CHAPTER II.

I had originally intended to proceed from Coniston
Water Head, by Hawkshead and Bowness to Ambleside. When I found myself at the foot of so fine a
mountain as the Old Man, I was strongly tempted to
ascend it in the morning, before setting out on the
easy ride I had planned for the day, as the views
from the top of a mountain are to me far more
delightful than any to be had in the valleys. But I
had long had a hankering after the ascent of Scawfell
Pikes, the highest mountain in England, which,
from its situation, and the ruggedness of its surface,
is rarely ascended. I began therefore to calculate whether it was practicable to proceed from
Coniston Water to the head of Great Langdale, go up
the mountain from that place, and afterwards ride to
Ambleside in the evening. I found by the map
that the ascent would be a long one, as Scawfell
Pikes lay at a considerable distance from the head
of Langdale, and another range of hills appeared to
intervene. But I had not the least doubt of being

able to accomplish it, if I should find a person to serve as a guide in climbing the mountain; which was somewhat doubtful, as I should come down into Langdale by a cross-road just at the head of the valley, where there were only two or three farmhouses. At Coniston Water Head I could find no one who had ever been on Scawfell Pikes, and indeed the natives of this country never ascend a mountain for pleasure; except, perhaps, on a hunting expedition, when the fox often betakes himself to the tops of the hills, and is followed thither by his eager pursuers.

The only persons who know the mountainous tracts are the farmers' servants, who have to tend the sheep upon them; and they know scarcely any thing beyond their own sheep-walk: the next hill-side is to them a *terra incognita*. Indeed, there is an astonishing ignorance of the geography of the country amongst the peasantry; they have no notion of acquiring knowledge for its own sake, and would spend their lives at the foot of a mountain without asking its name. The only paths which a young fellow is acquainted with are those that lead to his sheep-walk or to the house of his sweetheart.

Having determined on making the expedition, I breakfasted early, and provided myself with sandwiches and brandy, as I expected to find no place of refreshment till I arrived at Ambleside in the evening. About half-past eight o'clock on a hot and cloudless morning, I left Coniston Water Head, passed through the delightful grounds of Mr. Knott, and found my way through a wood into the valley of Yewdale. This valley is probably so called from a row of yews which there is in the fields, clipped into stiff and odious forms, and which may be many centuries old; or from a single yew-tree in another part of the valley, which is remarkably tall and beautiful. I passed along under a range of stupendous crags, called Yewdale Crags, whose picturesque horrors were rendered almost amiable by the bright illumination of the sun, and the tufts of fresh green which sparingly embossed the face of the precipices. I soon entered the valley of Tilberthwaite, where the fells on either side might be thought one mass of blue slate, from the great number of quarries made in them for its extraction. This material constitutes the riches of the valley, which is otherwise most barren and desolate. At Tilberthwaite I asked my way to Blea-tarn, and was directed to go over a considerable hill to my left, with the assurance that I could not miss my way, as there was " nae ither gate." This assurance is very often given in these parts, and should always be taken with some grains of allowance. It does not mean in the absolute sense that there is no other road, but only that there is none which a man would be fool enough to take—the informant always presuming that a traveller knows more about the roads than is generally the fact. It may be that there is one road to the right and another to the left; but the peasant, knowing that one of them leads only to a quarry, or to some place far away from where the traveller wishes to go, concludes that he cannot possibly take that, and therefore gives him no warning against it. Thus I found it in the present case, and I was obliged sometimes to trust to my own sagacity in choosing my route. The track is steep and rugged, but commands some fine views of the valley, in which the ruggedness of the crags and quarries is relieved by larch-forests of the most vivid green. The road comes down into Little Langdale at a farm called Fell-foot. It may be right to mention, that in inquiring for the farms of Wall End and Style End at the head of Great Langdale, the traveller would do well to ask for *Wo* End and *Steeal* End.

At Fell-foot I entered Westmoreland, and, crossing the valley of Little Langdale, ascended a slack which conducts to Great Langdale. In this slack, between two considerable mountains, faced with tremendous crags, lies Blea-tarn, with a single farm-house near it, and a plantation of fir and larch on each side. I have more fully described this interesting spot and the grand view in descending to Great Langdale, in the Family Tour. (*Page 99.*)

I came down to Langdale-head at the farm of Wall End, and, inquiring for a guide to the mountain, I found that all the men had gone out to some distance, to mend the roads. I then rode to another farm a little lower down, where the only person who knew Scawfell Pikes had been lamed the day before in pulling down a wall. As a last resource, I went to Style End, a mile further, and the ultimate habita-

tion in the valley—exactly at the foot of Bowfell.
Here I found a young farmer harrowing potatoes,
and, learning that he had often been on Scawfell, I
asked him to accompany me. He seemed to have no
particular objection, but put what I thought a high
price on his services. He was a shrewd bargainer:
having ascertained that I could get no one else but
himself to go with me, he expressed his earnest wish
that I would find another guide, said he would much
rather not go, and declared that he was " thrang, varra
thrang." As the fellow had the monopoly of the
market, he put a monopoly price on his guidance,
and such was my need of the commodity, that I was
obliged to yield to his terms. After all, I believe he
was an honest, hard-working man, and he appeared to
maintain his family with decency. Having put my
horse in his stable, and got a little bread and milk
from a very comely young woman, his wife, I set out
with my guide for the mountain. He was well
accoutred for the expedition, having on a light jacket,
and a stout staff in his hand; his sheep-dog followed
him. I lightened my pockets as much as possible,
took off my cravat, and opened my waistcoat; and
thus, with a good stick in my hand, began to climb
this formidable hill under a meridian sun.

The farmer had determined, after some deliberation
with himself, to take me to the top of Bowfell, whence
he intended to go along the summits of the hills to
Scawfell Pikes. I suspected that this would not
prove the easiest, if it were even the shortest route;

but I acquiesced in his plan, both because I was myself
ignorant of the place, and because, if his route were a
little longer or more arduous, I should be repaid by
having ascended two mountains instead of one. We
began our journey in the most deliberate manner,
keeping on the ridge which rises immediately from
Style End to the very summit of Bowfell. As we
proceeded, the sheep-dog was very active in chasing
the sheep; and my guide told me that his master (for
he is employed by a gentleman to farm his land at a
fixed salary) had not less than five hundred sheep on
Bowfell. The whole of the mountain does not belong
to him, but he has a great part of it, and his sheep-
walk is separated from those of his neighbours by a
ravine, a gill, or some such boundary. The great
business of the sheep-dog and the farmer's man—for
there is no regular shepherd—is to prevent their
neighbours' sheep from straying into their pasture.
The sheep often go out of bounds, not from ignorance,
but "a truant disposition;" for the moment a dog
runs up to a mingled company of muttons, each
scampers off with all his might to his own territory.
A good sheep-dog knows his master's sheep as well as
the shepherd himself,* and will in a very short time
scour a large tract of mountain, over crags, bogs, and

* I am bound to confess that the evidence of a shepherd at Seathwaite, in Borrowdale, contradicted that of my Langdale guide on
this point; having told the former that I understood there
were dogs which knew their master's sheep, he replied—" They're
nobbut (only) thin i' this country, sic dogs as thae."

torrents, yelping aloud his notices to quit, and
expelling every intruder.

When we had been walking an hour, we sat down
to contemplate what had already been achieved. We
had almost attained the elevation of the pike o' Stickle,
and were above the Stake—the mountain-pass which
communicates between Langdale and Borrowdale.
The Stonethwaite branch of Borrowdale was visible
over the pass, and Skiddaw and Saddleback beyond.
In the opposite direction, that is, on our right as we
looked down Langdale, was the Pike o' Bliscoe, Wrynose, (which my guide pronounced *Rainuz*) Wetherlam,
and many a ridge of heath-covered fells. In front, on
the far horizon, was the not-to-be-mistaken head of
Ingleborough. The farmer here complained, like
myself, that it was "*terrible het;* I thought he
applied the adjective "terrible" appropriately enough,
if not grammatically, in this case, but I found that
he made as indiscriminate a use of it as the French of
their *bien;* for when I remarked that I had never
ascended a mountain on a clearer day, he replied that
it was "terrible clear." A quarter of an hour more
gave us a view of Windermere, opening out beyond
the valley of Langdale, and enabled us to see, over the
Stickle Pikes, the whole extent of the Borrowdale
and Langdale fells, Helvellyn, Fairfield, and many
other hills. Shortly after, we saw the lofty mountains
of Grasmoor and Grisedale Pike, to the north. My
guide undertook the ascent of the precipitous crags
which form the forehead of Bowfell; and I had no

difficulty in following him as he wound amongst them, though, looking at the place from below, I should have thought it madness to attempt scaling them. A stranger, indeed, could not have done it alone without peril.

At half-past twelve, being an hour and three-quarters after leaving Style End, we found ourselves on the summit of Bowfell. The view was glorious, but the first object we looked for gave us little comfort. Scawfell Pikes appeared at least as far from us as we were from the valley, and, though we were within two hundred and fifty feet of their elevation, many thousand feet of cruel rocks separated us from them. My guide's theory had been delusive, and it afforded another proof how defective a knowledge these men have of their own immediate neighbourhood. He had at different times tended sheep on Bowfell, Scawfell, and the surrounding hills, but there was a great want of combination in his knowledge : the plans of his sheep-walks lay in his head like separate portions of a dissecting map, which he could not put together. We had to descend many hundred feet, to make a long circuit, and then to re-ascend before reaching the point, an inch short of which I was determined not to rest. Whilst we were climbing the last and steepest part of Bowfell, and had been too much engaged in looking to our safety to observe any thing but the rocks around us, the sky had become completely overcast. My guide now prognosticated rain, but I suspected him of doing so from a wish to return ;

I thought it would still hold up, at least till we could reach Scawfell. In the south, there was a small ragged cloud hanging down from the rest over the Bay of Morecambe, and if the wind had changed to that direction, we were very likely to have rain. I held up my handkerchief to see the direction of the wind, but not a breath of air was stirring even at that elevation. Then the farmer talked about thunder: but as I observed that the clouds were still considerably higher than the mountain-tops, I slighted his evil auguries. However, no time was to be lost, and, after I had myself taken, and given to him, a taste of brandy, we prosecuted our enterprise. When we reached the top of Bowfell, we had so husbanded our strength, that I was as fresh as when I set out; but our apprehensions of the rain now made us push on with all our vigour, and our walk over the rocks and hill-tops was a severe effort till we reached the summit of our ambition. At the top of Bowfell we passed out of Westmoreland into Cumberland. We had first a long descent, in which we skirted the top of tremendous precipices, till we came to the slack called Ash-course, overlooking the head of Eskdale. Here I saw clearly the direction we ought to have taken, and which would have saved us a long ascent and descent. We now went up the east side of Great End, and, passing over the top, again descended a considerable distance. From this place to the top of the Pikes, the summits are composed of huge blocks of stone, just painted with the lichens

which cleave to their weather-worn surfaces, and,
except in one spot, with no other symptom of vegetation. The last ascent is very steep, but I climbed
it · with hearty good-will, as it placed me on the
highest summit in England.

Scawfell Pikes command the best view of the
mountainous region of Cumberland, Westmoreland,
and Lancashire, and perhaps a more extensive range
of prospect beyond it than any other hill. Its central
situation, as well as its height, give it this advantage : it is midway between Skiddaw and Black
Comb, and something more than midway betwixt
Ullswater and the sea. Nearly all the great valleys
branch off from Scawfell and Great Gavel, as Mr.
Wordsworth has observed, like the spokes of a wheel
from the axle. Here I became cicerone, and the
farmer listened whilst I traced over the geography of
the district. Looking northward, Sty-head with its
tarn lay immediately beneath us, and I saw the spot
at the top of the long descent into Wasdale, where
George and I last year sat down to admire the sublime
mountain on which I now stood. Borrowdale
stretched away beyond, but was partly hid by
Great End : from Ash-course we had had a view of
the whole valley, and of the charming lake of Derwentwater with its islands. Skiddaw and Saddleback
rose beyond, and betwixt the former and Grisedale
Pike we saw, over the lake of Bassenthwaite, part of
the level country, and faintly discerned Solway Frith ;
but the haze prevented us from seeing the Scotch

mountains.   Turning eastward, we saw Helvellyn and
his range, High-street, Hill Bell, and the vast group
of mountains which encompass Hawes Water.   Langdale ran due east, and discharged itself into the vale
of Windermere, but was hid from us by Bowfell.
The head of Windermere and Esthwaite Water were
visible, and the never-failing Ingleborough beyond
them.   Coniston Old Man, Wetherlam, Wrynose, and
all that group, lay to the south-east.   Immediately
south is the summit of Scawfell, within about sixty
feet of the elevation of the Pikes, and separated from
them by the great chasm of Mickle Door.   The beautiful vale of the Esk runs down on the left to the
sea, and Donnerdale also conducts the eye to the
broad mouth of the Duddon.   Morecambe Bay and all
the coast of Lancashire are seen due south ; and, had
the day been clearer, the Welsh mountains would
have appeared in the extreme distance.   Turning to
the south-west, Black Comb came within view, and
the wide expanse of the Irish sea swept round the
horizon as far as the north-west, only broken in one
part by the hills of the Isle of Man, which appeared
over the foot of Wast Water.   Deep, deep below us
lay the " Den of Wasdale," with its lake : beyond,
apparently within arm's length, the rival height of
Great Gavel, and, stretching to the left, the ridges of
Kirkfell, Yewbarrow, Seatallan, the Hay Cock, and
the Pillar, some of which excluded from our view the
lake and vale of Ennerdale.   Proceeding northward,
High Crag and High Stile, which rise over Butter-

mere, and Grasmoor and Grisedale Pike, on the east
of Crummock Water, were proudly conspicuous; and
from Great End we saw the foot of the last-mentioned
lake.

Though the day was now far from being "terrible
clear," we saw all these objects with distinctness.
The clouds had not lowered since we noticed them
from Bowfell, and a slight breeze had sprung up in
a quarter which dissipated my apprehensions of rain.
We sat down under the shelter of the pile of stones
erected on the highest Pike, and divided our sandwiches and brandy. The ascent had been made in
three hours and five minutes, and we had lost fully
half an hour by crossing Bowfell. Having seen in
the progress of our ascent nearly all the objects which
were visible from the summit, we did not tarry long
to survey the entire panorama. The descent cost us
an hour and fifty minutes, though we ran a good part
of the way; but, being exceedingly thirsty, we often
stopped to drink at the fresh streamlets. From Ash-
course we kept to the left, and descended an easier
path to the level of Angle-tarn, which lies at an
awful depth beneath the precipitous summit of Bowfell. The descent into Langdale is by an excessively
steep and savage gill, called Rosset gill; and when we
reached the valley, we had to walk about a mile to
the farmer's house. The route which we took in our
return is that by which we ought to have ascended.
The young farmer, though habituated to the mountains from his childhood, was nearly as much fatigued

as myself by our five hours' walk. My shoes and
stockings were soaked with the water of the bogs
we had crossed, and when I took them off to dry
them, I found that my toes had lost some of their
skin, from constant pressure against the shoe in
coming down the hills: If my shoes had not been
both strong and roomy, I should have suffered much
more. The young and pretty wife of the farmer had
spied us at a distance, and had prepared for us some
eggs boiled as hard as stones, and tea, or rather warm
water tinged with a spoonful of tea. Poor as the
beverage was, we drank it with eagerness, and I took
a couple of glasses of home-brewed beer into the
bargain, being fully of the opinion of the blooming
matron, that it was " varra dree wark climmin
t' fells."

I could not but reflect on the all-pervading power
of commerce, which brings into these deep recesses
of the mountains, and to the use of the ignorant
peasant, the luxuries of the most distant climes :
he comforts himself on the sheep-walk with a
soothing quid from Virginia, and is refreshed after
his day's labour with an infusion of the plants of
China, sweetened by the sugar of the Indies. His
rude pepper-box is filled with the produce of Java ;
the nutmeg of Borneo is a plaything for his children ;
and his careful spouse dresses their hurts with the
spermaceti of the Antarctic Ocean.

A ride of about ten miles down the beautiful tract
of Langdale, and past the small lake of Elterwater,

brought me to Ambleside. The day's journey might be about thirty-two miles, reckoning twelve or thirteen for the mountain, and nine from Coniston Water to Style End. I was a good deal fatigued, and needed the repose of the following day, which was to me emphatically a Sabbath.

CHAPTER III.

BOWNESS——ESTHWAITE WATER——HAWKSHEAD——MR. WORDS-
WORTH'S, RYDAL MOUNT——KESWICK——HONISTER CRAG——
WATENDLATH——PENRITH——CARLISLE——THE CASTLE——THE
CATHEDRAL——NEIGHBOURING MANSIONS——CONCLUSION.

Having now described at some length that district
of the Lakes which was omitted in our Family Tour,
the rest of my Excursion will be very briefly sketched,
as it was, with few deviations, over the same ground
as I have attempted to describe in the former part of
the volume.

On Monday morning I rose early, and rode along
the banks of Windermere to Bowness, where I breakfasted. From Bowness I proceeded over the Ferry to
the Lancashire shore, intending to make a circuit by
Esthwaite Water and Hawkshead to Ambleside. In
descending the hill which separates Windermere from
Esthwaite Water, there is a charming view of that
small lake and its beautiful valley, and of Bowfell,
the Langdale Pikes, and the other mountains amongst
which I had been on Saturday. Esthwaite Water,
though it has nothing of grandeur, has much lively
beauty : the extreme prettiness of the woods and

meadows on its borders are refreshing to the eye after
the almost cloying richness of Windermere. The
lake is about two miles long, and beyond the head of
it is a pool which contains a floating island, bearing
several considerable trees and shrubs. I was assured
by "mine host" of the Red Lion, Hawkshead, that
he had seen this island several times floating from
one side of the pool to the other, as the wind
changed. When I was there, it was close to the
eastern shore.

Hawkshead is an ancient town, beautifully situated
on the hill-side half a mile from Esthwaite Water.
The walks round it command fine views of the
mountains at the head of Windermere, as well as
of the Langdale mountains, and interesting excursions may be made from it in every direction. My
stay here was short, and I returned to Ambleside to
dinner.

In the evening, about five o'clock, I set out for
Keswick, being accompanied by a friend from Ambleside, who was kind enough to introduce me at Mr.
Wordsworth's, of Rydal Mount. The poet himself
was not at home, but we saw some of the family, who
gave us an obliging reception. His youngest son
accompanied us into the gardens in front of the house,
which command two distinct views, each of them
amongst the most delicious at the Lakes. The first
is from a grassy terrace which looks down upon the
woods of Rydal-park, and along the valley of Ambleside to Windermere. From no other point does this

N

valley appear nearly so beautiful. The second view bursts upon you, after passing along a shady walk, when a door is opened at the extremity. The lake of Rydal, of which you have not hitherto had even a glimpse, and the fine woody valley in which it is embosomed, lie beneath in the most fascinating beauty and the sweetest repose. This lake, with its tufted islands, possesses nearly every attribute of the picturesque; and the suddenness with which it was presented to me, combined with its perfect loveliness and the unearthly stillness of the scene, produced on my mind the effect of a fairy vision. I was informed that the walk which commands this prospect was constructed by Mr. Wordsworth himself and his sons.

The hour forbad me to linger here, and I rode on through the valleys of Grasmere and Wythburn to Keswick. Here, as well as at Ambleside and Bowness, I found a considerable number of visiters, the season having apparently commenced the preceding week.

From Keswick, on the following day, I rode to Buttermere and Crummock Water, through the Vale of Newlands, and proceeded by Gatesgarth and Honister Crag, over the hawse, into Borrowdale. The passage from Buttermere to Borrowdale was new to me, and I was much impressed by the stupendous crag of Honister, which, though not the highest mountain, is by far the boldest rock in Cumberland. Its total elevation is 1700 feet, and it rises from

Gatesgarth-dale in a single precipice of 1500 feet, imparting to the pass a character of grandeur not equalled by any other in the country. It reminded me of a pun of Matilda's, who said she supposed the crag was called Honister on account of its perfect uprightness and loftiness of character. The track on both sides of Borrowdale-hawse is excessively rugged and steep. The views from it are, however, noble and interesting. One-horse cars occasionally pass this way, but it must be attended with great fatigue to the horse and danger to the vehicle.

When I had descended Borrowdale as far as Rosthwaite, I crossed the hill on my right to see the small lake and vale of Watendlath, one of the most secluded in the country. At Rosthwaite I passed the beck, which was now almost dry, and then began to climb a long, winding, and excessively steep path, which may be ascended by horses, but not by any kind of carriage. The trouble is compensated by the fine views which the hill affords of the upper part of Borrowdale, as far as the village of Seathwaite, of Scawfell Pikes, and Great Gavel, Glaramara, and the awful crags of Stonethwaite. The descent to Watendlath is still more rugged than the ascent from Rosthwaite.

The valley of Watendlath is not deep, but most impressively lonely. On the banks of its small lake, or tarn, are a few cottage-houses of great antiquity, and built of dark stone; and besides these there is not a habitation within view. The children stare at a traveller with wonderment, as if they had never before seen a human being out of their own families; and a troop of terrier dogs, more clamorous than Mustard and Pepper at Charlie's-hope, bark as if a beast of prey were descending into the valley. The stream of Lowdore flows out of the tarn over a torturing bed of rocks, and runs two miles down this elevated valley before it forms the cataract of the same name. I followed its course nearly the whole distance, and parted from it on a hill which overlooks the hamlet of Lowdore, where the vale of Watendlath opens out on that of Keswick. Here, as from a raised platform, I had a splendid view of Derwentwater, Skiddaw, and the whole " subjected plain." The road, which is very rugged, descends rapidly by the farm of Ashness, and in the rear of Barrow-house, to the highway round Derwentwater. I reached Keswick between six and seven o'clock.

On Wednesday I rode to Penrith to dinner, and in the evening to Carlisle. On leaving Penrith, I witnessed a fine effect of the partial storms which may often be seen in this country. I followed just in the rear of a thunder-storm, which was passing over Inglewood Forest in the direction of north-west; and from the hill about a mile from Penrith I saw the country before me obscured with the falling rain, whilst the extensive and beautiful plain behind was perfectly clear. But the most striking contrast was on the mountains to the left. The group of Saddleback, Skiddaw, and Carrock Fell was shrouded in tempest; whilst Helvellyn and all the mighty hills round Ullswater, without a vapour hanging near them, appeared brighter in their tints and better defined in their outline than I had ever seen them. When I had proceeded some miles further, another storm gathered on Black-law, the range of hills to my right, which was soon entirely obscured, though the Scotch hills on the northern horizon appeared with perfect distinctness. The rays of the setting sun reddened the clouds which brooded over Black-law, and gave to them such an effect as would be produced by a vast and distant conflagration.

The entrance of Carlisle is adorned by two magnificent circular towers, which in their form and dimensions more nearly resemble the famous tomb of Cecilia Metella, near Rome, used as a fortress in the middle ages, than any other structure that I have seen. They are the county court-houses, and were erected in 1812 on the site of two towers which formerly defended the " English-gate" of Carlisle. I was struck with the spacious, handsome, and cleanly streets of this ancient city. It has of late years considerably increased in extent, from the effect of its flourishing manufactures. A great part of the city walls have disappeared, but the Castle continues in a defensible condition, and is a fine piece of antiquity. It is supposed to have been the site of a Roman fortress: Egfrid, king of Northumberland, is believed to have erected a castle here in the seventh century, and the massive buttresses of the north battery are ascribed to William Rufus, who rebuilt the castle of Carlisle, and erected that of Newcastle, " to bridle and render insecure the possession of the Scottish kings in the two northern counties."* The strong central keep is of unknown date. Mary Queen of Scots was imprisoned here for some time after her landing in England, and the rooms she occupied are still shown. The walls command a beautiful view of the fertile country round Carlisle, and of the Eden and the Caldew, which form their confluence near the city. The fine bridge over the Eden, and the race-course, are seen from the castle. The cathedral is a venerable pile, but inferior in dimensions and magnificence to many of the English cathedrals. Its east window, however, is the largest in the kingdom. The choir part was built in the reigns of Edward III. and Richard II. and is a beautiful specimen of architecture. The edifice was much injured and curtailed of its proportions in the time of the Commonwealth. An abbey was attached to the cathedral, finished by Henry I. and the part called the Fratry still remains. It is a beautiful building, and was honoured as the seat of a parliament in the days of Edward I.

In the neighbourhood of Carlisle are many ancient castles and mansions, built in the times when the incursions of the Scotch made the frontier residences liable to frequent attack. Rose Castle, the seat of the Bishop of Carlisle, Naworth Castle, the seat of the Earl of Carlisle, Corby Castle, the residence of Henry

* Sir Walter Scott's History of Scotland.

Howard, Esq., and the beautiful remains of Lanercost Priory, are well worthy of notice. From Carlisle I returned to Penrith, and rode the same evening through the grounds of Dalemain to Ullswater, and along the borders of that noble lake to Patterdale. The following day a long journey brought me through Ambleside and Kendal, to Lancaster.

Having been much favoured by the weather, I enjoyed my Excursion highly; but my days' journeys were perhaps too long, and the rapidity with which I passed through the country would have been very unsatisfactory to a person who had not previously seen it. The mode of travelling, however, is agreeable, and each tourist can regulate his journeys according to his taste, strength, or convenience. He who wishes to see much in little time would accomplish that object by following nearly in my footsteps.

NOTE.—Since my account of the journey *over-Sands*, from Lancaster to Ulverston, was written, the proprietors of the coach have taken it off that route, and it now goes round by Miln-thorpe and Newby-bridge. This change was made owing to the accidents which occurred in crossing the Sands.

FIRST

EXCURSION ON FOOT.

INEXHAUSTIBLE ABUNDANCE OF SCENES AND OBJECTS AT THE LAKES—PEDESTRIAN EXCURSION FROM KENDAL—BOWNESS—TROUTBECK—KENTMERE—ASCENT OF HILL BELL AND HIGH STREET—LONG SLEDDALE—BELATED AMONG THE HILLS—MARDALE-GREEN—HAWES WATER—LOWTHER—PENRITH—ULLSWATER—PATTERDALE—KESWICK—SKIDDAW—DERWENTWATER—WALLOW CRAG—WATENDLATH AND BORROWDALE—GRASMERE—LOUGHRIGG—AMBLESIDE—KENDAL.

THE mountainous region of Westmoreland and Cumberland is so extensive, and every part of it so abounds in striking objects and grand or beautiful scenes, that it cannot be exhausted even by the most active and inquisitive traveller. The principal lakes may be seen, and a few of the highest mountains ascended, in a short space of time; but after this has been accomplished, there remains a vast variety of objects for the admirer of the picturesque,—valleys, mountains, crags, waterfalls, lakes, tarns, and streams, which the adventurous may explore with even greater pleasure than is derived from the more frequented scenes. A tourist always values himself most for those objects which he has seen exclusively—for what there has been of rare and uncommon in his rambles ; and to entitle himself to this pleasure, he must quit the carriage and the high road, and leave even his horse behind, whilst he penetrates by rugged paths into the mountain-fastnesses, where he will often be repaid by some "little unsuspected paradise," some view of surpassing grandeur, some interesting trait of character amongst the retired dalesmen, or some curious legend obtaining among a rude and simple peasantry.

In the summer of 1829 I set off from Kendal, to ramble through some parts of the Lakes which I had not yet visited. I was accompanied by a young friend, who was now making his first journey to this part of the country, and for whose sake we took a horse, he not being able to bear the fatigue of a pedestrian excursion among the mountains. I accomplished the tour almost entirely on foot, but the saddlebags we took saved me the encumbrance of a knapsack.

After a streaming morning the weather cleared up about two in the afternoon, and we set out from Kendal to Bowness. The views of the mountains were fine, and we arrived in time for a pleasant excursion on Windermere. We visited the Station and Belle Isle, with which my companion was greatly delighted, and which yielded me (though I had seen them so often) undiminished gratification.

The following morning the weather was coquettish

N 3

—smiling and lowering alternately; yet, after some deliberation, we thought we might safely enter upon the long day's journey we had contemplated. Our design was to skirt the eastern side of the valley of Troutbeck, and, ascending Applethwaite-common, to cross the hill into the valley of Kentmere; thence to ascend the fine mountains of Hill Bell and High Street, leaving our horse at Kentmere; to cross afterwards into the valley of Long Sleddale, and to make our way to Mardale Green, at the head of Hawes Water. We found the journey long and rather arduous, but it was so interesting as amply to repay us for the fatigue.

We took the road to Ambleside till it joined the turnpike-road from Kendal to that town, near Oresthead. Instead of turning into the latter, we kept straight forward up a beautiful lane, which leaves Elleray to the right; and for three or four miles we continued to ascend along the side of Applethwaite-common, with Hill Bell directly before us, and Troutbeck on our left. In this part the views are delicious and splendid. The whole of Windermere, from Loughrigg to Newby-bridge, lay under our view, an the islands formed a group in the centre, of the most fascinating beauty. In the direction of Low Wood the landscape was rich and varied to the highest degree; a considerable extent of fertile land, undulating in beautiful lines, clothed with green meadows, yellow corn-fields, and woods, and gradually sloping down to the lake, constituted the fore-ground; Windermere lay in placid beauty in the mid distance; and, as the background, Great Langdale stretched up to the heart of the mountains—Bowfell and the Pikes being wrapped in one of those partial storms which often add interest to a summer's prospect. As we proceeded, the valley of Troutbeck came more immediately under our eye: it is not seen from Windermere, owing to its own windings; the vale is fertile and lively, and the village, which stands on the side of the opposite hill, is picturesquely irregular. A neat whitened chapel stands near the beck, in the midst of the valley. The hill that rises above Troutbeck is Wansfell, along the side of which we traced the road that leads from Troutbeck-bridge to Kirkstone and Patterdale. Hill Bell descends into the valley with one long, steep, and regular slope, and is clad in a coat of lively verdure.

After a long and patient ascent, we reached nearly the highest part of Applethwaite-common, and, turning sharp to the right by a stone wall, we shortly came in view of Kentmere, a valley which runs parallel with Troutbeck on the eastern side of Hill Bell and High Street. From this part we might easily have ascended Hill Bell, being already half-way up the mountain; but, not thinking it safe to take the horse on a mountain where we had never been before, we very reluctantly descended a long, steep, and rugged path to the village of Kentmere, in order to leave the animal. Had we not had this encumbrance, we might have greatly abridged the

day's journey, not only by ascending Hill Bell and
High Street from Applethwaite Common, but by
descending from High Street direct to Mardale
Green, at the head of Hawes Water, instead of returning to Kentmere. It is indeed practicable to
take a horse over this mountain range, which is tra-
versed by the ancient road from Kendal to Penrith;
but the attempt would be very unsafe for a person
who was not well acquainted with the mountains.

Kentmere is a pretty valley, containing a small
lake, and a castellated house called Kentmere-hall;
but there is nothing very striking in the scenery. We
asked and obtained permission to put up our horse at
the first farm we came to, and the good woman of
the house sent her " lile lad" to show us part of the
way up the mountain. We took the bull by the
horns, beginning to climb a very steep part of the
hill betwixt stupendous crags. When we reached
the top of the crags, after half an hour's toil, the lad
pointed out to us the course we were to pursue. We
were to make straight for the top of the ridge on our
left, which led up in a long slope over an inferior
summit to the highest point of Hill Bell: having
attained that elevation, we were to proceed along
the ridge that connects Hill Bell with High Street:
from the latter mountain we were to return,
sweeping round the head of Kentmere, to Nan-bield,
a remarkable gap lying between High Street and
Harter-fell, and intersected by a sharp ridge of rocks;
from which place a pathway would bring us past a

slate quarry into the valley, and back to the village of Kentmere.

What boots it to tell how we toiled patiently—and sometimes impatiently—through the long heath, over bogs and rocks, or up the slippery sward? It is the old story of the ascent of a high mountain. Suffice it to say, that in two hours after leaving Kentmere, we stood on the green and pointed summit of Hill Bell, at the height of at least two thousand five hundred feet above the level of the sea. My young friend had thought the ascent the most wearisome thing in the world, but the view from the summit repaid all, being beyond comparison the most novel, interesting, and wonderful prospect he had ·ever beheld. We traced the valleys of Kentmere and Troutbeck through all their windings, and the larger valleys into which they fall, as far as the sea. The town of Kendal and nearly the whole of Windermere were visible, as were the estuaries of the Kent and the Leven, Morecambe Bay, and the hills of Yorkshire and Lancashire, even beyond Ingleborough and Pendle-hill. We saw the fells of Cartmel and Furness, Black Comb, Coniston Old Man, Wetherlam, Bowfell, Scawfell Pikes, Great Gavel, Langdale Pikes, Wansfell, Kirkstone, Scandale, Fairfield, Helvellyn, High Street, Harter-fell, the Shap-fells, and the country beyond Penrith terminated by Cross-fell. Place-fell, Patterdale, and the upper reach of Ullswater, as well as Hays Water-tarn, under the north-west side of High Street, were also visible. The weather was now perfectly clear, and continued so during the remainder of the day.

Whilst enjoying this magnificent prospect, we lunched on the sandwiches and brandy which we had brought with us from Bowness; and after a short rest, we pursued our walk along the undulating ridge which connects Hill Bell with High Street. We had to descend several hundred feet and to re-ascend twice or thrice, and the distance was very considerable—more than we had calculated upon. On the side of Troutbeck the mountains have a smooth swelling outline, and are clothed with a thick carpet of grass, on which many sheep are fed: but on the side of Kentmere the ridge shelves down abruptly in awful precipices, which have a terrific appearance to a person walking along the top. The head of Kentmere, indeed, is remarkably grand, from the amazing height of the mountain walls which stand round it. Along the side and over the summit of Hill Bell and High Street a green road may be traced, which is believed to be the line of an old Roman road from Kendal to Penrith. That it was a road in use when pack-horses were the chief mode of conveying goods, is certain. This, like many other old roads in England, has been carried over the highest ground, evidently on the jealous principle of disturbed and warlike times, when it would have been unsafe to travel along the valleys, from the liability to be surprised and overpowered by an enemy in possession of the heights. An annual meeting of the shepherds formerly took place on High Street, which is centrally situated betwixt several valleys; they gave each other information concerning the sheep that might have strayed, and the meeting was cheered by a merry-making, when races and other sports took place on the broad summit of the mountain, at an elevation of 2700 feet above the level of the sea.

When we reached the most elevated part of High Street, we found that it was three hours and a half since we had left Kentmere. From hence Skiddaw and Saddleback, and the Scotch mountains, were visible, in addition to the objects we had seen from Hill Bell. Kidsay Pike, we perceived, was joined to High Street, as that mountain was to Hill Bell; and it appeared to us of greater elevation than either; but neither our time nor our strength permitted us to extend our mountain range, and we made the best of our way to Nan-bield. In proceeding to this point, the lake of Hawes Water for the first time greeted our eyes, and its apparent nearness excited our regret that we had to make so long a *detour* before we should reach it. A tarn also, called Small water, was seen in a hollow of the mountain under Nan-bield. At the latter place we rested, and ate the remainder of our sandwiches; after which we descended rapidly into the valley, and walked three miles to the village of Kentmere. The whole walk had cost us six hours; we were a good deal fatigued, and quite prepared for the plain but hearty dinner that awaited us at the public-house.

Had we been acquainted with the country, our best plan would have been to get a person from Kentmere to take our horse to Nan-bield, whilst we ascended the mountains, to meet us there at an appointed hour, and thence to conduct us down the steep but practicable descent into Mardale. The neglect to do this cost us a round of many miles, and nearly occasioned our being benighted among the hills. It was after seven o'clock in the evening when we set out from Kentmere to cross the hill into Long Sleddale, a valley running parallel to that of Kentmere, and which seemed by the map to lead without any intervening hill to Mardale at the head of Hawes Water. When we came down into Long Sleddale the shades of evening were coming on, and we therefore pushed on vigorously, scarcely allowing ourselves time to admire the bold and craggy mountains which enclose the vale. We could not, however, but be struck with the vast crags of Crowbarrow on our right, which rear their enormous bulk perpendicularly from the vale. To our surprise we found that the valley ran up among the hills, without the outlet we had expected towards Mardale : and after toiling up a long ascent, we found ourselves on an elevated moor betwixt higher mountains, and not knowing which way to pursue. Two slacks appeared to lie before us, but still considerably above, one to the left and the other to the right. My impression was that Mardale lay to the right, but the track we were upon led up the hill to the left. It was now half-past nine, and darkness was coming on ;

we were several miles from any human habitation; there was little time to deliberate; we both mounted the horse, and urged him up the narrow and stony pathway, in hopes that we might reach the top of the slack before night had so far advanced as to prevent our seeing Hawes Water. The animal seemed to understand the emergency: he trotted briskly up a rugged ascent, pricking his ears, and snuffing up the wind. At length we reached the top of the slack, (which I afterwards found was called Salset-brow) and the path began to descend: we looked down into a deep and narrow valley, at the head of which gloomy and awful precipices towered to a mountain-height: we could not see Hawes Water, but it was evidently our safest plan to proceed as rapidly as possible along the track, which must certainly conduct us to some habitation, either in Mardale or in another valley. We dismounted and ran down the hill, I leading the horse. We had not descended far, when, to our unspeakable relief and joy, we saw Hawes Water in the valley below us, which assured us that we were in the right road, and were near our place of rest for the night. It was now ten o'clock, and by half-past ten we reached the White Bull at Mardale Green. Mr. Thomas Lambley, the host, had retired to bed, but we roused the family, and obtained supper and comfortable accommodation for the night, both for our good horse and ourselves.

I have mentioned these particulars as a warning to the future rambler not to judge of the distance he has to travel and the difficulties he has to conquer merely by the map, but always to obtain the fullest information possible from persons acquainted with the country. I also strongly recommend him never to deviate from the beaten track when he is doubtful of the way. Peat tracks and paths connected with quarries may often appear to him to lead more directly to his destination than the track which he is upon; but it is always the safest to prosecute the main track, which, though perhaps not wider than the other, is constructed with greater solidity, being generally formed by a bed of small stones.

Mardale is a lively, fertile, and beautiful valley, with very few habitations, at the head of Hawes Water, but terminating in utter barrenness and desolation at the foot of Harter-fell. It lies between Branstree on the east, and Chapel-hill on the west, and at the upper part the mountains are steep, naked, and craggy—especially Harter-fell, whose stupendous and furrowed precipices frown over the head of the dale. A sharp and barren ridge runs up from Mardale to High-street, and has given to a branch of the valley the name of Riggindale; that mountain and Kidsay Pike are seen from the valley, and in front of the latter, looking upon the head of Hawes Water, is a prominent and lofty rock called Castle Crag. The mountain which rises immediately on the western side of Hawes Water, is Whelter, and at its upper end is a grand mass of rock called Whelter Crag.

We left Mardale Green about noon, and a mile brought us to Hawes Water, a beautiful lake three miles in length and half a mile in width. The western side of the lake has a margin of cultivated fields, the effect of which is lively and beautiful. On the eastern side the hill rises steeply to a considerable elevation, and is covered with herbage, plentifully bestrewn with fine natural wood. Round the head the mountains are sublime and awful. Hawes Water is nearly divided into two lakes by a beautiful promontory of cultivated and wooded ground, that shoots into it on the western side near the village of Measand; and opposite this point, on the eastern shore, is a stupendous crag, named Wallow Crag, whose sides are feathered with wood.* The lower part of the lake is rich, graceful, and negligently elegant. One of the branches of the river Lowther flows out of it in a clear and rapid stream, which winds through the valley.

Below Hawes Water the valley opens out to a considerable width, and quite loses its boldness, but continues highly fertile and beautiful. We proceeded

---

* A characteristic legend is connected with this crag: the vulgar believe that the spirit of " Jemmy Lawther," (as they familiarly call the Sir James Lowther who was remarkable for his penuriousness) is imprisoned in the dark womb of the rock; and I was gravely told by two natives of the valley that when Sir James died he could not *roost* (rest),—that various incantations were tried by the learned vicar of Bampton to *lay* his ghost,— that the reverend gentleman was roughly handled by the refractory spirit,—but that at length, having " sent for more books," the vicar fairly succeeded in lodging him in Wallow Crag !

forward to Askham, a distance of five miles from
Hawes Water; and having dined at the public-house,
we entered the splendid domain of Lowther park.
We saw the interior of the castle, and then proceeded
through the grounds to Penrith.

The remainder of this Excursion was over ground
which has been already described, though we made
several deviations from the former routes. It will
only be necessary for me to mention our days' journeys, for the guidance of those who may take a similar
excursion. From Penrith we went, by Yanwath and
Tirrel, to Pooley Bridge, seeing Arthur's Round
Table and Mayburg on the way. Proceeding by land
to Patterdale, we were overtaken by a storm, and
were obliged to take refuge and dry our clothes at
Lyulph's Tower: we were again drenched in going
thence to Patterdale.

The following day we sent our horse to Lyulph's
Tower, whilst we rowed to the same place in a boat;
and the weather being fine, all that glorious scenery
was revealed to us, which had been shrouded in clouds
the previous evening. We saw Airey Force to great
advantage, as the stream had been swelled by the rain.
We proceeded to Keswick by Dockwray, and over the
elevated moor which lies on the north of the Helvellyn
range. The views ascending the hill from Gowbarrow
Park to Matterdale, were superb. Our road led us
across the valley of Wanthwaite, which is part of the
Vale of St. John, and we took the new road to
Keswick. A thunder-storm raged over the town

after we had arrived, and the peals were fearfully reverberated from the surrounding mountains. In the evening, when the storm was passing off southward, we walked to Friar Crag, the promontory on Derwentwater, whence we saw the distant lightning playing awfully over Scawfell, and heard the thunder mutter and growl among the mountains with a sublime depth of sound.

From Keswick we ascended Skiddaw on foot, and rowed round Derwentwater, in one day ; we also saw the waterfalls of Barrow and Lowdore, and landed on several of the islands: the weather was clear, and the views extremely fine.

The next day we went to Watendlath and Borrowdale. I ascended by Castlerigg to the top of Wallow Crag, and walked along the Derwent fells to the farm of Ashness, where I met my friend, who had ridden on horseback along the high road. The views from Wallow Crag, of Derwentwater and its islands, and of the surrounding valleys and mountains, are most interesting and splendid. We crossed from Watendlath to Rosthwaite in Borrowdale, and returned by Bowder Stone and Lowdore to Keswick. The same evening we proceeded to Grasmere, I taking advantage of the mail. At the snug and comfortable inn, the Red Lion, we found excellent accommodation and provision, and felt much more at home than we had done in large and crowded inns.

On the following morning I climbed Helm Crag, which commands very fine and extensive prospects :

we then rowed round Grasmere Water, and afterwards took the road over Loughrigg and by Clappersgate to Ambleside.   In our way we ascended to the top of Loughrigg-fell, from which, owing to its central situation, there is a splendid panoramic view.

Stockgill-force, the Rydal waterfalls, and Windermere detained us the greater part of a day, and the evening brought us back to Kendal.

Our excursion had occupied ten days, during which we had travelled about a hundred and sixty miles, ascended three high mountains and several considerable hills, and seen ten lakes, and five or six of the principal waterfalls.   The tour was full of gratification both to myself and to my young companion, and it contributed to our health as much as to our pleasure.

SECOND

EXCURSION ON FOOT.

HAVING made a short pedestrian excursion in the
autumn of 1833, I shall sketch such parts of it as
have not been comprised in my previous tours.

I set out from Ambleside in the morning of Saturday, the 28th of September, with the intention of
ascending Rydal-head, passing over the summit of
Fairfield to that of Helvellyn, and, after this long
mountain ramble, descending into the valley of Wythburn near Thrispot, and proceeding to Keswick. The
weather prevented the execution of this design.

Fairfield was capped with clouds, and I was compelled to trudge along the valley amidst rain; but, as some compensation, the woods of Rydal and the verdure of Grasmere had their brilliancy heightened by the showers. As I climbed the long hill to Dunmail Raise, the clouds rose and broke, giving me hopes that I might still ascend Helvellyn from Wythburn. But the promise was not realized: when I reached the Horse Head, though the rain had ceased and the clouds risen, the sky was too dubious to justify so serious an undertaking. However, that I might not wholly lose the opportunity of tasting the mountain air, I resolved to cross the Thirlmere fells to the valley of Watendlath, and thus to make my way to Keswick. I had not before been upon these fells, which are as dark and savage as any in Cumberland; but, being little more than half the height of Helvellyn, I hoped they would continue clear, though the clouds should descend and wrap the loftier hills in their mantle.

At half-past one I quitted the high road, and passed through that ancient hamlet near the head of Thirlmere lake, called the City of Wythburn. Whether in any former age, as during the independence of Cumbria, this was the site of a city,—whether the name has been given by some humourist among the statesmen of Wythburn,—or what else may have been the origin of such a designation,—I must leave antiquarians to explore or to conjecture. At present the City is a little hamlet of rude architecture, and the *citizens* as unpolished as their habitations. One of them, however, gave me directions how to find my way over the fell. He pointed out a path which took me nearly to the top of the hill, and told me that when I got fairly upon the moor, I should see a ruined stone fence at some distance before me and a little to the right, and that I must aim at that, and proceed keeping it on my right hand. The direction I was to take was, as I knew, an oblique one, holding to the right; that is, I was to go in a north-westerly direction, which would bring me in three or four miles to the secluded valley of Watendlath. I am particular in specifying these directions, as they may be important to others, especially if overtaken by clouds or by evening; but I strongly recommend no one to cross these fells except in favourable weather and in broad day.

The ascent of the fell side is what a dalesman would call *a strong clim*. I took it with all coolness and patience. The less you hurry in such a task, the sooner you seem to yourself to leave the vale below. Cool down your expectations, and just keep moving; your progress will outstrip your hopes. It is so on a Cumbrian fell, and it is the same in climbing the hill of life: not the impetuous and the eager, whose efforts are sudden and violent, gain the highest elevation, but those who keep quietly and steadily onward, never wandering from the path. The reader must pardon me if I sometimes moralize; nothing so much allures to moralizing as a solitary ramble on the mountains.

o

In half an hour I had a sublime view.   I was yet
winding up the rugged breast of the hill, but was
sufficiently high to see Wythburn below me as on a
map.   The green valley, and the black (because overshadowed) mere, had shrunk into a very narrow
though lovely string, drawn round the base of the
vast and soaring Helvellyn.   The road, seen for miles
through the valley, was a mere white line, and its ups
and downs were reduced almost to nothing.   As the
objects below diminished, Helvellyn swelled into a
mightier and loftier mass.   To those who travel along
the valley, but a small portion of him is seen at any
one time ; and his sides rise so steeply that the eye of
the traveller does not reach the receding upper parts
of the mountain.   I was now just at the proper distance and elevation to comprehend his enormous outline.   However scarred and rugged may be the surface
of such a mountain, the general contour is always
smooth and flowing.   The ravines which so deeply
seam the hill are nearly lost in the vastness of a bulk,
which spreads along for miles on either hand, and
swells upward into an expanse certainly the most
sublime presented by any mountain in England.   In
the lower half of the mountain, which is bestrewn
with shale, the grass is very scanty, and the grey predominates over the green ; on the upper half, where
the slope is less precipitous, the herbage is thicker,
and the green has there the predominance, though
here and there cloven by deep slate-coloured ravines,
radiating from the summit.

For about three quarters of an hour after I began the ascent, the top of Helvellyn was free from clouds, or only occasionally and partially obscured. But soon I saw reason to rejoice that I had not attempted to grapple with the giant. Vapours gathered upon Seat Sandal, and gradually stole along the sides of Helvellyn. At first they were not thick, but by and bye Seat Sandal became gloomy, and substantial clouds, big with rain, rolled streaming over the surface of Helvellyn, at little more than half the elevation of the mountain—the top still continuing visible. Though this afforded an unpleasing indication, I could not but admire the view of Helvellyn, round whose breast the clouds sailed, not much more considerable, when compared with this "monarch of mountains," than so many cock-boats or canoes paddling round the hull of a first-rate man of war. For some time he had merely a zone of clouds, with a thin vaporous veil drawn over his head, almost as transparent as gauze ; but the clouds continually increased in size and density, till they wholly shrouded him from view.

The reader will believe that my eyes, though often attracted to the opposite mountain, not less frequently turned in the direction of Steel-fell, the higher part of the hill I was myself ascending, and which lay to my left, that is, to windward. The clouds were already lower on Helvellyn than the top of the Thirlmere fells ; and though sometimes the clouds embrace and cling to the larger masses of hills, and leave the smaller ones without a visit, yet I could scarcely hope that this would long be the case to-day, as the wind was southerly and very moist. I had now lost sight of Wythburn, from having passed over the brow of the hill which overlooks the valley, and had got upon the heath-covered, boggy, and rocky moor that lies between that valley and Watendlath. But I had by no means attained the highest part which I had to cross; so that when the clouds began to tip the fell on my left, my coolness and sentimentalizing soon left me, and I knew it was my business to push on as fast as my legs could carry me, in order to get a peep at Watendlath ere the clouds descended. The rain began to fall smartly: the clouds lowered, but happily not fast. I had seen the old ruined wall which the good citizen of Wythburn directed me to look for, and at length I reached it, after tasting of several bogs, though I kept as much as possible along the rocky ridges which cross the moor. To be in a hurry among the long heath, bogs, and rocks, is no enviable thing. I startled the meagre, black-faced sheep, which bounced off for some distance, and then stood and stared at me as I leaped and splashed along. I had kept my shirt dry in ascending out of Wythburn, but now it became almost as wet as my stockings. It would not have been prudent to spare myself till I had got over the crown of the fell, and seen my way down into a habitable region.

At three o'clock, an hour and a half after leaving the City, I came in view of the hills beyond Borrow-dale. In a few minutes more I had the high gratification to obtain a view down the valley of Watendlath, at the embouchure of which I saw the lovely lake of Derwentwater; and immediately after, just beneath me, the little tarn-like water of Watendlath came into view. The clouds were now gathering fast at my heels: in fact they chased me down the hill, the descent of which was by no means easy, owing to its steepness and slipperiness. The rain fell in torrents, and made the path—for I had again come to a sheep-track—excessively unpleasant. This, however, I felt to be nothing, as the danger of being surrounded by clouds on the fell was altogether past.

It was half-past three when I reached the hamlet of Watendlath, and I went into the first house to exchange a few words with the inhabitants. They asked me if I had met two gentlemen on the fell, whom they had a little while before set on their way to Wythburn. When I told them I had not, they expressed some fears lest the travellers should have missed their way, and should be caught in the clouds, which now rested on the whole fell. I never heard whether this was the case or not, but I have no doubt that the travellers ultimately got either to Wythburn or back to Watendlath. The houses here are rude, dark, dirty, and comfortless. Uneven floors, old crazy furniture, and patched windows,—a lump of peat just smoking in the hearth, as an apology for a fire,—the women habited in coarse woollen garments and wooden clogs, —the men in tattered fustian,—an antique spinning wheel in one corner, on which the old woman spins yarn for their stockings, from the locks of wool picked up by herself and the children on the hill-side, and carded at Keswick,—the men and women hard-favoured, cold-looking, and unintelligent, as might be expected from the drudgery in which they spend their lives in this inhospitable, out-of-the-world place;—all form a picture very much the reverse of what poets love to feign concerning the abodes of shepherds and shepherdesses, and little suited for the theme of any muse except that of Crabbe.

As there is no place of refreshment at Watendlath, I pursued my way down the valley to Lowdore, two miles distant. Having just come off the misty moor, I was exceedingly struck with the beauty of the scenery about a mile down the valley. On the right, the green hill-side is besprinkled with trees of delicious foliage, and the vivid green and brown tints are contrasted with the silver grey of the rocks: on the left, stupendous precipices rise from the valley to the Borrowdale fells. The atmosphere was rendered only more transparent by the aqueous vapour it contained; and the gloom of the shrouded hills heightened by contrast the freshness, the lively colours, and the variegated beauty of this upland vale, which Nature has decked in her own inimitable way.

A mile and a half below Watendlath, before coming to the farm of Ashness, I turned off the road to the left, crossed a wooden bridge over the stream, and descended by a steep winding path into the plain of the Derwent, to the hamlet of High Lowdore. There are few prospects more striking than that obtained from the elevation above the cataract, looking towards Derwentwater. The foot of the lake and its islands are seen through a chasm formed by two lofty rocks, one of them called Shepherd's Crag and the other Gowder Crag,—the former perfectly bare, and the latter made shaggy with natural wood. The distant lake is all softness, elegance, and repose : the crags are wild and savage.. I could not help comparing the scene to two hideous giants, keeping guard over sleeping beauty. It is betwixt these crags that the stream makes its awful leap, forming the fall of Lowdore. I went to see the cascade, now swelled by the heavy rain, and the quantity of water was greater than at any former visit.

Having obtained some refreshment at the inn, I walked on to Keswick, where I arrived at six o'clock, wetted from top to toe. The reader will judge of my *satisfaction* on hearing that my portmanteau, which contained all my clothes except those on my back, instead of having been left by the coach at Keswick, had been taken on to Whitehaven, whence it could not be obtained till the Monday ! If an occurrence of this kind is not included in the " Miseries of Human Life," I recommend it to the consideration of the author in preparing a new edition. Moreover, as a supplement, he may add that no dry clothes were to be obtained but those of a gentleman twice as corpulent as myself ; and that in order to go out on the Sunday, I was obliged to put on my own shoes, which,

not having lost the memory of the bogs, gave me a
sore throat.

From Saturday to Tuesday, Skiddaw wore his
cloudy hood, and the greater part of the time an
ample cape, which descended so low as to be quite
fashionable.* On Monday I walked to Buttermere
and back, through the vale of Newlands ; on Tuesday
I lay by, to cure my throat: and on Wednesday I
formed one of a party to ascend Skiddaw. Old Neddy
Birkett, an ex-guide, and Joe Brown, one of the present guides, spent part of an evening with me.   We
fought a good many battles o'er again, and as Birkett
is now eighty-six years of age, he could tell of some
long and hard campaigns, without at all drawing
upon his invention.

Thursday was a glorious morning, and I set off
for Borrowdale, having marked out the ascent of Great
Gavel for that day's work, and the ascent of Langdale
Pikes for the following day. When passing under
Falcon Crag, about half way up the lake, one of the
richest and loveliest pictures ever seen or dreamed
of presented itself. The lofty and steep slope of
Catbells, decked in all those hues with which October
invests the hills, rich brown and lemon colour, mingled
with green, and streaked here and there like a dove's
neck from the effect of slate and metallic ore, was
illuminated by a brilliant morning sun ; and the

* *Nota bene :* This will not apply to the next season, as the
milliners will no doubt speedily retrench the ladies' capes, to cut
out fresh work for themselves.

whole hill-side was reflected from the mirror of Derwentwater without a wrinkle. The inverted image was actually brighter than the hill itself, as it received a lustre from the glassy surface on which it was painted.* As I proceeded towards Barrow-house, the richly wooded islands, with their mellow autumnal foliage, the beautiful vale of Newlands, the embrowned ridge of Swinside, the plantations of Derwent-bay and Derwent-bank, the black horn of Causey Pike, and finally the whole mass of Skiddaw with his azure peaks, were successively, and at length all together seen reflected from the surface of the lake,—the most glorious and inimitable picture I ever witnessed. If the reader can imagine a sheet, not of canvas, but of crystal, three miles in extent, painted with the warm tones of Cuyp, and with the exquisite finish and softness of Gerard Dow or Carlo Dolci, he may imagine something which would be but a rude mockery of this heavenly-tinted and divinely penciled landscape. I knew not how to leave it.

Borrowdale, which I had never before seen in October, was now in its perfection of beauty, from the rich variety of hues which the trees and the hills

---

* Though any comparison of Nature's work with Man's must to a certain degree be derogatory, it may convey a more exact impression of the effect if I say, that the only difference between the appearance of the hill-side itself and the reflection in the water was that which exists between a painting when unvarnished, and the same painting softly and delicately varnished.

assume at this season.   The splendour of the weather
made my walk through such scenery delightful.   I
halted at Rosthwaite merely to bespeak a bed for the
night, and then proceeded to Seatoller.

I had not previously had the pleasure of an acquaintance with the family of Mr. Fisher, the principal
statesman of Borrowdale: but as we had common
friends, and as I knew well the character of Seatoller
for old English hospitality, I took the liberty to call and
introduce myself.   The kindness of my reception
more than answered my expectations.   Mr. and Mrs.
Fisher and their sons knew my name, and were familiar with my rambles among their native mountains.
They pressed me to stay dinner, which was at the
good old-fashioned hour of half-past twelve; and
though it is quite contrary to rule to dine before
ascending a mountain, yet for the sake of enjoying
their company a little longer, I accepted the invitation.
As we were dining, the company was swelled by the
arrival of two young ladies and a young gentleman,
the son and daughters of an estimable clergyman
residing at Buttermere, who had come with their
ponies over Borrowdale-hawse to see their friends at
Seatoller.   Their reception was as kind as possible.

After dinner one of Mr. Fisher's sons was so
obliging as to accompany me to the Wad Mines, and
he would have gone with me on to Great Gavel if a
particular engagement had not prevented.   However
it was arranged that I should take tea at Seatoller on
my return.

The celebrated Wad Mines, where the useful mineral called plumbago or black lead is found, are situated at a considerable elevation on the ridge called Gillercoom, connected with Seatoller-fell, and overlooking the valley of Seathwaite. In walking along the foot of the hill before we began to climb, we saw several fine yew trees, one of which is of magnificent growth; its trunk measures twenty seven feet in girth, and, though centuries must have passed over its head, it is still in undecayed strength and beauty.

The ascent to the Wad Mines is steep, and we were obliged to take it very slowly, lest we should heat ourselves, and make it dangerous to enter the cold subterraneous passages of the mine. We found at the entrance the son of Mr. Dixon, the steward, who accompanied us into one of the levels conducting to an old working, and also into a new working higher up the hill, where a plentiful supply of the mineral had lately been discovered. The earth in the level is of a red colour, as our shoes and trowsers sufficiently testified on our return out of the wet and cold gallery. This level is two hundred and twenty yards in length, and we penetrated to the extremity, each carrying a candle; but there is little here to repay the trouble and unpleasantness, as the workings are abandoned.

At the new working higher up the hill, we descended by ladders about four yards, and then went along a short level, to the part where the miners are employed. The sides of the mine are covered with shining black

mineral, and the workmen detach it from the rock or
earth in which it is embedded; other workmen cut or
scrape off any portion of stone which may adhere to it,
after which the lead is ready for the market. It is
sawn into the form proper for pencils, by the manufacturers in London and Keswick. The lead in this
new working is not of good quality. The purer the
mineral is, the lighter it weighs; when mixed with
stony or earthy particles, it is of course gritty, and
its specific gravity is increased. Few lumps of the
mineral that I saw were more than three or four
inches long. The rock in which the mineral is found
is grey wacke, but a soft black earth surrounds the
lead in the parts where the miners were then working.
The black lead does not lie in veins, so as to admit of
its being easily traced, and the supply calculated, but
in sops or bellies, ramified like a tree, and surrounded
with hard rock, so that it is often lost, and the miners
penetrate the hill at hazard in search of a new supply.
Before this sop was discovered, the lead had been lost
for some time, and the miners had tried before in the
same part of the hill without hitting upon the mineral.

Mr. Green informs us that " this lead is a source of
almost incredible wealth to the owners of the mines: upwards of twenty-eight tons have been procured from one
of these bellies, of a quality worth from thirty to forty
shillings a pound, besides a great quantity of an inferior sort." Mexican black-lead, however, is now
superseding English for most purposes except making
the finest pencils: the quality of the Mexican is con-

siderably inferior, but its price is not more than a
hundredth part that of the Borrowdale lead. One half of
the property of the mines belongs to Henry Bankes, Esq.
formerly member for Dorsetshire, and the other half
to a company in London. These mines have been
known from an ancient date. They are mentioned by
Camden, who wrote nearly two centuries and a half
ago ; and before his time the shepherds used the
mineral for marking their sheep. They afford the
best black-lead in the world, and the proprietors
sell it at a monopoly, that is, at an arbitrary price.
This mineral is used not only for making pencils,
but for polishing iron, in the composition of cruci-
bles, and in making an anti-attrition paste to prevent
the friction of machinery.

After leaving the Wad Mines, Mr. Fisher ascended
to the top of the ridge with me, in order to point
out the best way to Great Gavel, and at three
o'clock in the afternoon I left him on my expedition.
Following his directions I kept up an elevated valley,
leaving the valley of Seathwaite on my left hand,
and excluded from my view by a high ridge. I soon
came to one of those large piles of stones and broken
crags, called fox-bields, from the foxes making their
holes amongst them. Passing this, I kept along the
right side of the valley, and climbed the hill at a green
slack, where the ascent was the most gentle. When
I had got upon the ridge, where the valley of Ennerdale and its high mountains came into view, I turned
to the left, and in a quarter of an hour more I gained

the summit of Green Gavel, where the loftier summit of Great Gavel rose in frowning and fearful majesty before me. It is a few hundred feet higher than Green Gavel, but from the latter you see the sheer descent of Great Gavel from the summit down into the head of Ennerdale, and the sight of those precipices is awful. Nor is it very consoling to look down into the deep ravine which separates the two mountains from each other, and to the almost perpendicular ascent which must be climbed on the other side to reach the top of Great Gavel. When Mr. Fisher told me afterwards that he had often run across this ravine, which is filled with sharp stones, barefoot, and carrying his shoes and stockings in his hand, in order that he might the more quickly pursue the fox into his mountain retreats, I thought this was a kind of fox-hunting which would appal the best Yorkshire and Leicestershire Nimrods.

The view from Green Gavel is superb, but I did not long pause to enjoy it. I went down into the ravine, and climbed up a scarcely perceptible track on the steep and rocky hill-side beyond, keeping to the left,—an ascent which it would hardly be prudent for a person who has not a tolerably good head to attempt. At half past four, that is, in an hour and a half after leaving the Wad Mines, I found myself on the pointed summit of Great Gavel, at an elevation of 2925 feet above the level of the sea.

The whole region of the lakes lay beneath my view, though most of the lakes themselves, and the more beautiful parts of the valleys, were shut out from my sight by the swelling ridges which run off from Scawfell Pikes and Great Gavel like radii from their centre. The sun was rather too near his setting, and a slight degree of haziness prevented me from distinctly perceiving the sea. The tarns and little sheets of water on the black mountains betwixt me and the sun, glittered like diamonds. Every considerable hill from Black Comb to Solway frith, and from the sea to Shap fells, was distinctly visible. Nearest to Gavel, and separated from it by what seems a narrow space, Scawfell Pikes, with their lofty Man, girt with the most awful precipices, and separated from Scawfell by the deep chasm of Mickle Door, have a truly sublime effect. Wast Water was visible from the summit, but I had to walk a few yards in order to see Wasdale-head, whose green strip, with its few houses and enclosures mapped upon it, and shut in between enormous hills, had a singularly beautiful effect. Betwixt Seatallan and the Pillar, the Hay Cock swells to an enormous bulk, little corresponding with its name. The lonely valley of Ennerdale, with the almost inaccessible heights of the Pillar and other steep mountains rising above it, runs off from the base of Gavel itself: but the lake of Ennerdale, which I had seen from Green Gavel, was not visible from the higher summit. Nearly the whole of Crummock Water, with the beautiful valley at its foot, was visible; but only a small angle of Buttermere lake appeared over the top of the Hay

Stacks. Borrowdale and the valley of Watendlath lay open to view; and Latrigg, Wallow Crag, and Grange fell were conspicuous, but Derwentwater lay hid behind the hills. The vast ranges of Grassmoor, Skiddaw, and Helvellyn were the giant features of the prospect on the north and east. Langdale Pikes and the head of Windermere appeared to the left of Bowfell, and, much nearer, Sprinkling-tarn lay deep beneath the crags of Great End. The Calder, the Irt, the Nite, and the Esk were seen issuing out of their respective valleys westward, and meandering through the plain to the sea. To specify all the mountains visible from this elevated spot, would be to name nearly every mountain in Cumberland and Westmoreland.

At the top of Great Gavel is a small triangular hole in a rock, containing about a gallon of water; and though it is supplied only by the rain, yet so slow is the evaporation at this height that the reservoir has never been known to be dry, except (as I was informed by Mr. Fisher) on one occasion, when Mr. Tyson, of Wasdale-head, saw his fox-hounds lap up the whole contents. The water of this cloud-supplied well served to dilute the stronger liquid I had brought with me.

I remained on the summit an hour, which was as long as I durst stay; for, it being then half-past five, the sun was within a few minutes of setting, and he and I had a hard race. Happily the side of Great Gavel towards Sty-head, by which I descended, is so soft, (except just on the top) and of such a regular descent, that I was able to run the whole way down to Sty-head tarn : I therefore accomplished a descent of nearly 1700 feet in nineteen minutes. Keeping up a quick pace over Sty-head, and down the steep side of the hill to the head of Borrowdale, I reached Stockley-bridge, above Seathwaite, forty-two minutes after leaving the summit. About two miles and a half down the valley brought me to the hospitable roof of Seatoller, where I arrived at a quarter to seven o'clock, not before dark.

Seatoller unquestionably furnishes the finest bread and the sweetest honey I ever ate : and I am sure I took enough of both with my tea to enable me to form an opinion. The honey is of that kind called heath honey, the bees which produce it feeding on the heath-flowers : it is of a darker colour and a much finer flavour than the honey produced by bees which feed on garden flowers ; and the two kinds are made within a short distance of each other, as, for example, the heath-honey at Ashness, above Lowdore, and the other honey at Barrow, at the foot of the same hill. Holm-honey, which is that produced in the level country, is inferior to both.

After spending some time with the family of Mr. Fisher, and receiving from them the truest hospitality and kindness, I took my leave; but one of the sons walked with me to the village of Rosthwaite, where I spent the night.

On the following (Friday) morning, I set out a few

minutes after eight o'clock, to cross the Stake and
Langdale Pikes into Great Langdale, and thence to
Ambleside. The sun had risen in splendour, but the
clouds gradually lowered so as to cap the highest
hills; and though the day passed over without rain,
the clouds continued to rest on all the hills above two
thousand feet in height, with occasional fluctuations
from the effect of the wind. Leaving Borrowdale
chapel on my right, I went through the village
and up the valley of Stonethwaite; and having at the
village been put into the most convenient path, (which
should be inquired for,) I passed through a wood and
over some rocks into a valley which runs due southward, called Langstreth. The views in this part are
of the richest picturesque, from the combination of
towering hills and crags, with woods, streams, and
branching valleys. Eagle Crag is a stupendous pile
of rock, soaring above the separation of the Langstreth
and Greenup valleys.

Above Borrowdale Chapel, the wide valley or small
plain of Borrowdale branches off into three, having
some rude resemblance to the forks of a trident,—the
Seathwaite branch being that to the right, the Greenup
branch to the left, and the Langstreth branch in the
centre, but much nearer the left than the right.
The two latter join about a mile above Stonethwaite.
Through the valley of Greenup and over the fells,
travellers may pass into Easdale and Grasmere; •
through Langstreth, and over the Stake, into Langdale. I turned into Langstreth, leaving Eagle Crag

immediately on my left, and, crossing the bridge, kept up the left side of the valley, along a faintly marked path, for nearly three miles. On entering Langstreth, all cultivation ceases, and not a single habitation is to be seen : yet the valley, though most impressively lonely, has not a gloomy character, as there is herbage in the bottom and on the sides of the hills, sparingly besprinkled with fine yew trees, of graceful form, and whose dark green foliage is of incomparable richness.

Something more than a mile above the bridge is a large detached rock, bearing a striking resemblance to a ruined tower : it appears from a distance to be covered with ivy, but when you approach, you perceive that it has a covering of ling or heath, whence it is called the Lingy Stone ; it has also the names of Black Cap and Hanging Stone. Above this rock, on the left, rises the magnificent crag called Sergeant Crag, on the same ridge with Eagle Crag. The path goes immediately beneath Lingy Stone. At the head of the valley is the dark and lofty mass of Bowfell, but the clouds rested upon it, so as to prevent me from seeing the summit.

Three miles from the entrance, the valley makes a gentle curve to the right, and at this place a mountain streamlet comes dashing down the hill on the left hand, joining the main stream, (which flows from beneath Bowfell,) at a *wash-fold*, that is, a fold where the sheep undergo the operation of washing. This is the commencement of the pass called the Stake. A zigzag path leads up the hill to the left,

besides the gill or stream which I have mentioned,
and which tumbles over great masses of slate rock, so
as to make a succession of falls.   The mountain-ash,
whose leaves had now turned scarlet and crimson, and
the graceful birch, overhang the gill.

   At a quarter past ten, two hours after leaving
Rosthwaite, I reached the top of the hill, though not
quite the highest part of the Stake, and Pike o'
Stickle came into view.   I proceeded on the path as
far as a small pile of stones, which is exactly at the
crown of the pass, and which marks the division of
Cumberland and Westmoreland.   On one side of this
boundary the water flows down into Langdale, and
on the other into Langstreth and Borrowdale.   Here,
according to the directions I had received, I quitted
the path, and went over a boggy moor in an oblique
direction to the left, aiming directly at the Pike o'
Stickle.   It caused some apprehension to perceive that
the clouds occasionally tipped the Pike in their
passage; but as they again cleared off, and as on the
best observation I could make they were not just at that
time lowering, I determined to persevere.   Yet I
thought it prudent to notice, as closely as I could, the
course of the gills, so that if the clouds should come
down on the mountain, I might by following the water
retrace my steps to the Stake.   Again and again both
Harrison Stickle and Pike o' Stickle were capped for
a little while, but the wind carried off the clouds, so
that I pressed on, and exactly at eleven o'clock I stood
upon the pointed summit of Pike o' Stickle.

The view down into Langdale is enough to make a person of good nerves tremble, though the top of the Pike is not so sharp a point as it seems from a distance. However I only stayed here a few moments. Harrison Stickle, which rises on the other side of a little elevated plain, and is four hundred feet higher than the Stickle Pike, smoked as though he was on fire ; and I could not with entire complacency find my head just touching the clouds, on a hill top of which I knew almost nothing, except that on two sides it was surrounded with frightful precipices. I therefore made all the haste I could to reach Harrison Stickle, which was still occasionally clear, and in twenty-five minutes more I sat down on his sublime throne. The view was not only transcendantly grand, but, from the clouds struggling with the sunshine on the elevated ranges of hills, it was of a most peculiar character. The tops of the high mountains, as Helvellyn, Fairfield, and Bowfell, were cut off by the clouds ; but immediately beneath the stratum of vapour, through occasional openings, there poured in floods of sun-beams, which illuminated large portions of the mountains ; and as the wind carried about the clouds, there was a continual shifting of light and shadow in vast masses, alternately revealing and shrouding hills and crags, like a phantasmagoria. It was a scene at once fascinating and wonderful. Whilst on Harrison Stickle the clouds were several times far beneath me, but they were so transparent, that I could see Windermere and most other distant objects through them.   At a fearful depth beneath the summit lies the Stickle-tarn on one side, with the stupendous precipices of Pavey Ark skirting it, and at the other side the more awful depth of Great Langdale.

The view from the Pikes is very extensive. That fine sheet, the head of Windermere, Esthwaite Water in its whole extent, Blea-tarn, Elterwater, a small part of Rydal Water, Loughrigg-tarn, Stickle-tarn, the river Leven running to the Bay of Morecambe, that extensive Bay itself, and the stream of the Brathay serpentizing through the whole length of Great Langdale,—such are the forms of water that are visible.   The mountain-view is even more imposing than from a higher elevation, because you have the advantage of seeing the fine outlines of the highest mountains rising above you, instead of looking down upon every other, as is the case from Scawfell Pikes.   The noble masses of Bowfell, Scawfell Pikes, and Great Gavel were unfortunately hidden on this occasion: but all that splendid range on the east, from Ingleborough southward, by the Sedbergh fells, the Shap fells, Hill Bell, High Street, Scandale, Fairfield, and Helvellyn, quite to Saddleback in the north, were seen, with the exception of the highest points of Helvellyn and Fairfield.   Here I saw below me, as in Langstreth I had seen above me, a falcon making his sublime circles in the mid-air, keenly watching for prey, but I did not chance to see him stoop.   The height of Harrison Stickle above the sea is 2400 feet, but his form is at least as bold as that of any other mountain in these counties.

Betwixt Pike o' Stickle and Harrison Stickle rises a third peak, called Gimmer Crag, high enough to hide Pike o' Stickle from spectators in many situations eastward, and bearing a considerable resemblance in its pointed form to that Pike. All the three summits are seen from Low Wood and the entrance to Great Langdale: but near Elterwater, and also at Rayrigg-bank on Windermere, only Harrison Stickle and Gimmer Crag are visible,—Pike o' Stickle being further back than either, and hid by the intervention of Gimmer Crag. The Stickle Pike is seen to the greatest advantage from Langdale-head, where it looks like a pillar of the skies; it is also distinctly seen from Skiddaw: but from all points eastward, owing to its situation, its elevation appears less than it really is.

After remaining about ten minutes on Harrison Stickle, as the clouds still occasionally gathered and lowered, so as partly to hide the valley from me, I thought it expedient to descend. The descent to the tarn is exceedingly steep, and the precipices on either hand are terrific. Leaving Stickle tarn (famous for its excellent trout,) on my left hand, I followed the course of the stream which issues from it; the descent into Great Langdale requires caution and patience, as the hill is not only steep, but its surface is very hard and slippery. At a quarter before one o'clock, I reached Millbeck, in the valley, seven miles from Ambleside.

At Chapel Style, two miles further down the valley, I made a dinner of eggs, cheese, oat-cake, and butter; and I received, moreover, a severe scolding from the landlady of the public-house, for going on the fells in such weather, and so late in the season. " You'll never be cured till you're lost," she said, " and then you'll learn :" and she told me of several persons who had been enveloped in clouds on the fells, and had narrowly escaped with their lives. There was as much real kindness as plainness of speech in the good lady; and as it was then too late for me to profit by her advice, seeing that my tour was at an end, I record it for the benefit of all adventurously disposed travellers who may honour these pages with a perusal.

About four o'clock I re-entered Ambleside,—having in the last three days ascended three high mountains, Skiddaw, Great Gavel, and the Langdale Pikes, and passed through some of the most magnificent valleys in the district of the Lakes.

THE END.

AN

ITINERARY OF THE LAKES,

INCLUDING

A DESCRIPTIVE ACCOUNT OF THE TOWNS AND VILLAGES,
NOBLEMEN'S AND GENTLEMEN'S SEATS, MOUNTAINS,
LAKES, WATERFALLS, AND OTHER OBJECTS WORTHY
OF NOTICE: FOR THE INFORMATION AND GUIDANCE
OF TOURISTS.

Made from actual Survey, and corrected to 1834.

CONTENTS.

P

LANCASTER to KENDAL, by KIRKBY LONSDALE, 30 miles.

	From Lancaster.			From Lancaster.
Miles.	Miles.	Miles.		Miles.
5 Caton	5	2 Tunstall		13
2 Claughton............	7	2 Burrow		15
2 Hornby	9	2 Kirkby Lonsdale		17
2 Melling	11	13 Kendal		30

LANCASTER, the capital of the county palatine of Lancaster, is an ancient town, very finely situated on a hill rising abruptly from the river Lune, which falls into the bay of Morecambe at the distance of seven miles. On the summit of the hill is the castle, a majestic structure, originally built by Roger de Poictou, in the 11th century, and re-edified by John of Gaunt, Duke of Lancaster, in the 14th. It has been repaired and greatly enlarged in modern times, and now serves as the county gaol; it is one of the most secure and best regulated prisons in the kingdom. The Assizes are held in the castle, and the Nisi Prius Court is a spacious and beautiful Gothic hall. The parish church of St. Mary's, an ancient structure with a lofty tower, stands on the castle-hill; it consists of a nave and two side-aisles, and contains some curious monuments and specimens of antiquity. There are several other episcopal and dissenting places of worship in the town. The principal public buildings are, the town-hall, in the Market-place; the custom-house, on St. George's Quay; the assembly room, and the theatre. The County Lunatic Asylum, on Lancaster Moor, a mile to the east of the town, is a handsome building, capable of accommodating 300 patients: it is near the race-course. The workhouse is in a commanding situation on the Lancaster side of the same hill. The foreign commerce of Lancaster, though very considerable thirty years since, is now much circumscribed, having been injured by the competition of Liverpool. The navigation of the Lune is difficult at neap tides, in consequence of the sand-banks; and the larger ships generally unload at Glasson Dock, distant five miles from the town. Lancaster is connected with the principal towns of the county by a canal ninety miles in length, which is carried over the Lune, a mile from the town, by a magnificent aqueduct of five arches, erected by the late Mr. Rennie. In consequence of the recent communication made between this canal and Glasson Dock, and of the erection of large warehouses at the latter place for the reception of grain and other commodities, a great part of the Irish trade of Kendal and Preston, as well as of Lancaster, is now carried on through Glasson and the canal, and the trade is annually increasing. Packet boats of a new construction, very long, narrow, and flat-bottomed, are drawn on these canals by horses at the rate of eight or nine miles an hour, and form a cheap and pleasant mode of travelling. A steam-packet passes weekly, and frequently twice a week, between Lancaster and Liverpool, and conveys both passengers and goods; but it is irregular in the days of departure. The principal manufactures are, mahogany furniture, cordage, sail cloth, cotton goods, candles, hats, &c. The new bridge is a fine structure of five arches. There is a salmon-fishery in the Lune, which has of late years been much less productive than formerly. Lancaster is incorporated under a mayor, aldermen, &c., and sends two representatives to parliament. It is a great thoroughfare, and has numerous stage-coaches. Population 12,613; market-days, Wednesday and Saturday; inns, *King's Arms* and *Royal Oak.*

*** To Liverpool 53 m.; to Manchester 53 m.; to Preston 22 m.; to Kirkby Lonsdale 15 and 17 m.; to Kendal 22 m.; to Carlisle 66 m.; to Ulverston 21 m.; to London 239 m.

The following seats are near the town, in addition to those mentioned on the northern roads:—S. of the town, Springfield, Henry Hargreaves, Esq.; 1 m. Aldcliffe-hall, Edward Dawson, Esq.; 2 m. Stodday-lodge, Henry Borron Fielding, Esq.; 3 m. Ashton-hall, the Duke of Hamilton; 4 m. Thurnham-hall, John Dalton, Esq.; 5 m. the Lawnd, James Clarke, Esq.; 5½ m. Ellel-hall, unoccupied. E. of the town, 7 m. Wyerside, late John Fenton Cawthorne, Esq. N. E. 2½ m. Halton-hall, Robert F. Bradshaw, Esq.; 4 m. Halton-park, Thomas H. Bateman, Esq. W. 3 m. Poulton-hall, Anthony Eidsforth, Esq.

Caton, 1¼ m. before, and 3¼ m. from Lancaster, is an extremely fine view, from a field above the road, of the beautiful and fertile vale of the Lune, with Ingleborough towering over its head. 2 m. before, on the r. Quernmore-park, Mrs. Gibson; entering, on the r. Grass-yard-hall, Thomas Edmondson, Esq.; on the l. Miss Barrow.

Claughton, the ancient hall, on the r. of the village, is now inhabited by a farmer. ½ m. before, on the r. West End, Samuel Still, Esq.

Hornby, on an eminence on the r. Hornby-castle, the heirs of John Marsden, Esq.: part of the castle is ancient, and formerly belonged to the Barons Monteagle: on the l. Hornby-hall, John Murray, Esq.

Melling, on the r. Melling-hall, Wm. Gillison Bell, Esq.: beyond, on the r. Crow Trees, Reginald Remmington, Esq., 1 m. on the r. Wennington-hall, Misses Salisbury.

Tunstall, ½ m. before, on the r. Thurland-castle, Richard Toulmin North, Esq. 1 m. before, on the r. Cantsfield-house, Richard Tatham, Esq.

Burrow, on the r. Burrow-hall, Mrs. Smith; 1 m. on the l. beyond the Lune, Whittington-hall, Thomas Greene, Esq. M.P.; 1 m. beyond, on the r. Summerfield, Trotter Tatham, Esq.

¼ a mile from Kirkby Lonsdale, cross the Lune, and enter Westmoreland.

KIRKBY LONSDALE, a small neat town, beautifully situated on the west bank of the Lune.   The church-yard is celebrated for the fine views it affords of the valley.   The bridge over the Lune is very old, and is an admirable structure, though inconveniently narrow: it is lofty, and has three arches beautifully ribbed.   The mills are singularly situated, on the side of a steep bank, and one above the other, so as to receive in turns the fall of water from a brook which is conveyed through the town: seven wheels are turned by the water in its descent into the valley. Population 1686 ; market-day, Thursday ; inns, *Rose and Crown, Green Dragon.*

*** To Kendal 13 m. ; to Lancaster 15 and 17 m. ; to Settle 17 m. ; to London 252 m.

1 m. on the r. Casterton-hall, Wm. Wilson Carus Wilson, Esq. ; ½ m. on the l. Underley-park, Alexander Nowell, Esq. ; on the r. entering, Lune-field, Mrs. Carus ; 3 m. up the Lune, Rigmaden-park, Christopher Wilson, Esq.

KENDAL, or *Kirkby in Kendal,* is a neat and flourishing town, the largest in Westmoreland, standing on the banks of the river Kent.   It is situated in a very agreeable valley, beneath a lofty scar or cliff, which rises over the west side of the town.   On the opposite side of the river are the remains of the ancient castle, situated on a considerable elevation, and commanding a beautiful prospect: the castle formerly belonged to the family of Parr, and Catherine, the last Queen of Henry VIII. was born there.   On the western side of the town is an artificial mound, called Castlelaw-hill, on which the inhabitants, in 1788, erected an obelisk to commemorate the glorious revolution of 1688.   The church is a spacious Gothic structure, and has three chapels, memorials of the ancient dignity of three neighbouring families, the Bellinghams, Stricklands, and Parrs.   There are several other places of worship in the town.   Besides the public buildings of long standing, are recently erected the White-hall, in Lowther-street, a large handsome building : a handsome structure, situate in Highgate, for the purpose of carrying on the concerns of the Westmoreland Joint Stock Bank ; and near Abbot-hall gates, an imposing building in the Gothic style, for the residence of a limited number of spinsters.   Kendal has long been famous for a manufacture of coarse woollens, called *Kendal cottons,* linseys, serges, druggets, hats, leather, and especially of knit worsted stockings.   The manufacture of these articles has, however, of late years greatly declined, and they have been succeeded by finer manufactures, principally of fancy waistcoatings.   The trade of the town is facilitated by its canal communication with the principal rivers and towns of Lancashire, Yorkshire, and the centre and south of England. It is a great thoroughfare to the north, and most of the visiters to the Lakes pass through the town. Kendal is a corporate town, governed by a mayor, 12 aldermen, and 20 capital burgesses. It received the right of sending one member to Parliament under the Reform Act, and its first member was James Brougham, Esq., on whose death John Barham, Esq., was elected. Population (including the township of Kirkland) 11,753; market-day, Saturday; inns, *King's Arms*, *Commercial Inn.*

*** To Lancaster 22 m.; to Kirkby Lonsdale 13 m.; to Newby-bridge 12 m. over Cartmel-fell, and 17 m. by Levens-bridge and the New Road; to Bowness 9 m.; to Hawkshead 13 m.; to Ambleside 13½ m.; to Penrith, 26 m.; to Appleby 23 m.; to Ulverston 20 m. over Cartmel-fell, and 27 m. by Levens-bridge and the New Road; to London 261 m.

1 m. before on the l. Helme-lodge, Wm. Dilworth Crewdson, Esq.; Watts-field, William Walker, Esq.; ½ m. before, on the l. Collin-field, Anthony Yeats, Esq.; entering on the r. Abbot-hall, Edward Wilson, Esq.; 1 m. on the Penrith road, Mint-house, Isaac Metcalf, Esq.; 4 m. N.E. Shaw-end, Arthur Shepherd, Esq.; 5 m. N.E. Mosedale-hall, James Thompson, Esq.; 6 m. N.E. Holme Park, Rev. T. Airey; on the r. going out on the Ambleside road, Green-bank, Benj. Atkinson, Esq.; 2 m. on that road, on the r. Tolson-hall, John Bateman, Esq.; 1 m. E. Park-side, R. Benson, Esq.; Birklands, Edward Wakefield, Esq.

LANCASTER *to* KENDAL, *by* Milnthorpe, 21¼ m.

Miles.		From Lancaster. Miles.	Miles.		From Lancaster. Miles.
2¾	Slyne	2¾	½	Beetham	12½
1¼	Bolton-le-Sands	4	1¼	Milnthorpe	13¾
2	Carnforth	6	1¼	Heversham	15
2	Junction of the Milnthorpe and Burton roads	8	1½	Levens-bridge	16½
4	Hale	12	1½	Sizergh	18
			3¼	Kendal	21¼

On leaving Lancaster cross the Lune, and a mile from the town cross the Lancaster canal.

1 m. from Lancaster, on the l. Lune-villa, Robert Gawthrop, Esq.; 1½ m. on the l. Cross-hill, Richard Clark, Esq.; 1½ m. on the r. Beaumont-hall; a little further on the r. Beaumont-castle, Rev. R. Gibson; Hest-bank lodge, Mrs. Salisbury.

Slyne, on the r. Slyne-house, R. Green Bradley, Esq.

Bolton-le-Sands; before and beyond the village, very fine view are obtained of the bay of Morecambe and the mountains of Westmoreland and Cumberland.

DUNALD MILL HOLE, 2 m. to the r. of Carnforth is the remarkable cave, called Dunald Mill Hole, into which a considerable brook sinks by several cascades, and runs under ground till it rises again at Carnforth. Visiters may descend into the cave, and follow the course of the stream for several hundred feet; the remarkable rocks of the cave, the fantastic masses and stalactites pendant from the roof, and the roar of the waters in their rocky channel, render this place highly interesting.

Carnforth, 2 miles beyond, on the r. is Borwick-hall, partly in a ruinous state; 2½ miles on the right, Caponwray, Colonel Marton; 2¼ miles beyond, on the left, Hyning-hall, John Bolden, Esq.; 3 miles beyond, on the left, Leighton-hall, Richard Gillow, Esq.; 3½ miles beyond, on the left, Morecambe-lodge, John Ford, Esq. 1 mile beyond, cross the Keer.

Hale, 1 mile before, enter Westmoreland; 1 mile on the right, Elmsfield, William Cotton, Esq.

Beetham, ¼ mile before, on the left, Beetham-hall; Beetham-house, William Hutton, Esq.

MILNTHORPE, a small market-town, on the estuary of the Kent; it is the only seaport in Westmoreland, and has trade to Liverpool, Glasgow, &c. Population (with Heversham) 1509; market-day, Friday; inn, *Cross Keys.*

⁎ To Burton 4½ miles; to Newby-bridge 14 miles; to Ulverston 22 miles; to Bowness 14 miles, (3 miles nearer than by Kendal); to Kendal 7½ miles; to London 253 miles.

Half mile to the left, Dallam Tower, George Wilson, Esq.

Heversham, on the r. Plumtree-hall, ⸺ Wilson, Esq.

Levens-bridge; cross the Kent; the roads to Bowness, Newby-bridge, and Ulverston, turn off to the left. There is a beautiful walk from the bridge, through Levens-park, and by the shaded banks of the Kent, to Kendal, 5½ m. On the left, Levens-hall, the Hon. Fulk Greville Howard; 1½ mile beyond, on the left, Eaves-lodge, James Gandy, Jun. Esq.

Sizergh; on the left, Sizergh-hall, Thomas Strickland, Esq.; on the right, across the river, Sedgwick-house, J. Wakefield, Esq.

Kendal, see p. 316.

LANCASTER to KENDAL, by BURTON, 21¾ m.

From Lancaster.		From Lancaster.	
Miles.	Miles.	Miles.	Miles.
10¾ Burton	10¾	2¾ Barrow's Green	18¾
4¾ Crooklands	15¼	3 Kendal	21¾
½ End Moor	16		

8 miles from Lancaster, leave the Milnthorpe-road to the left. (see p. 317.)

BURTON, a small market-town in Westmoreland ½ m. beyond the Lancashire boundary; population 733: market-day, Tuesday: inns, *King's Arms, Royal Oak*.

*** To Kendal 11 m.; to Kirkby Lonsdale 6½ m,; to Milnthorpe, 4½ m.

1½ m. before, on the l. Buxton-house, Mrs. Burrow; 1 m. on the r. entering, Dalton-hall, Edmund Hornby, Esq,; on the r. Burton-house, Mrs. Atkinson, the Vicarage, Rev. Byran Waller; on the r. going out, Church-bank, John Williams, Esq.; Curwen Woods, Thomas Collon, Esq.

End Moor, ½ m. before, on the l. Old-hall, —— Vincent, Esq.

Kendal, see p. 316.

———

LANCASTER *to* ULVERSTON, over Sands, 21 m.

From Lancaster.			From Lancaster.	
Miles.		Miles.	Miles.	Miles.
3¼	Hest Bank	3¼	1¼ Flookburgh	15
¼	Lancaster Sands	3½	½ Cark	15¾
9	Kent's Bank	12½	¼ Leven Sands	16
1	Lower Allithwaite	13¾	5 Ulverston	21

2¼ m. from Lancaster, turn off the Milnthorpe-road on the left.

Hest Bank, a bathing place, agreeably situated on Morecambe-bay.

LANCASTER SANDS. At the ebb of the tide, the shores of Morecambe-bay are left dry to the extent of several miles from land; and, the sands being very firm, it is common to pass over them in going from Lancaster to Ulverston, as this route is 15 miles shorter than that by Milnthorpe and Newby-bridge. The tract varies, as the channel formed by the sea is sometimes nearer and sometimes further from the shore: in June, 1828, and for some months previous, the track was 11 miles in length, though it is frequently not more than 9, and sometimes only 7. The principal danger is in crossing the rivers Keer and Kent, which run over the sands to the sea; and here, therefore, Guides are stationed, (appointed by the Duchy of Lancaster) whose duty it is to conduct travellers safely across the rivers. The guides receive a small stipend, but it is customary for travellers to give them a few pence. The guide at the Keer is on foot, as the river is very shallow; at the Kent the guide is on horseback, the river being considerably wider and deeper. The latter has obtained the name of *the Carter*, the duties of the guide having been performed by a family of that name for many generations. The sands can only be crossed when the tide is out, and should never be attempted without the guides: at high water the track is covered by from 9 to 19 feet of water. A coach formerly passed over the sands, between Lancaster and Ulverston, but the sands having become increasingly dangerous, it was discontinued. The views here are extremely fine, comprising the whole coast of the bay of More-cambe, Pile Castle at its entrance, the bold crags of Warton and Arnside-fells on the right, Ingleborough to the east, the finely broken and wooded shores of the Kent, and a noble range of the Westmoreland and Cumberland mountains.—Arnside-tower, once a mansion of the Stanleys, is seen under the fells of that name; and Castlehead, the elegant seat of the late John Wilkinson, Esq. (now of Robert Wright, Esq.) at the pyramidal hill, three miles above Kent's Bank, on the western shore.

Kent's Bank; 2 miles on the r. Blawith Cottage, Thos. Holme Maude, Esq.

Lower Allithwaite; 2 miles to the r. is

CARTMEL, a small market-town, containing 347 inhabitants; there is a spring of medicinal qualities, from two to three miles distant, called Holy Well; the church is an ancient and handsome structure; it was formerly a priory, and contains some interesting monuments. Near the town are Bigland-hall, George Bigland, Esq.; Broughton-hall, Gray Rigge, Esq.; Broughton-house, John Atkinson, Esq.; Broughton-grove, Richard Machell, Esq.; Aynsome, Reverend Thomas Remington; Green-bank, John Wilkinson, Esq.; Ivy Cottage, Jonathan Lodge, Esq.

Cark, ½ mile on the r. is the finely-situated mansion of Holker-hall, the Earl of Burlington, where there is a valuable collection of pictures.

LEVEN SANDS. The estuary of the Leven, ½ m. beyond Cark, is three miles across, and is left dry at low water, except the channel which conveys the united waters of the Leven and the Crake to the sea. A guide on horseback is stationed here, and is very necessary, as the channel of the Leven shifts frequently, and renders the sands dangerous. The views in crossing are splendid; on one side are the woods of Holker-hall, on the other the grounds of Conishead-priory, and to the north the estuary conducts the eye to a grand amphitheatre of mountains round the head of Coniston Water and Windermere. There is a small island below the ford, called Chapel Island, on which are the ruins of a chapel originally dependent on Conishead Priory.

ULVERSTON, a well-built and flourishing market-town, the capital of Furness, is situated at the foot of green and sloping fells. It has two handsome churches, one recently built by a subscription of £5000, and a grant of the Parliamentary Commissioners. The town is the mart for the agricultural and mineral productions of Furness, and its market on Thursday is extremely well attended. The manufactures of cotton and linen are carried on to a consider-able extent, and great quantities of blue slate, limestone, and iron oré, extracted from the neighbouring fells, are shipped here. The canal which connects the town with the Leven and Morecambe-bay is 1¼ mile in length, and is said to be the shortest, widest, and deepest in England, admitting vessels of 200 tons burthen. 1 m. to the S. W. of the town is Swarth Moor-hall, once the residence of George Fox, the celebrated founder of the sect of Quakers, and near it is a meeting-house built by Fox, and still used by the Friends, whose number and respectability are great in these parts: the old hall is inhabited by a farmer, and is considerably dilapidated. The principal iron mines of Furness are at Whitrigs, 3 m. on the Dalton-road, and they yield the richest ore found in the kingdom: great quantities of it are shipped at Barrow, within the port of Ulverston, 2 m. below Furness Abbey. There is a coach daily to and from Lancaster, by Newby-bridge and Milnthorpe; and a one-horse car goes daily to Whitehaven, through Brough-ton, Ravenglass, and Egremont. Population 4876: inns, *Sun, Braddyll's Arms.*

** To Lancaster, (over Sands,) 21 m. (by Cartmel,) 33¼ m. (by Newby-bridge,) 36 m.; to Newby-bridge 8 m.; to Bowness 16 m.; to Kendal 27 m.; to Ambleside, by Coniston Water, 22 m.; to Hawkshead (by Coniston Water) 19 m.; (by Pennybridge) 16 m.; to Broughton 9½ m.; to Whitehaven 44 m.; to London 260 m.

2 miles south of the town are the delightful grounds of Conishead Priory, Thomas Richmond Gale Braddyll, Esq. who is now rebuilding his mansion on a scale of great expense and splendour. The traveller who passes through Ulverston should not omit visiting Conishead Priory, and especially the hermitage in the park. Near Ulverston, on the S. Little Croft, William Gale, Esq.; Belle Vue, Mrs. Dodgson; Spring-field, Rev. John Sunderland; going out on the W. Fair View, Charles S. Kennedy, Esq.; ½ m. on the E. the Lund, Benson Harrison, Esq.

FURNESS ABBEY, whose interesting and magnificent remains ought to be seen by every visitor to the Lakes, is 6 miles S. W. of Ulverston, and 1 mile beyond Dalton. The Abbey was founded A.D. 1127, by Stephen, Earl of Mortaign and Boulogne, afterwards King of England, and was endowed with the lordship of Furness, and many royal privileges. The monks were of the Cistercian order. The Abbey is situated in a close valley, called "the glen of the deadly night shade." The remains amply attest the former magnificence of the structure: the walls of the church, the chapter-house, the refectorium, and the school-house, are still in a great part remaining, and show fine specimens of Gothic architecture; the chapter-house, 60 feet by 45, has been a sumptuous apartment; the roof, which was of fret-work, was supported by six channeled pillars. The great east window, the four seats near it adorned with Gothic ornaments, and four statues found in the ruins, are particularly worthy of notice. A few years ago, the late

Earl of Burlington,* the proprietor, caused the rubbish which choked up many of the apartments, to be cleared away, and the effect of the ruin is now greatly improved, besides that many beautiful fragments of sculpture and of columns and capitals were discovered during the operations.

The small town of *Dalton* was formerly the capital of Furness : it has an old square tower, the remains of a castle.   Population 759; market-day, Saturday.—In returning from Dalton, the traveller may take the Urswick road, and pass over Birkrigg, the top of which commands a most extensive prospect of the sea and the mountains, stretching to Wales and the Isle of Man, and may visit Conishead Priory in his return to Ulverston.

ULVERSTON to HAWKSHEAD, by CONISTON WATER-HEAD, 19 m.

Miles.	From Ulverston. Miles.	Miles.	From Ulverston. Miles.
6	Lowick-bridge 6	8	Coniston Water Head 16
2	Nibthwaite 8	2	Hawkshead 19

Lowick-bridge ; 1½ m. before, at the separation of the Broughton and Hawkshead roads, a very fine view is obtained of Coniston Water and the mountains.   The Old Man towers over the head of the lake, flanked by Wetherlam on his right and Walna Scar on his left; in the extreme distance, Scawfell Pikes appear more to the left, and the range of Helvellyn and Fairfield to the right.   1 mile before, on the left, Lowick-hall, inhabited by a farmer. Cross the Crake, which flows out of Coniston Water.   ¼ mile below the bridge, Bridgefield, Joseph Penny, Esq.

Nibthwaite ; 1 mile before, on the left, the iron forge of Messrs. Harrison, Ainslie, and Co.; ¼ mile beyond, on the left, Water Park, Benson Harrison, Esq. : an extremely fine view of Coniston Water and the mountains from this point.   The road follows the eastern bank of

CONISTON WATER.   This lake, sometimes called *Thurston Water,* is 6 miles long, and ¾ mile in its greatest breadth; it has two small islands, both of them near the shore : its greatest depth is 27 fathoms, and it abounds in trout and char.   The shores of the lake are very beautiful.   The Old Man rises near the head of the lake to the height of 2657 feet ; on the summit of the mountain, which commands a most extensive prospect, are three heaps of stones, called the Old Man, his Wife, and Son, and a beacon has formerly been there.

Coniston Water Head ; there is here a good inn, delightfully

---

* Since the "*Companion*" was printed off, the Earl of Burlington who was formerly Lord George Cavendish, is deceased, and his grandson has inherited his title and estates.

situated at the head of the lake, (a mile from the village of Coniston): 2½ miles before, on the right, Brantwood, Mrs. Copley; 2 miles before, on the left, Coniston-bank, William Bradshaw, Esq.: ¼ mile before, on the left, Tent-lodge, Mrs. Smith; ½ mile on the Coniston road, Thwaite-house, John Beever, Esq.; above the inn, Waterhead, Michael Knott, Esq.

HAWKSHEAD, a small, neat market-town, the principal place in Furness Fells, is situated in a warm and sheltered valley, near the head of the beautiful lake of Esthwaite. The views round it are very fine; the mountains of the Coniston and Langdale districts, with those round the head of Windermere, may all be seen. Hawkshead-hall, 1 mile from the town, in which the abbots of Furness formerly held a court, is now tenanted by a farmer. Population 797; market-day, Monday; inn, *Red Lion.*

*** To Ambleside 5 miles; to Ulverston 16 miles; to Bowness 5½ miles; to Kendal 13 miles; to Newby-bridge 8 miles.

ULVERSTON *to* BOWNESS, 16 m.

Miles.	*From Ulverston.*	Miles.	Miles.	*From Ulverston.*	Miles.
3	Green Odd	3	1	Newby-bridge	8
3	Low-wood	6	8	Bowness	16
1	Backbarrow	7			

Green Odd—cross the river Crake at its confluence with the Leven. ½ mile on the left, at Penny-bridge, James Penny Machell, Esq.

Low-wood—at this place, on the river Leven, is a considerable manufactory of gunpowder, carried on by Messrs. Daye Barker and Co; ½ mile before, on the right, Hollow Oak, Miss Machell; 3 miles distant, on the left, Oxen-park, John Robinson, Esq.; Whitestock-hall, George Romney, Esq.

Backbarrow—cross the river Leven: here is an extensive cotton manufactory, carried on by Messrs. Ainsworth, Catterall, and Co.; and Backbarrow iron-works, carried on by Messrs. Harrison, Ainslie and Co.

Newby-bridge; here is an excellent inn, charmingly situated at the foot of Windermere. On the right, James Machell, Esq.; 1 mile beyond, on the left, Fell-foot, James Starkie, Esq.; Landing, John Harrison, Esq.; 1 mile further, on the margin of the lake, Townhead, William Townley, Esq.; 3 miles from Newby-bridge, Gill-head, John Poole, Esq.

From Town-head to Bowness, 6 miles on the borders of Windermere, there are beautiful views of the lake and of the Coniston and Langdale mountains.

Bowness; 2 miles before, Storrs-hall, John Bolton, Esq.; 1 mile before, Belfield, Andrew Henry Thomson, Esq.; Ferney-green, Robert Greaves, Esq.   (For Bowness, see p. 325.)

HAWKSHEAD *to* AMBLESIDE, 5 m.

1 mile from Hawkshead, on the right, Belmont, unoccupied; 1 mile on the left, Field-head, unoccupied; a little above, Borwick Lodge, unoccupied.

Ambleside, 1½ mile before, on the right, Brathay-hall, John Harden, Esq.; 1 mile before, on the left, Howsley-cottage, Mrs. Freeman; on the right, Croft lodge, James Brancker, Esq.; 3 miles to the left, in Great Langdale, Elterwater hall, John Huddlestone, Esq.

(For *Ambleside* see p. 326.)

HAWKSHEAD *to* BOWNESS, 5½ m.

Sawrey 2 miles; Windermere-ferry 2 miles; Bowness 1½ m.—Total 5½ miles.

ESTHWAITE WATER, a beautiful lake, 2 miles in length, and half a mile in breadth, skirted by woods and meadows. In a small pool nearly adjoining the upper end of the lake, is a floating island, on which are several trees and shrubs: the island is moved from side to side of the pool by the changing wind. 1 mile down the west side of the lake, Esthwaite-lodge, Thomas Alcock Beck, Esq.; 1 mile down the east side, Lake-bank, William Towers, Esq.

Sawrey—Mount, John Eccles, Esq.; Sawrey-house, Thomas Beck Towers, Esq.; Lake-field. Rt. M. Frazer, Esq.; Cottage, James Watson, Esq. In ascending the hill which separates Esthwaite Water from Windermere, there is a splendid view of the Coniston and Langdale mountains; in descending on the other side there is an equally fine view of Windermere.

Windermere Ferry; here is a good inn, delightfully situated; horses and carriages pass by the Ferry. Above the inn is a pleasure house, called the Station, belonging to Henry C. Curwen, Esq., whence some of the most charming views of Windermere are to be had. 4 m. below, on the w. side of the lake, Graythwaite-hall, Miles Sandys, Esq.; Low Graythwaite-hall, John Job Rawlinson, Esq.

(For *Bowness* see p. 325.)

KENDAL *to* AMBLESIDE, *by* BOWNESS, 15 m.

	From Kendal.			*From Kendal.*
Miles.	Miles.	Miles.		Miles.
3 Bonning Yate............	3	2 Bowness...		9
2½ Quaker's Meeting house	5½	2½ Troutbeck bridge 11½		
		2 Low Wood Inn 13½		
1½ Clay Barrow	7	1½ Ambleside 15		

The road from Kendal to Bowness possesses nothing of interest, except the views of the distant mountains, Coniston Old Man, Bowfell, Langdale Pikes, &c. till, at the distance of a mile from Bowness, the traveller comes within view of

WINDERMERE, or *Winandermere*. This is the largest of the English lakes, and its scenery is of the most exquisite beauty, rising towards the head into magnificence. It is 10½ miles in length, measured down the middle, and its greatest breadth is more than a mile. In some places it is 35 fathoms deep. The lake is principally fed by the rivers Brathay and Rothay, which fall into it at the head, and by the stream of Troutbeck, on the eastern side : its waters discharge themselves by the Leven at Newby-bridge. Windermere is adorned with no less than fourteen islands, called holms, the largest of which is Belle Isle, near the centre of the lake, opposite Bowness. It contains thirty acres, and was beautifully laid out in groves, lawns, and walks, by the late John Christian Curwen, Esq., who also built a handsome house upon it, in which his son, Henry C. Curwen, Esq. the present proprietor, resides. The lake abounds in trout, perch, pike, and char, the last being a rare and delicate fish, found only in the deepest of the lakes. Many handsome villas have been built on the shores, and the groves and pleasure-grounds attached to them add to the natural elegance of the scenery. The whole of the western shore of Windermere, and nearly half of the eastern, are in Lancashire, but the lake is considered to belong to West-moreland. There is a ferry over the lake, a mile below Bowness, which is the direct way to Hawkshead, distant four miles. Pleasure-boats may be engaged at all the principal places on the borders of the lake.

Bowness is charmingly situated near the centre of Windermere, on its eastern bank, and at the bottom of a small bay. It is the chief port on the lake, and has a few fishing vessels and a trade in charcoal. From its admirable situation it is much frequented by visiters, and has excellent accommodation for them in two good inns, the *White Lion* and the *Crown*, as well as in lodgings.

Rayrigg-bank, 1½ m. above Bowness, the Station, Belle Isle, and the hill above the village, afford the finest prospects.

In addition to Storrs-hall, Belfield, and Ferney-green, mentioned p. 324, and Belle Isle, there are, in or near the village,

Holly-hill, Mrs. Bellasis; The Villa, — Rudd, Esq.; the Rectory, Edward Swinburn, Esq.; and the houses of the Hon. Mrs. Carpenter, Captain Butcher, Captain Beaufoy, and G. A. Aufrere, Esq.; 2 m. up the lake, on the west side, Belle-grange, Edward Curwen, Esq; 3 m. the Wray, — Wilson, Esq.; and 1 m. on the Ambleside road, to the l. Rayrigg-hall, Rev. John Fleming.

Troutbeck bridge; from the elevated parts of the road before and beyond the bridge, splendid views are obtained of the head of Windermere and of the mountains, which appear in the following order, proceeding from left to right—Coniston Old Man, Wetherlam, Scawfell Pikes, (in the extreme distance,) Bowfell, Great Gavel (in the same distance,) Langdale Pikes, Loughrigg-fell, and Fairfield. The valley of Troutbeck is worth visiting, on account of its picturesque buildings. Half a mile before on the right, The Wood, the Misses Watson; 1 mile on the right, St. Catherine's, the Earl of Bradford; 2 miles on the r. The Howe, John Wilson, Esq.; just beyond, on the left, Calgarth Park, Rd. Luther Watson, Esq; half a mile to the right, Briary Close, Captain Greaves.

Low Wood Inn, an excellent inn, delightfully situated on a small bay, from which the head of Windermere opens out magnificently, with Brathay Park and the valley of Great Langdale beyond, and the mountains above mentioned forming the back ground. Many visiters take up their abode here for some time. Boats may be had at the inn, and the views from the surface of the lake are very fine. Half a mile beyond, Waterside, Thomas Jackson, Esq.; and Waterhead, Wm. Newton, Esq.

AMBLESIDE, a small town, romantically situated in the valley of the Rothay, a mile from the head of Windermere. It stands on the side of the hill, and is irregularly built, but commands charming prospects of the valley, the parks of Rydal and Brathay, and the lake of Windermere. From its central situation, Ambleside is frequently made the head-quarters of tourists for some time. There is a superior boarding school here. The town was formerly a Roman station, and faint traces of a fortress are to be seen in a field at the head of Windermere. Population, 1095; market-day, Wednesday.

*** To Kendal 13½ miles; to Hawkshead 5 miles; to Coniston Water Head, 8 miles; to Ulverston 24 miles; to Newby Bridge 14 miles; to Keswick 16¼ miles; to Patterdale 10 miles; to Penrith 25 miles; to London 278 miles.

In and near the town, The Cottage, H. T. Lutwidge, Esq.; The Oaks, Ford North, Esq.; Belle Vue, Miss Dowling; Green Bank, Benson Harrison, Esq.; Foxghyll, Mrs. Luff; Covey Cottage, Robt. Partridge, Esq.; Gale-house, Edward Pedder, Esq.; Broadlands, Rev. John Dawes; Hill-top, Thomas Carr, Esq.; Rothay-bank, Mrs. Claude; Croft-lodge, James Brancker,

Esq.; Brathay-hall, the property of — Redmayne, Esq., occupied by John Harden, Esq.; Oak-bank, Mrs. Carleton; Fox-howe, Dr. Arnold, (of Rugby.)

STOCKGILL FORCE, one of the most beautiful cascades among the Lakes, is in a deep glen, half a mile in the rear of the town. The fall is 150 feet in height, and the water is divided into two portions by a crag in the centre of the precipice.

KENDAL *to* AMBLESIDE, 13¾ m.

Miles.		From Kendal. Miles.	Miles.		From Kendal. Miles.
5	Staveley	5	1½	Troutbeck Bridge	10
1¼	Ings Chapel	6½	2	Low Wood Inn	12
2	Orest-head	8½	1¾	Ambleside	13¾

Orest-head; on the right, Orest-head, John Braithwaite, Esq.; on the left, Birthwaite, George Gardner, Esq.; a little beyond, on the right, Elleray, Professor Wilson; The Wood, Miss Watson; St. Catherine's, Earl of Bradford. An extremely fine view of Windermere is obtained from the brow of the hill.

Troutbeck Bridge, &c. (see p. 326.)

Many very interesting EXCURSIONS may be made from Ambleside. The finest is the *Langdale Excursion,* and parts of it may be taken in a carriage, but it is not uncommon to perform the whole excursion in carts. The traveller may proceed first to Skelwith-bridge, 3 miles, a little above which is the cascade of Skelwith Force; then, by a road which commands a fine view of Elterwater and Great Langdale, he may proceed to Colwith-bridge, above which is the waterfall of Colwith Force, 5 miles from Ambleside. Then, proceeding up Little Langdale, nearly three miles, he may turn to the right over a *slack,* in which lies Blea-tarn. Descending the hill to the head of Great Langdale, the Langdale Pikes appear before him, and Bowfell on his left, in the utmost sublimity. The conical pike is called Pike o' Stickle, and the broad-headed pike Harrison Stickle. He will come into Great Langdale at the farm house of Wall End, whence he might either ascend Bowfell, or pass the Stake into Borrowdale; but the regular excursion will bring him down the valley to Mill-beck, where he may see the curious waterfall of Dungeon Gill. Still descending the valley, he may turn to the left when he comes in view of Elterwater, and cross the hill by High Close to Grasmere, enjoying splendid views of Windermere and Langdale on one side, and of the lake and vale of Grasmere on the other. A road which leaves Grasmere and Rydal Lakes on the left will bring him back to Ambleside. This forms a circuit of eighteen miles ; but many content themselves with going to Skelwith Force, and then crossing Great Langdale, and passing over into Grasmere. Coniston Water, Hawkshead, and Bowness, may also be visited from Ambleside. Some pass over Kirkstone to Patterdale, at the head of Ullswater, 10 m.; but this is not the best way of seeing that noble lake. There are also mountain excursions to Rydal-Head, Fairfield, and to Wansfell Pike, which present very fine and extensive views.

AMBLESIDE *to* KESWICK, 16¼ m.

	From Ambleside.			*From Ambleside.*
Miles.	Miles.	Miles.		Miles.
1½ Rydal 1½		4	Smalthwaite-bridge ...12¼
3½ Swan, Grasmere......... 5		3	Castlerigg 15¼
2 Dunmail Raise 7		1	Keswick 16¼
1¼ Horse Head, Wythburn 8¼			

Rydal; on the right, Rydal-hall, Lady le Fleming ; in the grounds are two beautiful cascades; just above, Rydal Mount, Wm. Wordsworth, Esq. one of the most charming situations amongst the Lakes, looking down upon the vale of Ambleside and the lake of Windermere on the one hand, and the lake of Rydal on the other : the house and gardens are in the best taste ; the latter have assumed their present form in a great measure under the poet's own hand. Beyond, on the right, Ivy-cottage, Major Hamilton ; Rydal Cottage, Sir Thomas Sabine Pasley, Bart.

RYDAL WATER, one of the smallest of the lakes, being only a mile in length, but one of the most beautiful from its woody islands and picturesque shores.

GRASMERE WATER, a mile beyond Rydal Water, is about the same length as that lake, but wider, and has one considerable island, covered with verdure, in the centre. The views on every side of this lake are splendid, from the grand ampitheatre of mountains by which it is surrounded. Rising above the head of the lake is the lofty conical hill, called Helm Crag ; the summit is composed of vast rocks, in whose forms fancy has discovered a resemblance to a lion and lamb, and to an old woman cowering.

On the south side of the lake are Dale-end, Mrs. Carter ; Wyke, James Greenwood, Esq.; Gell's Cottage, T. Parry, Esq. ; and Allan Bank, J. Crump, Esq. The Rectory, the Rev. Sir Richard Fleming, Bart. On the north side of the lake, Hollins-grove, Mrs. Ashworth.

Swan, Grasmere : this inn is on the road side, a quarter of a mile from the village : travellers may be well accommodated here and at the Red Lion in Grasmere.

DUNMAIL RAISE, a considerable cairn of pebble stones, which marks the boundaries of Westmoreland and Cumberland, and was erected by Edmund I. King of England, when, he had defeated Dunmail, the last King of Cumbria, A. D. 945; Dunmail and his four sons were put to death, and his dominions given to Malcolm, King of Scotland. The views from this monument are extremely fine,—on the one hand the lake and vale of Grasmere—on the other the lake of Thirlmere and valley of Wythburn; with Helvellyn on the right, Thirlmere-fells on the left, and Skiddaw in the distance.

Horse Head, Wythburn, the half-way house, at the head of Thirlmere; 2 miles beyond, on the lake, Dalehead hall, Thomas Stanger Leathes, Esq. ; on the opposite side of the lake, Armboth · house, John Jackson, Esq.

THIRLMERE, often called *Leathes Water,* from the family to whose estate it belongs, and *Wythburn Water,* from the valley, is a narrow and deep lake, more than two and a half miles in length, little ornamented by trees or meadows, and lying betwixt the steep and rugged sides of Helvellyn and the Thirlmere-fells. It is five hundred feet above the level of the sea, which is higher than any of the other lakes. Near the foot of the lake, on the west side, is the dark and stupendous rock called Raven Crag, and higher up are Bull Crag and Fisher Crag.

HELVELLYN, one of the highest mountains in Cumberland, being 3055 feet above the level of the sea. Its summit, on which is a pile of stones, can only be seen at a considerable distance. The mountain may be ascended either from Wythburn or from Thrispot, near the 6th mile-stone from Keswick, or from Patterdale; the ascent is very steep, but not dangerous, except in the part called Striding-edge, on the Patterdale-side, and this part may be avoided by passing along Swirrel-edge. The view from the summit on a clear day is prodigiously extensive, comprehending the mountains of Wales and Scotland, and the Irish Sea.

Smalthwaite-bridge, cross the Greta, which issues from Thirlmere lake; leave St. John's Vale on the right.

Castlerigg; a splendid view is obtained from the brow of the hill, of the vale of Keswick, with Bassenthwaite Water four miles distant in front, Derwentwater at the foot of the hill on the left, Skiddaw and Saddleback on the right, Grisedale Pike, Grassmoor, and Causey Pike in front beyond the vale of Keswick, and the entrance of Borrowdale at the extreme left.

A DRUIDICAL TEMPLE lies half a mile to the right, consisting of 48 rude stones, some prostrate and some upright, disposed in an oval figure, 34 yards by 30.

KESWICK, a small market town, in a magnificent situation, between the foot of Skiddaw and Derwentwater, and near the river Greta. It may be considered as the capital of the Lakes, and is frequented by a great number of visiters during the season, who make excursions from it to the surrounding lakes, valleys, and mountains. The town is old, and most of the houses white-washed; it has a manufacture of coarse woollens, flannels, blankets, kerseys, &c. Black-lead pencils are also extensively made here, the mineral being found in the mines of Borrowdale. The parish church, called Crosthwaite church, is at a distance of a mile from the town. Crosthwaite's and Hutton's Museums, Mr. Green's Exhibition of Views of the Lakes, and several collections of minerals, are to be seen here. Guides and horses may be had for the excursions, and all the accommodations for visiters are very good. Population 2159. Market-day, Saturday; Inns, *Royal Oak* and *Queen's Head.*

₊ To Ambleside 16¼ m.; to Penrith 17¼ m.; to Cocker-mouth 13 m.; to Whitehaven 27 m.; to Workington 21 m.; to Carlisle (by Penrith) 36 m.; to Pooley-bridge 18 m.; to Patter-dale 22 m. (carriage road) 15 m. (horse-road); to Buttermere (by Newlands) 9 m.; to London 294 m.

Taking the circuit of Derwentwater, 2 miles from Keswick, on the eastern side of the lake, Barrow-house, Joseph Pocklington, Esq.; returning by the western side, 2½ m. from Keswick, Der-wentwater-bay, Alex. Hoy, Esq.; and Derwent-bank, Mrs. Bla-mire; 1¼ m. from Keswick, on the l. Derwent-lodge, Miss Keer; on the r. 1 m. from Keswick, Derwent-hill, Mrs. Turner; ap-proaching the town on the l. The Dove Cote, Jas. Stanger, Esq.; on the l. The Vicarage, Rev. James Lynn, (Rev. —— Whitesides;) Greta-hall, Robert Southey, Esq. LL.D.; Vicar's Island, in Derwentwater, Major-General Peachy; Greta-bank, Anthony Spedding, Esq.; l. m. Penrith road, on the r. Chesnut hill, G. Dare, Esq.; Ormathwaite-hall, (under Skiddaw) Capt. Joseph Dover; Skiddaw-lodge, Rev. Chauncey Hare Townsend.

DERWENTWATER, at a distance of half a mile from Keswick, is upwards of 3 m. in length, and 1½ in breadth: its greatest depth is 14 fathoms. It is adorned by several considerable islands, richly clothed with wood—Lord's Island, containing six acres, so called from having been the site of a house belonging to the Earls of Derwentwater; the Vicar's Isle, containing five acres and a half, so called from having belonged to Fountain's Abbey, and sometimes called Derwent Isle, on which is the house of General Peachy; St. Herbert's Island, near the centre of the lake, cele-brated as the residence of that holy man, who, according to Bede, died A.D. 678; Rampsholm; Otter Isle, in a bay near the head of the lake; and three islets. At the south-east corner of the lake, about 150 yards from the shore, is a floating island, which is generally under water, but occasionally rises to the surface, and appears for several weeks or months, when it again sinks. It has appeared seven times in the last twenty-six years. The lake is principally fed by the Derwent and Lowdore, which flow out of the valleys of Borrowdale and Watendlath. The scenery around Derwentwater is varied, and on every side magnificent. On the

north towers the simple and majestic form of Skiddaw ; on the
east are Wallow and Falcon Crags and the Derwent-fells ; the
savage valley of Borrowdale opens on the south, and conducts the
eye to Glaramara and Scawfell Pikes ; Catbells, Causey Pike, and
Grisedale Pike, overlook the western shore, and the delightful
vale of Newlands runs up betwixt them.   The best views of the
scenery are from the surface of the lake, from Castlehead—a
conical hill half a mile from Keswick, Crow Park, the Vicarage,
Latrigg, Wallow Crag, and Swinside.   All the land on the north-
east of Derwentwater formerly belonged to the Earls of Derwentwater, but was confiscated on the death of the last Earl, who was
beheaded for taking part in the rebellion of 1715, and until within
the last two years belonged to the Trustees of Greenwich Hospital, by whom it was sold, along with the extensive manorial
rights, to John Marshall, Jun., Esq. M. P. for Leeds.

SKIDDAW rises in a vast pyramidal form from the vale of Keswick.   It is 3022 feet in height, and is not difficult of ascent ; the
distance from Keswick to the summit is six miles, and ladies may
ride up on horseback, though not without considerable fatigue.
This mountain commands prospects of astonishing extent and
variety.   Cumberland lies as on a map beneath the eye : the Isle of
Man and the Scotch and Yorkshire mountains are distinctly visible.
Bassenthwaite Water lies immediately under the eye, but most of
the other lakes are hid by intervening mountains, and even Der-
wentwater by one of the summits of Skiddaw himself.   Scawfell
Pikes are distinctly seen due S., Helvellyn and Ingleborough
S. S. E., Grisedale Pike S. W., Cross-fell E., and Criffell, in
Scotland, N. W.

EXCURSIONS FROM KESWICK.

To BORROWDALE and ROUND DERWENTWATER, 12 m.

Miles.		Total Miles.	Miles.		Total Miles.
2	Barrow-house	2	1	Return to Grange	6
1	Lowdore	3	4½	Portinscale	10½
1	Grange	4	1½	Keswick..................	12
1	Bowder Stone	5			

Barrow-house, Joseph Pocklington, Esq. ; behind the house is a
beautiful cascade, 122 feet in height, in two falls.

LOWDORE : behind the inn, in a ravine betwixt Gowder-crag
and Shepherd's-crag, is the fine waterfall of Lowdore, falling over
and amongst a jumbled pile of rocks, to the depth of one hundred
and fifty feet.   In dry weather there is very little water here, but
after heavy rain it is a magnificent cataract.   In a meadow in front

of the inn is a remarkable echo, and a cannon is kept there to be discharged for the gratification of visiters.

Grange is situated in the Straits of Borrowdale.

BORROWDALE ; at Grange the grand and savage scenery of this valley commences. The valley is strewn with rocks of enormous size in the wildest disorder, and seems like the breaking up of nature. The river runs in a deep channel with rocky banks, and the mountains rise on either hand in rugged and awful crags. Numerous slate quarries, which yield excellent slate, are worked in the sides of the hills. Beyond Castle Crag and Bowder Stone the valley opens out into a small plain, which is equally fertile and beautiful, and in the midst of which is the village of Rosthwaite. The valley of Seathwaite forms the highest part of Borrowdale.

BOWDER STONE is a rock of extraordinary dimensions, which has fallen from the crags above, and is pitched on the edge of a precipice overhanging the river. The stone is 62 feet long and 36 high : its circumference is 89 feet, and it weighs 1971 tons. From this point a fine view of the upper part of Borrowdale is obtained, with Castle Crag on the right, the village of Rosthwaite, Eagle Crag and Glaramara in front, and Scawfell Pikes in the extreme distance. Travellers seldom proceed further than this, unless they intend visiting Buttermere and Wast Water. Return to

Grange, where the traveller may cross the Derwent, and return to Keswick by the western side of the lake, passing Derwentwater-bay and the entrance of the vale of Newlands.

To BORROWDALE *and* BUTTERMERE, 23 m.

Miles.		Total Miles.	Miles.		Total Miles.
5	Bowder Stone	5	2	Buttermere	14
1	Rosthwaite	6	9	Keswick, by New- lands	23
2	Seatoller	8			
4	Gatesgarth	12			

Seatoller is a hamlet in the upper part of Borrowdale, where John Fisher, Esq. has a house. A carriage may proceed as far as this place, but here begins the ascent of Borrowdale-hawse, and the road is so narrow, rugged, and steep, that cars pass with extreme difficulty. When the summit of the hawse is reached, Honister Crag on the left, and Yew Crag on the right, come in view. Honister springs from the vale in one enormous precipice 1500 feet high. The track descends through a desolate valley betwixt these mountains, to the hamlet of Gatesgarth and the vale of Buttermere.

BUTTERMERE. The lake of this name is a beautiful sheet, a mile and a quarter in length, and nearly half a mile in breadth. It is bordered on the east by fine woods and meadows, and overhung on the west by the rocky steeps of High-crag, High-stile, and Red-pike. In this secluded valley is Haseness, inhabited by the Rev. James Bush, a mile from the inn.

CRUMMOCK WATER is three quarters of a mile below Buttermere lake; it is nearly three miles in length, and three quarters of a mile in breadth, and lies between the mountains of Melbreak on the west and Grassmoor on the east. The head of the lake is highly beautiful, the middle part stern and grand, and the foot richly adorned with wood. Near the head is Woodhouse, Mr. Robert Jopson.

SCALE FORCE, on the west side of Crummock Water, is generally visited from Buttermere. The road being very boggy, it is usual to take a boat on Crummock Lake, row about a mile down the lake, and land at the opposite side, whence a rocky path of half a mile conducts to the waterfall. It is situated in a deep chasm, and the water falls at a single leap 156 feet; including a smaller fall below, the height of the cascade is nearly 200 feet.

*** Crummock Water and Buttermere may be visited more easily in a carriage by the route of Whinlatter and Lorton : this would make the distance to Buttermere 16 miles, and, if the same route were taken in returning, to avoid climbing the steep ascent of Buttermere-hawse, the day's journey would of course be thirty-two miles : many travellers go to the inn at Scale-hill, near the foot of Crummock Water, twelve miles from Keswick, and take a boat up the lake to Scale Force and Buttermere.

To WASDALE, ENNERDALE, and LOWES WATER.
A Two Days' Ride.

Miles.	From Keswick.	Miles.	Miles.	From Keswick.	Miles.
6	Rosthwaite	6	6	Strands, Nether Wasdale	20
2	Seatoller	8	4	Gosforth	24
1	Seathwaite	9	3	Calder Bridge	27
3	Sty-head	12			
2	Wasdale-head	14			

Second Day.

Miles.	From Calder Bridge.	Miles.	Miles.	From Calder Bridge.	Miles
7	Ennerdale-bridge	7	2	Scale-hill	16
3	Lamplugh Cross	10	4	Buttermere	20
4	Lowes Water	14	9	Keswick	29

Rosthwaite. The ride up Borrowdale to Seatoller has already been described, but, for this journey, it may be desirable to mention that at Rosthwaite is the last public-house before coming to Strands, in Nether Wasdale.

Seathwaite, the last village in Borrowdale ; on the hill to the r. are the celebrated wad-mines, from which the mineral vulgarly called black-lead and wad is extracted : these are the only mines of the kind in England.

Sty-head : a mile above Seathwaite, cross a bridge, and ascend the mountain, following the zig-zag track, and keeping the stream which flows out of Sty-head tarn on the right, till the path crosses it on the top of the hill and leaves the tarn to the left hand. The view down Borrowdale is extremely fine. Crossing Sty-head, the traveller has Great Gavel on his right and Great End on his left ; and when he comes to the descent into Wasdale, there is a magnificent view of Scawfell Pikes immediately before him.

SCAWFELL PIKES, the highest mountain in England, rise in one vast concave sweep from Wasdale Head, to the height of 3166 feet above the level of the sea. The summits are surrounded by frightful precipices, and the highest is crowned with a conical pile of stones built for the purpose of the trigonometrical survey. Scawfell has two principal summits, separated from each other by a deep chasm, called Mickle Door : the southern summit, which is 66 feet lower than the other, is called Scawfell, and the northern summit Scawfell Pikes. The latter may be most easily visited from Seathwaite in Borrowdale, and the former from Wasdale or Eskdale. This mountain is much more difficult of ascent than Skiddaw or Helvellyn, the top being composed of great blocks of stone, with scarcely a symptom of vegetation. Nevertheless, a good pedestrian may accomplish it with a guide, and will be repaid by the most complete prospect to be any where had of the mountains of Cumberland and Westmoreland. This is the highest and central point, from which the principal valleys diverge on every side. The Welsh mountains, the Isle of Man, the Scotch, Northumbrian, and Yorkshire mountains are all within view.

WAST WATER. After descending the steep and painful track from Sty-head, and walking nearly two miles down Wasdale-head and by the hamlet of that name, the traveller comes to Wast Water, a lake three miles long, half a mile broad, and forty-five fathoms in depth, lying along the foot of a high ridge called the Screes. The scenery is grand and desolate. At the foot of the lake, Wasdale-hall, Stansfeld Rawson, Esq. ; one mile below, Stang Ends, late the residence of Robert Wilkinson, Esq.

Strands, a village containing two comfortable inns, a mile beyond the lake. Here the mountains terminate, and the road passes over a comparatively level country, open to the sea, to

Calder-bridge ; a most delightful village on the river Calder, 9 miles south of Whitehaven. There are two excellent inns ; and contiguous to the village, on the left, in a spacious park, stands Ponsonby-hall, the seat of Edward Stanley, Esq., M.P. A mile to the eastward are the beautiful remains of Calder Abbey. Close to its lofty and ivy-covered ruins is the residence of Thos. Irwin, Esq., and though the exterior is tastefully modernized, it originally formed part of the ancient Abbey: internally there is sufficient proof of this having once been the case.

On the morning of the *Second Day*, the tourist may cross the bleak fells of Copeland Forest, with Dent on his left, to

Ennerdale bridge : descending the hill to this place, there is a view of the fertile valley of Ennerdale, and of the lake stretching up to the high mountains. There is a public-house here, where refreshments may be obtained.

ENNERDALE WATER is 2½ miles in length and ¾ of a mile in breadth. It is deficient in wood, and the mountains shelve rapidly to the water. Above the lake, in the lonely valley of Gillerthwaite, are the high mountains of the Pillar and the Steeple: from the head of the valley, a pedestrian may cross to Buttermere (over Scarf-gap) or to Wasdale-head, (over Black Sale,) and there is a track from the lower part of the valley, by Flouterntarn, to Crummock Water. How-hall is advantageously situated on the hill-side near the foot of the lake.

LOWES WATER. 7 miles of road through an open country brings the traveller from Ennerdale to Lowes Water, where he re-enters the mountainous district. This lake is about a mile in length, and is surrounded by noble mountains, the lower parts of which are richly clothed with wood. The waters of the lake flow into Crummock Water, distant two miles. The tourist may proceed from Scale-hill, at the foot of that lake, up its eastern side to Buttermere, and by the vale of Newlands to Keswick ; or he may take the shorter route of Lorton and Whinlatter to the same town. (See p. 333.)

Scale-hill, before, on the l. Godfred, Thomas Smith, Esq. ; Foulsike, Josh. Skelton, Esq. ; Kirkgate, John Hudson, Esq. ; the Park, Jonathan Pearson, Esq. ; three miles N. Lorton-hall, Raisbeck L. Bragg, Esq.

The Borrowdale Excursion may be varied by taking in the secluded and interesting valley of WATENDLATH, which runs parallel with Borrowdale, on the east. At Rosthwaite the traveller may ford the river, and ascend a steep winding path-way for upwards of a mile, enjoying fine views of the upper end of Borrowdale and the mountains beyond. Another mile brings him down to the edge of the small lake or tarn of Watendlath, and the lonely hamlet of that name, the houses, of which bear every appearance of great antiquity. Crossing the stream which supplies the cataract of Lowdore, he may go down the narrow valley for three miles, till he comes into the high road round Derwentwater, by Ashness. Above the fall of Lowdore, the view of the lake of Keswick is very fine. This excursion may be made on horseback.

A drive round BASSENTHWAITE WATER may be made in 18 miles, by Castle Inn, Ouse-bridge, and Peel Wyke. At the northern extremity of the lake is Armthwaite-hall, Sir Francis Fletcher Vane, Bart. ; at the southern, Spring-bank, Isaac Lancaster, Esq.; at Lissick, under Skiddaw, the Rev. John Monkhouse ; at Mirehouse, on the E. side of the lake, John Spedding, Esq.

Bassenthwaite Water, otherwise called Broad Water, is four miles in length, and near the foot more than a mile broad. The vale of Bassenthwaite is beautiful, and Skiddaw rises majestically above it. The best view is from Ouse-bridge.

WHITEHAVEN to KESWICK, 27 m.

Miles.	From Whitehaven.	Miles.	Miles.	From Whitehaven.	Miles.
2	Moresby	2	5	Cockermouth	14
2	Distington	4	2½	Embleton	16½
2	Winscales	6	6½	Thornthwaite	23
3	Little Clifton	9	4	Keswick	27

[This route has not before been introduced into guide-books for the Lakes : but, owing to the great number of travellers who now visit this district by means of the steam-packets from Liverpool, which land them either at Whitehaven, within 27 miles of Keswick, the capital of the Lakes, or at Workington, within 21 miles of that town, the route is here described.]

WHITEHAVEN is, after Carlisle, the largest town in Cumberland, and has risen from a mere hamlet to its present rank as a seaport within 190 years, chiefly owing to its valuable coal-mines. It is situated on a bay, and the harbour has been greatly improved by art : the town is built with uncommon regularity, the streets are spacious and the houses neat. The Earl of Lonsdale, who is lord of the manor and the proprietor of the coal-mines, has a commodious residence here, called the Castle, where there are some fine paintings. The harbour is large and convenient, and sheltered with several stone piers : one of them the new west pier, forms a most delightful promenade, and is as splendid a piece of masonry as the country can boast of. The plan was furnished by Sir John Rennie, and the work constructed under his superintendence. There are light-houses both at the extremity of the old quay, near the entrance of the inner harbour, and at the extremity of the new west pier. The light-house on the new quay is now used as a station, on which the half-tide flag, as it is termed, is exhibited. This flag is hoisted every tide as soon as there is sufficient water for ordinary sized vessels to enter the inner harbour, which is about half flood, and lowered again when the harbour is not accessible, which is about half ebb. This harbour is still being further improved : an extensive pier is at present in the course of erection on the north side of the harbour, under the same distinguished engineer who projected the west pier. There are three churches in the town—St. Nicholas, the Holy Trinity, and St. James ; a Scotch church, several dissenting meeting-houses, and a handsome theatre. The coal mines are very extensive, and some of them not less than 310 yards in depth. They extend in various directions under the town and harbour, and the workings from more than one of the pits extend to a distance of more than a mile in a direct line under the sea. Upwards of 150,000 chaldrons of coals are said to be annually exported from these collieries, chiefly to Ireland, exclusive of the home consumption. There are not less than half a dozen ship building yards at this place, which has long enjoyed a high character for the fine model and faithful construction of the vessels built at it. There are three roperies, and until of late years a considerable quantity of sail-cloth was manufactured here : latterly, however, the business in this particular department has very much declined. There is also an extensive earthenware manufacture at White-haven. Four miles south of Whitehaven is St. Bees, celebrated for its ruined priory, and its grammar school, and in modern times for its clerical institution, or college. There are steam packets twice weekly between Liverpool and Whitehaven, which leave the former place about the time of high water, and reach Whitehaven the succeeding flow, not unfrequently completing the voyage in from eight to ten hours. These packets are commodiously fitted up for passengers ; and a traveller by this conveyance proceeds from Liverpool to within 27 miles of the capital of the lake district—but to within half that distance of some as fine lake and mountain scenery as the county can boast of—for a few shillings, a distance of nearly one hundred and fifty miles by land. Whitehaven sends one member to Parliament, and its present representative is Matthias Attwood, Esq. Population of the township of Whitehaven 11,393 ; of Preston Quarter, which forms part of the town of Whitehaven, 4,323 ; total 15,716 : this, too, is exclusive of seamen. Market days, Tuesday, Thursday, and Saturday ; inns, *Black Lion, Golden Lion,* and *Globe.*

*** To Keswick 27 miles ; to Cockermouth 14 ; to Carlisle 41 ; to Workington 8 miles ; to Egremont 6 miles ; to Ravenglass 16 miles ; to London 320 miles.

Q

1 m. S. Hensingham-house, Lady Senhouse; 2 m. Summer Grove, Major Spedding; 3 m. Keekle Grove, Robert Jefferson, Esq.; 3 m. Linethwaite, Major Carlisle Spedding; Ingwell, Joseph Gunson, Esq.; 4 m. Spring Field, Captain Ponsonby, R. N.; 5 m. Gillfoot, Thomas Hartley, Esq.; 7 m. Hail-hall, John Fisher Ponsonby, Esq.; 9 m. Ponsonby-hall, Edw. Stanley, Esq., M.P.; Calder Abbey, Thomas Irwin, Esq.; Ponsonby, Sampson Senhouse, Esq.; 13 m. Park Nook, Capt. Caldecott; 14 m. Holm Rook Hall, Skeffington Lutwidge, Esq.; 15 m. Carleton-hall, Joseph Burrow, Esq.; 16 m. Muncaster Castle, Lord Muncaster; Irton Hall, Samuel Irton, Esq. M.P. (All these places are to the south of Whitehaven, and at the distances stated.)

Moresby, Rose Hill, Milham Hartley, Esq.; Roseneath, Mrs. Solomon; Richmond Hill, Mrs. Wheelwright.

Distington, ¼ m. Prospect, Henry Jefferson, Esq., Esq.; 1¼m. Gilgarron, James Robertson Walker, Esq.

Little Clifton, 4 m. beyond, at Brigham, The Hill, John Wilson, Esq.

COCKERMOUTH, a borough town situated upon the Cocker, where it falls into the Derwent : the streets are spacious, and, generally speaking, neatly built. On the summit of an artificial mount are extensive remains of the ancient Castle, which belongs to the Earl of Egremont. There are here manufactures of hats, coarse woollens, coarse linens, and leather. The town sends two members to Parliament, and the present Members are H. A. Aglionby, Esq., of Newbiggin-hall, and F. L. B. Dykes, Esq. of Dovenby-hall.—Population 4536 ; market-day, Monday ; inns, *Globe, Sun.*

⁂ To Whitehaven 14 miles ; to Workington 8 miles : to Keswick 13 miles ; to Wigton 16 miles ; to Carlisle 27 miles ; to London 306 miles.

Derwent-bridge end, Captain Senhouse ; at Papcastle, Major Skelton, and Thos. Knight, Esq. ; at Bridekirk, H. T. Thompson, Esq. ; Dovenby-hall, Fletcheville Lawson Ballantine Dykes, Esq. M.P. for Cockermouth ; Tallentire-hall, William Browne, Esq. ; Wood-hall, John Sanderson Fisher, Esq. ; Isel-hall, William Wybergh, Esq.

Bassenthwaite Water (see p. 336.) *Keswick* (see p. 329.)

WORKINGTON to KESWICK, 21 miles.

WORKINGTON, a seaport of Cumberland, situate at the mouth of the Derwent : it has a good harbour and a considerable trade in coal, from the collieries belonging to Henry Curwen, Esq. of Workington Hall, and several inland collieries, some of them at the distance of six or seven miles, belonging to different gentlemen, who cart this valuable mineral to Workington for exportation. The manor-house of the family of Curwen stands upon a fine eminence on the banks of the Derwent. It is an elegant quadrangular building, and is of considerable antiquity, but has been modernized. A steam packet has been established at this place within the last eighteen months; it performs one voyage weekly between that port and Liverpool, and one between Maryport and Liverpool. Population 6415; market-day, Wednesday; inns, *Green Dragon, New Crown, King's Arms.*

₊ To Whitehaven 8 miles; to Cockermouth 8; to Keswick 21; to Carlisle 35 miles; to London 314 miles.

2 miles E. Clifton-house, Richard Watts, Esq.; 3 m. Clifton Lodge, John Watson, Esq.

The road joins that from Whitehaven to Keswick 4 miles from Workington.

———

KESWICK to PENRITH, 17½ m.

From Keswick.		From Keswick.	
Miles.	Miles.	Miles.	Miles.
4 Threlkeld 4		3¼ Stainton 15	
7½ Penruddock 11½		2½ Penrith 17½	

Threlkeld, 1 m. before, on the l. the Riddings, Josh. Crosier, Esq. On the right is seen the interesting valley of St. John, at the upper end of which is a huge rock, called, from its resemblance to a fortress, the Castle Rock of St. John.

Penruddock, 2 m. to the l. is seen Greystoke-castle, Henry Howard, Esq., a fine and ancient structure, standing in a spacious park: near it, Greystoke-house, Rev. Henry Askew; 1 m. beyond, on the r. Hutton John, Andrew Fleming Huddleston, Esq.; 1 m. beyond, the road to Pooley-bridge turns off to the right.

Stainton, 1½ m. beyond, on the r. Skirsgill-house, Hugh Parkin, Esq.

PENRITH (often pronounced *Peerith*) is a neat and clean town, not regularly built, but containing some good streets and many handsome houses. It is situated in a wide and fertile valley, a mile from the confluence of the Eamont and the Lowther. It is a great thoroughfare, being on the road from Glasgow and Carlisle to the south, and many visiters to the Lakes approach them in this direction. Penrith and the neighbourhood abound in objects of antiquarian curiosity. The church was rebuilt in 1722, and connected with the ancient tower. In the church-yard is a monument of great antiquity, called the *Giant's Grave,* or *Giant's Legs,* consisting of two stone pillars, about 10 feet high and 13 feet apart, and four large semi-circular stones, two on each side of the grave, imbedded in the earth. The pillars are rudely carved, and a cross is said to be distinguishable on each. Tradition avers that this is the tomb of Sir Ewan or Hugh Cæsarius, a warrior of gigantic size, who reigned in this country in the time of Ida, one of the Saxon kings. At some distance is another stone pillar, six feet high, which, though not apparently connected with the grave, bears the name of the *Giant's Thumb*. The remains of the *Castle* stand on an elevation at the west side of the town. This was formerly a place of strength, was built about the reign of Edward IV. and dismantled in the time of the Commonwealth. It belongs, with the honour of Penrith, to the Duke of Devonshire. A mile from the town, on a hill which commands a splendid prospect of the vale and the Westmoreland and Cumberland mountains, is the *Beacon*, the property of the Earl of Lonsdale, a lofty stone building, erected in the times of frequent hostility between England and Scotland. *Brougham Castle*, a majestic ruin, which Camden supposes to be on the site of the Roman station *Brovoniacum*, stands on the south of the rivers Eamont and Lowther, at their confluence. This was anciently the seat of the Veteriponts, and from them descended to the Cliffords and Tuftons: it still belongs to the Earl of Thanet, hereditary high-sheriff of Westmoreland. The traces of a Roman encampment are distinctly visible, and the present high road here takes the line of the ancient Roman road.—Between the Eamont and and the Lowther is a curious relic of British antiquity, called *Arthur's Round Table;* it is a circular grass-grown area, 29 yards in diameter, surrounded by a broad ditch and an elevated mound, with two approaches cut through the mound, opposite each other. It is believed to have been an arena for tournaments in the days of chivalry, and some antiquarians suppose it to have been originally a castrensian amphitheatre of Roman construction.—A few hundred yards to the west of the Round Table, is an elevation, called *Mayburg*, or Maybrough, on which is a circular enclosure, 100 yards in diameter, made by a broad ridge of pebble stones heaped up to the height of 12 or 15 feet; in the centre of the circle is a massive pillar of unhewn stone, 11 feet high, and in one part 22 feet in circumference. This is believed to have been a place of Druidical judicature.—A much finer relic of Druidical times is the monument called *Long Meg and her Daughters*, on the summit of a hill near Little Salkeld, six miles north-east of Penrith, which is a circle three hundred and fifty yards in circumference, formed by 67 stones, many of which are 10 feet high, with one at the entrance 18 feet high. There is another remarkable monument called Carl Lofts, at Shap, ten miles south of Penrith, near the Kendal road; for an account of which see *Shap*, p. 306.—Two miles below Brougham Castle, on the rocky and perpendicular banks of the Eamont, is a huge cave, called the *Giant's Cave* or *Isis Parlis*, which tradition affirms to have been the abode of a gigantic freebooter, called Isir.—A mile and a half from Penrith, on the Appleby road, is a pillar called *the Countess's Pillar*, which was erected, according to the inscription, A.D. 1656, by Anne Countess of Pembroke, "in memorial of her last parting at that place with her good and pious mother Margaret Countess Dowager of Cumberland, the 2nd of April, 1616; in memory whereof she has left an annuity of £4, to be distributed to the poor within the parish of Brougham, every second day of April for ever, upon the stone hereby." Five miles north of Penrith, on the left of the Carlisle road, are the remains of a Roman station, supposed by Camden to be *Petriana*, and by Horsley *Bremetenracum;* the ruins are very considerable, and they go by the name of *Old Penrith*: for an account of them see *Plumpton*, p. 344. The inns in Penrith are excellent. Population of the parish 6059; market-day, Tuesday; inns, *Crown Hotel, George.*

₊ To Carlisle 18 m.; to Keswick 17½ miles; to Kendal 26 m.; to Appleby 12¾ m.; to Pooley-bridge 5 m.; to Patterdale 15 m.; to Ambleside 25 m.; to Glasgow 114 m.; to London 282½ m.

On the Kendal road, 1 m. from Penrith, on the left, Carleton-hall, John Cowper, Esq.; 1½ m., on the left, Brougham-hall, Lord Brougham and Vaux; 5 m. on the right, Lowther Castle, the Earl of Lonsdale; on the road to Ullswater, 3½ m., on the right, Dalemain, Edward W. Hasell, Esq; 4 miles east, Eden-hall-hall, Lady Musgrave; 4 m., n. e. Nunwick-hall, J. Richardson, Esq.; 5 m. on the Hesket Newmarket road, on the right, Hutton-hall, Sir Fras. Fletcher Vane, Bart.; 8 m. on the Temple Sowerby road, on the right, Newbiggin-hall, Wm. Crackenthorpe, Esq.; 6 m. on the Carlisle road, on the left, Inglewood-bank, Thomas M. Williamson, Esq.; 3 m. on the r. Bowscar, Colonel Youngson; in Penrith, Bishop-yard, John De Whelpdale, Esq.; 1½ m. Green Ways, James Parkin, Esq.

EXCURSIONS to ULLSWATER and HAWES WATER.

Ullswater, which is the second in size, and the first in grandeur and beauty of scenery amongst the English lakes, may be approached by various routes from Keswick and Penrith. From Keswick the nearest route is a bridle road, which leaves the Penrith road a little beyond the second mile-stone, crosses the vale of Wanthwaite, and passes over an exposed mountain side to Matterdale and Gowbarrow Park; this is about 11 miles, and brings the traveller to Ullswater at the distance of 4 miles from Patterdale. Carriages may proceed ten miles on the Penrith road, and then in 8 m. more reach Gowbarrow Park: this makes the distance to Patterdale 22 miles. Or they may go direct to Pooley-bridge, at the foot of Ullswater, 18 miles from Keswick. Adproaching from Penrith, travellers may go by Eamont-bridge, Yanwath, and Tirrel, and past the old tower of Yanwath-hall, in five miles to Pooley-bridge; or they may turn off the Keswick road beyond the second mile-stone, and pass through the beautiful grounds of Dalemain, coming to Ullswater near Pooley-bridge, in 6 miles, and to Patterdale in 15 m. It is believed that the best way of seeing Ullswater, approaching from Keswick, is to proceed to Gowbarrow Park, and thence to go to Patterdale, and return either by boat or along the shore, to Pooley-bridge; from which place a circuit may be taken by Lowther castle, or even as far as Hawes Water, to Penrith. Approaching from Penrith, the route may be reversed.

In proceeding from Keswick to Pooley-bridge, the traveller leaves the Penrith road 12 m. from Keswick, and, 3 m. before coming to Pooley-bridge, passes Dacre-castle, the remains of a very ancient mansion formerly belonging to the Dacre family, and now to Mr. Hasell, of Dalemain. In Dacre church-yard, are some rudely-carved monuments of great antiquity.

Pooley-bridge, a village at the foot of Ullswater, where there is a comfortable inn, but where post-horses are not kept. The hill of Dunmallet and the river Eamont adorn this place. Boats may be engaged here for going on the lake.

ULLSWATER is nine miles long and about a mile in its utmost breadth; its average depth is greater than any of the other lakes, and the deepest part is 35 fathoms. Its form is zigzag, resembling that of the letter Z. It has three small islands near the head. In sailing up the first reach of the lake, from Pooley-bridge, Swarth-fell is seen on the left, Hallen-fell in front, and a sloping shore, adorned with several villas, on the right. The second reach lies betwixt the hills of Hallen-fell, Birk-fell, and Place-fell, on the left, and Gowbarrow Parks on the right, with Helvellyn rising in great magnificence beyond the head. At the entrance of this reach is Hallsteads, the beautiful seat of John Marshall, Esq. Gowbarrow Parks are ancient deer-parks, belonging to H. Howard, Esq., of Greystoke Castle, having been bequeathed to him by the Duke of Norfolk. They comprise 1800 acres, and are divided into three parks—Glencoin Park, Gowbarrow Park, and the Low Park; the first and last of which are farmed off. Gowbarrow Park comprises 800 acres, and feeds 400 head of deer. Lyulph's Tower is a modern house, built in the castellated form, and inhabited by the gamekeeper. The cascade called *Airey Force*, one of the most beautiful amongst the Lakes, is in a glen, a quarter of a mile from the Tower: the water falls a perpendicular height of 80 feet through a chasm of the rocks. At the extremity of the park, and branching off to the right from the head of the second reach of the lake, is the valley of Glencoin, beyond which are the fine wooded rocks called Stybarrow Crag. The third reach presents the noblest view of mountain and valley, lake and wood, which is to be seen in Cumberland or Westmoreland. It lies between Place-fell on the left, and the outer ridges of Helvellyn and Fairfield on the right, St. Sunday Crag being finely conspicuous. (For Helvellyn see p. 329.)

The valley or district of *Patterdale* extends from Stybarrow Crag along the borders and partly round the head of the lake, from which it runs up two or three miles towards Brothers-water. Branching off from it, on the right, are the valleys of Glenridden and Grisedale. At the head of the lake is a comfortable inn, the King's Arms, Mr. Wilson's, where post horses may be had, and whence a rough carriage road of ten miles conducts, by Brothers-water and over Kirkstone-moor, to Ambleside. Above the inn is an extremely fine echo: a cannon being fired, the peal is returned on the ear six or seven times with great distinctness from the surrounding mountains. The whole of the southern shore of Ullswater, and part of the northern, are in Westmoreland; the rest is in Cumberland.

Near Pooley-bridge, Eusemere-lodge, John Charles Bristow, Esq.; on the opposite side of Dunmallet, Waterfoot, Colonel Salmond; and Dacre, Wm. Evans, Esq.; 2 m. up the lake, on the r. Rampsbeck-lodge, B. E. Stagg, Esq.; 3 m. up, on the r. Watermillock, J. Fallowfield, Esq.; a little beyond, Beau-thorn, Jonathan Scott, Esq.: still further, Hallsteads, John Marshall, Esq.; near Patterdale, Glenridden, Rev. Henry Askew; Patterdale-hall, William Marshall, Esq.; two miles beyond, Deepdale hall, Wm. Mounsey, Esq.

Lowther Castle, 4 m. from Pooley-bridge, and 5 m. from Penrith, the seat of the Earl of Lonsdale, is the most magnificent structure of modern date in the north of England. It stands on a fine elevation, amongst noble woods, and overlooks the vale of Penrith and all the surrounding mountains. The castle is quite modern, having been begun in 1808, and some of the interior parts are still in progress. The north front is in the style of the 13th or 14th century, and has towers and battlements: it is 420 feet in length: the south front is in the Gothic cathedral style, and looks upon a sloping vista of the park, enclosed by lofty trees. The interior is fitted up with splendour. The oaken wainscoting corresponds with the character of the building. The staircase, 90 feet high, and 60 feet square, is extremely fine.

Hawes Water, about 11 m. from Pooley-bridge, and th same from Penrith, is remarkable for the solemn grandeur of its rock and mountain scenery. It is 3 m. long, and only half a mile broad. Harter Fell, High Street, and Kidsay Pike are among the sublime mountains which rise above the head of the lake. There is a place of entertainment at Mardale Green, the White Bull. Hawes Water may also be approached from Long Sleddale and Troutbeck.

BROUGHAM HALL, near Lowther bridge, 1¼ m. from Penrith, the seat of Lord Brougham and Vaux, the Lord High Chancellor of England, is a plain, but lofty and venerable building, and, from the splendid prospect obtained from the terrace, has been called the Windsor of the North.—Clifton-hall, a dilapidated manor-house, the ancient seat of the Wyberghs, is half a mile distant.

PENRITH to CARLISLE, 18 m.

Miles.	From Penrith. Miles.	Miles.	From Penrith. Miles.
4½ Salkeld Gate	4½	4¾ Carlton	15¼
½ Plumpton	5	1 Harraby	16½
4¼ High Hesket	9¼	1½ Carlisle	18
1½ Low Hesket	10¾		

Salkeld Gate, on the r. Salkeld-lodge, Lieutenant-Colonel Lacy.

Plumpton; on the l. are the ruins of *Old Penrith*, formerly a Roman station, of which the vestiges of a fort, 132 yards long by 110 broad, and of considerable outbuildings, still remain. The station is 200 yards from the river Peteril: the ramparts are still very high, and the ditch round them almost perfect. The great Roman road, leading to the Picts' Wall, was on the line of the present high road. The station is supposed by Camden to have been *Petriana*, and by Horsley *Bremetenracum*.

High Hesket, 2 m. on the r. Armathwaite-castle, Rev. J. R. Hunton; 7 m. on the r. near Kirkoswald, the Nunnery, F. Y. Aglionby, Esq., the walks of which are the most romantic in this part of the country; and Staffold-hall, R. Lothian Ross, Esq.: beyond Hesket, on the r. Nordvue, Mrs. Dixon; on the l. Calthwaite-hall, T. Dixon, Esq. and Peteril-green, Christopher Parker, Esq.: Moorhouse-hill, Mrs. Lowden.

Low Hesket, 1 m. on the l. Barrock lodge, William James, Esq., M.P. for Carlisle.

Carlton, 1 m. before, Newbiggin-hall, H. A. Aglionby, Esq., M. P.; Woodside, Miss Losh; Briscoe-hill, Jas. Jardine, Esq.

CARLISLE, the capital of Cumberland, is an ancient city, and the see of a bishop. It stands on a gentle elevation at the confluence of the Eden, the Caldew, and the Peteril, within eight miles of the Scottish frontier, and is surrounded by a fertile and open country. Carlisle was a Roman station, and is within a quarter of a mile of the great Roman wall. It was anciently fortified, and in the wars between England and Scotland was a place of importance. Since the Union, it has greatly increased in trade and population. The streets are clean, and some of them very spacious and well-built. The castle is of unknown antiquity, but is said to have been built A. D. 680 : some very massive and antique buttresses on the north battery are ascribed to William Rufus: it is still kept in a defensible state, having been lately repaired, and has a small garrison. Mary Queen of Scots was imprisoned here in 1568, and the rooms she occupied, as well as her promenade, are shown. The cathedral is a venerable structure, partly of Saxon and partly of Gothic architecture: the east window is the largest in the kingdom: some old wooden screens in the aisles contain curious and ridiculous legendary paintings, representing events in the lives of St. Augustin and St. Anthony. The new gaol is an extensive and admirable building, situated at the southern entrance of the city, immediately contiguous to the county court-houses, (built in 1812) the principal features of which are two magnificent circular towers, the successors of two similar towers which in other days formed the defences of the " English-gate." The bridge over the Eden was finished in 1817, and is a solid and elegant structure, a quarter of a mile in length. A new bridge has been thrown over the Peteril at the south entrance to the town, and the hills on each side lowered thirty feet. Two churches in the Gothic style have recently been erected, and a County Infirmary has been completed at the head of English-street. A News-room, Reading and Billiard Rooms, have also been built, from a Gothic design by Messrs. Rickman and Hutchinson, of Birmingham, which contribute much to beautify the town. Carlisle has a flourishing manufacture of cottons, and also manufactures of woollens, linen, leather, and other articles: it is particularly celebrated for its whips and hats. Being within a few miles of the Solway, and having a ship canal to Bowness, its communications with Liverpool and all other parts are much facilitated by the steam-packets. A railway is commenced from this place to Newcastle, which may be expected still further to increase the prosperity of Carlisle. The city sends two repre-sentatives to Parliament, who at present are William James, Esq. of Barrock-lodge, and Philip Henry Howard, Esq. of Corby-castle. The county of Cumberland returns four members ; at present the Right Hon. Sir James R. G. Graham, Bart., of Netherby, (lately First Lord of the Admiralty,) and Wm. Blamire, Esq., of Thackwoodnock, are Members for East Cumberland ; and Samuel Irton, Esq., of Irton-hall, and Edward Stanley, Esq. of Ponsonby-hall, are the Members for West Cumberland. Population 20,006 : market-days, Wednesday and Saturday ; inns, *Bush, Coffee House.*

⁎ To Penrith 18 m. ; to Wigton 11 m. ; to Bowness 13 m. ; to Keswick 33 m. ; to Whitehaven 41 m. ; to Newcastle 57 m. ; to Glasgow 95¾ m. ; to London, 305 m.

7 m. S.S.W. of the city, Rose-castle, the Bishop of Carlisle ; 4 m. E. Warwick-hall, Mrs. Parker ; 5 m. E. Corby-castle,

Henry Howard, Esq., and Philip Henry Howard, Esq., M. P.;
11 m. E. Naworth-castle, (built in 1330,) Earl of Carlisle,
and near it the interesting ruin of Lanercost Priory, (built in
1169;) 7 m. E. Edmond-castle, T. H. Graham, Esq., and
Stonehouse, Col. Sir Hew D. Ross, K.C.B.; 3 m. N.E. Knells,
John Dixon, Esq.; 3 m. N.E. Houghton-house, Wm. Hodgson,
Esq.; Houghton-hall, Mrs. Ferguson; 3 m. N. Harker-lodge,
Rd. Ferguson, Esq.: 5 m. N. E. Scaleby-castle, James
Fawcett, Esq.; 5 m. N.N.W. Castletown-house, Robert Mounsey,
Esq.; 11 m. N. Netherby, Sir Jas. R. G. Graham, Bart. M. P.;
10 m. N. E. Kirklinton-house, Henry Farrer, Esq.; 3 m. S. W.
Dalston-hall, Wm. Sowerby, Esq.; 1 m. N. W. Morton-house,
Jno. Forster, Jun. Esq.

PENRITH to KENDAL, 26 m.

Miles.	From Penrith. Miles.	Miles.	From Penrith. Miles.
1	Eamont-bridge 1	5¾	Demmings 16
½	Lowther-bridge 1½	1	Hawse Foot...... 17
1	Clifton...................... 2½	2¾	Banisdale-bridge....... 19¾
2	Hackthorpe 4½	1¼	Gate Side 21
2½	Thrimby 7	1¾	Otter Bank 22¾
3¼	Shap 10¼	3¼	Kendal....................26

Eamont Bridge and Lowther Bridge—Arthur's Round Table
(see p. 340.) Brougham-hall (see p. 344.)
Hackthorpe.—Lowther castle (see p. 343.)

SHAP, a small market town, near the source of the river Lowther. A mile distant are the venerable and beautiful remains
of Shap Abbey. Near are many large upright stones inclosing
an area upwards of half a mile in length, and from 20 to 30
yards broad: the stones are of granite, three or four yards in
diameter, and ten or twelve yards distance; and at the upper
end is a circle of similar stones, about 18 feet in diameter.
This monument is called Carl Lofts (the liftings of the husband-
men,) and is thought to be of Danish origin: others suppose
it to be a Druidical temple. The market of Shap had sunk
almost into disuse, but has of late years considerably revived.
There is a spa, 3 miles south-east of Shap, of excellent medicinal
properties. It is the property of the Earl of Lonsdale, who has
recently built an extremely handsome inn, with hot baths, and
every accommodation in a superior style. For the last two years
the Spa has been well and fashionably attended, with considerable
benefit to invalids, and it promises to become a highly popular
resort. Population 1084; market-day, Wednesday; inns, *Grey-
hound, King's Arms.*

INDEX

OF ·

PLACES, SEATS, AND OBJECTS.

THE END.

EDWARD BAINES AND SON, PRINTERS, LEEDS.

Ino